IRONOPOLIS

GLEN JAMES BROWN

IRONOPOLIS

GLEN JAMES BROWN

Parthian, Cardigan SA43 1ED
www.parthianbooks.com
First published in 2018
© Glen James Brown
ISBN 978-1-912109-14-2
Edited by Edward Matthews
Cover design by Syncopated Pandemonium
Section Title Page Icons made by Freepik from www.flaticon.com
Glasses icon on Midnight title page by Allison Love @friendfriend.net
Typeset by Elaine Sharples
Printed in EU by Pulsio SARL
Published with the financial support of the Welsh Books Council
British Library Cataloguing in Publication Data
A cataloguing record for this book is available from the British Library.

For you, Sue

CONTENTS

Page 1
DAY OF THE DARK
(Una Cruickshank of Loom Street)

Page 77
THIS ACID LIFE
(Jim Clarke of Hessle Rise)

Page 153
MIDNIGHT
(Frank and Scott Hulme of Second Avenue)

Page 195
HEART OF CHROME
(Corina Clarke of Peelaw Bank)

Page 297
UXO
(Douglas Ward of Campbell Road)

Page 419
THE FINAL LEFT
(Henry Szarka of Sober Hall)

I believe that if we have a few more years at our disposal,
we shall have the best housing record of any nation in the world.

Aneurin Bevan, 1948

DAY
OF THE
DARK

Una Cruickshank of Loom Street

Dear Stephan,

Once, as a girl on holiday in Blackpool, I went on the Wild Mouse, this ride where you squashed into a fibreglass mouse that went screaming round a rickety wooden track. Never, ever again. Afterwards, I had to clamp head between knees to keep my candyfloss down, then spent the rest of the day holding the coats. You've probably never heard of the Wild Mouse, so maybe this wasn't the best way to start, but that was what reading your letter felt like.

In answer to your first question: yes, your 'detective work' was good. I still can't believe you went through the marriage records and wrote to everyone in the country with my old name. God knows what the ten other Jean Healys will make of this! I'm also struggling to wrap my head around the fact that Una named a painting after me. After what happened between us, I always wondered if she still thought of me. I suppose that answers that. I'll answer your questions about her as best I can, though I don't know how useful I'll be or how long it'll take. I'm not well you see, but I won't bore you with the details. The only thing drearier than illness is having to listen as others describe theirs.

You asked about when me and Una first met. Well, from the very beginning she was always around. Like I remember watching ants chew the legs off a woodlice (louse? I never know which) in the back yard, a line of ants carrying them away still twitching down a crack. Another time, I'm standing in the kitchen door with warm piddle running down my legs as Mam, her mouth full of wooden pegs, hangs the washing. I remember drowning my dolly Pree in a rain-filled pothole. I've got many raggedy shreds of sight and sound like that deep inside me, and in all of them Una is there somewhere, just out of frame.

Later, things get clearer: me and Una on the kerb tearing one of Mam's jam tarts apart with four hands. I see her twisting and popping her elbows to make the other Loom Street kids squeal (she was the most double-jointed person I've ever met). I remember sitting behind her in the bath as Mam tips soapy water over her head. Greasy black hair unkinking. Suds slipping down her spine. Back then you could still bathe another woman's child.

Una had no siblings but I had a sister, Agnes, five years older than me and pretty and popular and everything I wasn't. Plump, I suppose you would have called me (Agnes' name for me was 'suet'). I was shy, got picked on, and was convinced Mam loved me less because of it. Una would say, 'Sod Agnes, I'm your kin,' and at nights as I lay in bed listening through the wall while Mam did Agnes' hair, or pinned her a new dress, the two of them giggling away, I told myself it was true.

Then as now, kids like us didn't get an easy time at school. To give you an example I want to tell you about a specific P.E. class. Mr Thirsk was our teacher then, so we must have been eight or nine. I hated P.E. Whenever I think of those lessons now I see rain-filled skies, dead leaves skittering round my ankles. Nitheringly cold, too, our flimsy P.E. kits no match for the wind shrieking off the North Sea. School was split into houses based on history: The Stewarts were green, Hanover was red, Windsor blue, and yellow was The Tudors. I was a Tudor, Una a Stewart, and we were playing against each other in a netball match.

4

Netball terrified me because I thought if I caught the ball wrong I'd break my fingers. But Una was fearless: tall, stick-thin, lightning quick, spinning on her heel as she threaded the ball through waving Tudor arms. Elsie Stanger hated Una especially. Elsie was my team captain and worst bully, who had once squirted ink into my jam roly-poly and made me eat it. All through the game she'd been rolling her eyes and sniggering whenever I made a mistake (which was often) and as for Una, she stood on her heels and jabbed her in the back whenever Mr Thirsk wasn't looking. I heard Elsie hiss 'your mam's a crazy gypsy' as she and Una tussled for the ball, and as the game went on, Una's pale face darkened in a way that had nothing to do with exertion.

Near the end of the game, Una got the ball in the centre circle and Elsie saw her chance. She charged full tilt at Una with no intention of trying to win possession. No, Elsie wanted to flatten her. Una ignored her Stewart teammates as they yelled for her to pass, to save herself. Instead, she wound up and whipped the ball directly at Elsie's face. At almost the same second, a black streak shot across the playground and the ball exploded in a burst of feathers and an ear-splitting screech. Elsie, too, screeched as she tripped, skinning her hands and knees on the rough tarmac.

Stillness. Mr Thirsk blew his whistle. The rest of us blinked at each other.

The sparrowhawk lay smashed on the playground, one wing twisted under itself, the other unfurled and twitching. Its head was bent awfully to the side and a single golden eye stared up at us. The poor thing wasn't dead. Dappled brown feathers blew away in the cold wind. A few feet away, Elsie held her bloody knees with her bloody hands and whimpered. I didn't envy her. Her mam would be digging stones out of her with a hot pin for weeks.

'Take her to the nurse,' Mr Thirsk said. You could tell he wasn't sure what had just happened either.

Two girls hoisted Elsie up under her armpits and limped her away. Una stood in the centre circle alone, staring at the dying bird. Mr Thirsk blew his whistle again, and it sounded so thin and stupid against the wind. Lesson was over, he said, so we all headed back to the stinky cloakroom to change. The others in the class were whispering about Una and throwing suspicious glances over their shoulders at her. I turned back when I got to the door. Una was still on the playground, kneeling over the hawk. It looked like she was speaking to it. Then she wrung its neck. When she came over she had two feathers in her fist. She handed me one.

'Keep this,' she said.

Her eyes were pink, but dry. That was another thing: I never saw her cry. Actually, that's a fib. I did once, but many years later.

That sparrowhawk set the tone for Una at school. It was the beginning of the myth that grew darker and stranger the older she became. A myth which made girls like Elsie think twice before they messed with her. Because of this, I stayed as close to Una as I could. I included myself in her protective bubble, and while I may have succeeded, it meant the few other friends I did have soon drifted away. Until all me and Una had were each other.

So those are my earliest memories. My hand is cramping now. Can't write anymore. I'll post this tomorrow. I'm aiming to answer the rest of your questions as soon as I can, because I feel there's a lot more to come. You've jarred something loose, though whether that's good or bad, I can't say.

Sincerely,

Jean Barr

P.S. You said you're the boss of Ananke Acquisitions? Please send me the address, so I can direct future letters there. I'd prefer my husband not to wonder why I spend my days writing to another man. Things around here are tense enough as it is.

Dear Stephan,

You also wanted to know about her parents? Well, I've been sitting here all morning attempting to do just that but it's beyond me. Instead, I'll tell you about New Year's Eve 1958, and let it stand for all.

Even though you didn't get presents, I loved New Year's Eve better than my birthday or Christmas or anything. I think it was because everybody was the best version of themselves. People wore their best clobber and nicest perfumes. They had a drink, cracked a joke, and dropped their guards. It was wonderful to see. Teesside was a metal town back then, Ironopolis folk called it: over 40,000 people worked at the forges in their heyday, and the night skies burned red. But graft could be brutal. It could – and frequently did – swallow people whole, but for that one night everybody was changed. Our neighbours, but not.

We always threw a big party at our house for anyone who wanted to come. No invitation necessary. It was the only night of the year where we extended the dining table and Mam's special red and gold tablecloth came out. Seeing that cloth was like seeing an old friend. I was eleven, and I'd spent the whole day helping to make the food: sausage rolls, ham and pease pudding stotties, brandy snaps (bear in mind this was only four years after rationing and food like that was still the height of sophistication). I can still smell the Yardley's English Lavender and Old Spice and cigarette smoke as I walked through the party with trays. I loved how people sneaked looks at their watches, as if midnight was a big secret only they were in on.

8

I was also on coat duty, which I took seriously. I'd say, 'Good evening Mr and Mrs So-and-So,' trying to do my best radio voice, 'do come in.' There was a knock at the door but it was only Una. Her hair a violent charcoal scribble around her ghost face, those dark, taciturn eyes. I let her in without launching into my welcome-spiel.

'They're coming,' she said as she passed me.

I peered up Loom Street at the rapidly approaching figure of Talitha Cruickshank – Una's mother – clip-clopping towards me in a black dress and shawl that hung like a dead thing off her collarbones, her cleavage spilling out when she bent down to me on the front step. Her eyelashes were clumped together with mascara and her red painted mouth was a stab wound pressed hard to my cheek until I felt teeth. No perfume either, not like the other ladies. She reeked of sweat and her breath smelled like fruit turning black.

She raised her left hand, which was missing the ring finger, to the ceiling. 'The end is nigh,' she whispered. Never forgotten that. Then she said George would be along in two ticks, and with that she went into the party.

I shivered in the open doorway, straining my eyes up the street, but I couldn't see him. Maybe he'd forgotten something and gone home? Maybe he'd already come in through the back door? Like I said, I took my guest-welcoming seriously, but the December air was breadknives. I decided to keep the door open a crack just in case, and was in the process of wedging a shoe in the jamb when I saw him.

George Cruickshank came down the walk like a man in syrup. Shoe heels scraping the frosty path, arms loose at his sides. Minutes passed before he reached the house and my teeth rattled the whole time.

'Good evening, Mr Cruickshank,' I said when he finally arrived.

It took him a moment to realise where the voice was coming from. He looked down at me with watery eyes, and if you'd never met him before you'd think it was booze. But not me, I knew better.

'Hello, lass.' George pulled the words out like toffee.

'Your tie's untied, Mr Cruickshank.'

He put an unsteady hand on my head, but the tie remained loose around his throat.

When the party got off the ground I was allowed to play my favourite records. They're still in the loft somewhere: 'Tom Hark' by Elias and his Zigzag Jive flutes, and 'Endless Sleep' by Marty Wilde. (I still shiver when Marty sings: 'I heard her voice crying in the deep / come join me baby in my endless sleep'.) Dad and Uncle Neville had humped the settee onto the upstairs landing that morning, so there was space to cut a rug, and everybody was having fun. (I've got a diamond-edged memory of walking in on Mam and Dad kissing over the kitchen sink. When she saw me, Mam giggled and threw a tea-towel over Dad's head.)

Meanwhile, Talitha worked the room. She touched men's arms and laughed too-loudly at the things they said, while the wives of those men shot dark looks at each other. George sat on a stool against the wall with an untouched drink in his hand, lost in a spot on the carpet. I found Una upstairs on the settee with what looked like a glass of bitter lemon, but when I had a sip my mouth filled with spit.

'Gin in it,' she said, and popped her elbows.

Agnes shouted up the stairs that it was nearly midnight, so I pulled Una off the settee and we went down.

The last moments of the year are always the most exciting, don't you think? Someone lifted the needle off the record and snapped on the wireless, swizzling through the flying-saucer noise to the BBC announcer telling us we only had thirty seconds left. The adults bustled happily into a rough circle and crossed their arms, while the kids still on their feet at that hour formed another, smaller, circle inside theirs. I found myself across from Una, who was, I think, sozzled.

'Ten,' the announcer said.

TEN! – Everyone roared – NINE! – I mumbled – EIGHT! – Una didn't say anything – SEVEN! – The woman next to Talitha held her hand like you would a stranger's used hanky – SIX! – I looked around for George – FIVE! – he wasn't there – FOUR! – I caught a glimpse of him through the bodies, still on his stool, watching as his spilled drink soaked into the carpet – THREE! – TWO! – ONE! – **HAPPY NEW YEAR!**

The adults shook limbs to 'Auld Lang Syne', while we bairns substituted the words for 'daaaah daaaah dah dahs' while trying to yank each other's arms out of their sockets. Una put up no resistance. Her arms jerked painfully, her head bounced loose on her long neck. The adults broke apart, hugged and kissed and shook hands, and everything was perfect until an off-kilter wail silenced the room. Talitha had turned off the wireless. She clasped her hands between her breasts and stared with wild eyes. People instinctively gave her space, as you would a dog you don't trust. Someone tutted loudly.

Then Talitha smiled a wide, smoke-wrecked smile, closed her eyes and began to sing.

To this day I've never heard the like. How can I, with only this notebook and pen, begin to describe it? It was treacly and curdled and jagged all at once, and not in English. Smirking men elbowed each other while others (women, mostly) just glowered. Una slinked back upstairs with a freshly pilfered drink.

Talitha herself noticed nothing. She sang and swayed in the centre of the room like an animal caged so long its mind's gone, and only after the final trembling note faded did she open her eyes. Her mascara had run into mad black blurs like the ink-splot pictures they have at the loony bin.

The room was deadly silent until Mam led a half-hearted smattering of applause. Someone put a record on and the tension lifted a little. George's stool was empty. I went to the hall and the door was wide open, letting in the now-January bitterness. George himself was some way off up the street, shuffling away like an iron-booted diver across the seabed.

Back in the living room, Talitha was involved with some neighbours. I was out of earshot, but I could tell backs were up. Mary Eastbourne from Number 8 jabbed a finger at Talitha, who was grinning a grin laced with chaos. Mary lunged at her, but was held back. Mam stepped in and said something to Mary, who shook herself free and stormed into the kitchen. Then she spoke directly into Talitha's ear. I watched as Talitha's grin faded to an eerie Elvis lip hitch. Una's mother elbowed through the party towards me. I ran into the hall and opened the front door for her.

Talitha tugged her thin shawl across her shoulders. 'Everyone's a critic,' she said as she left.

Upstairs, Una's new drink was almost sunk. I said Happy New Year and she slurred it back. She smelled like unwashed bedsheets when I hugged her, and had to close one eye to focus on me.

'There's a kiss on your cheek,' she said as she passed out.

12

*

So those were her folks, Stephan. Make of them what you will. Next time I'll tell you about the riverbank. I know you are eager for me to get to that.

Sincerely,

Jean Barr.

Dear Stephan,

There's a racket downstairs. Vincent is shouting at Alan for not putting the washhouse key back on the hook. Alan is my son, Vincent my husband. Now I can hear Alan limping upstairs and shutting his bedroom door. Chopin – that's our dog – howls outside. Vincent stomps around. Now he's gone out and it's quiet.

I apologise. I didn't mean to tell you any of this, it's just it happens a lot. Alan is twenty-two and sensitive, something which Vincent finds difficult to accept. But then, you know about art, Stephan. I don't need to explain sensitivity to you.

Una was a born artist. Even as a bairn, she'd find some way to leave her mark – even just with her finger on a steamy bus window. Here's a story for you: one rainy weekend when we were about ten and mooching around the house – always my house – we saw Nana had nodded off in her chair. Una clocked her first, and went to the battered old sea chest my Dad still had from the war, where I kept my toys. She creaked the lid, got pencils and paper and stretched herself out on the hearth rug. Turning her head this way and that, sucking on the end of her pencil, she studied Nana. Then she started to draw. Her pencil scratched like mice in the walls, her eyes shining in their inkwell sockets.

I didn't want to be left out, so I got paper of my own, but when I looked at Nana…where did I start? The head, I supposed. Ms Fox in art class said that a face was a crucifix inside an oval, but Nana's face wasn't an oval. It wasn't any shape I could see. I glanced over at Una's page. Already, Nana was beginning to appear: her but not her, less the lines themselves but the spaces between them. I began my own drawing slowly. Each tiny, tentative stroke I made took me further from the picture in my head.

Una's blunted pencil rolled from her fist. 'Her ears are weird,' she whispered.

Her picture was…stunning. Proper art at ten years old. I tried hiding my own scrawl, but she tugged it from me with pinched fingertips.

'Don't,' she said.

Nana woke herself up in the usual way, by breaking wind. She always said the same thing: 'Oh deary me.' It creased us up, that. She wanted to know what mischief we were up to, and demanded we hand over our drawings. She held mine up to the window. The rain clicked softly against the glass.

'Oh, this is lovely,' she said. 'Just lovely.'

I could see my stupid drawing through the paper and said nothing.

Then Nana looked at Una's page and something passed across her face. She peered over the paper. Had Una drawn this just now?

Una nodded.

Nana looked at the page for a long time. 'I'm old, aren't I girls?' she said.

We said she wasn't, but I suppose she was.

Nana pinned our drawings on the wall above my sea chest, where they remained for many years, long after things had gone bad between the two of us. I would see them every day – an awful reminder of why they had.

*

When you said in your letter that Una had painted hundreds of the same scene, I knew exactly which one you meant. She used to do that riverbank over and over again. At first, I'd thought it was the river Tees, but later knew it wasn't. I can still see it: the black mud, the rustling reeds. The way you couldn't tell where the fog ended and the river began. Sometimes there would be shapes in the fog, just out of focus, or mostly off the page, but Una would never say what – or who – they were.

You asked if I knew why she was 'fixated'. Well, Ms Fox asked Una the same question after she had, for the umpteenth time, spent the lesson on her swirling blue-grey riverbanks. Una replied that it was a dream she had, actually the only dream she ever had. Ms Fox looked at her funny when she said that.

There's more to say about this, and it's to do with the Green Girl, but I can hear Chopin howling. That means Vincent's back, and I won't be able to relax until he and Alan have made peace. That's still my job, for now at least.

Sincerely,

Jean

P.S – No, I don't have any of her early work, sorry. Who knows where those pictures are now? Where does anybody's childhood go?

Dear Stephan,

You wanted to know who the Green Girl was in that one painting you described. Well, you're in luck.

Apart from art, the other thing Una loved was giving herself the heebie jeebies. Every other Wednesday, a man called Henry drove the mobile library down Loom Street and Una checked out as many ghost stories as her ticket allowed. Spooks floating down corridors, The Thing in the Cellar, those mad Victorian photos of ectoplasm coming out of the gypsy woman's eyes – Una ate it up.

Her favourite stories, though, were about being buried alive. You would not believe how often hospital patients used to wake up six feet under after some sackless doctor declared them dead, their long-buried coffins finally exhumed to show scratch marks on the inside of the lids. Or renovators turning an old castle into a swanky hotel knock through a wall and the mouldy bones of some bricked-up so-and-so rattle out. Or explorers going into an 'uncharted' South American cave system, only to find in the most inaccessible antechamber two human skeletons curled together like quotation marks.

Una's absolute favourite was about the luxury cruise liner that made a mysterious clanging below decks. Engineers combed the whole ship top to bottom but couldn't find the source. Years passed and the clanging got worse, got into the pipes, started echoing through the entire ship to wake up First Class, which was the last straw because once posh people got the hump, you knew about it. Unexplained fires began breaking out. Food supplies went rotten. A cabin boy was washed overboard by a freak wave on an otherwise calm sea. Word got around about the cursed cruise liner, and people stopped booking passage. Eventually the ship was scrapped.

Una had told me the story a dozen times, but still gripped my arm for the last part: 'and it's only when they prise the hull open that they find the riveter who went missing all those years before, during the ship's construction. Still in his overalls, mallet still in his bony hand. He'd been working in the hull when it was sealed up and nobody heard his cries for help. That's what the clanging was! His ghost hammering let me out! Let me out!'

Una was fascinated by what might have gone through the head of that doomed riveter during the days it must have taken him to die.

'He must have realised things,' she said to me once.

'Like what things?'

Una was serious. She leaned close so her lips brushed my ear. 'Like...**BOO!**'

Books aside, Nana was best for giving us the creeps. Whenever me and Una got too rambunctious for our own good, or didn't come back for tea on time, or ran our gobs during Hancock's Half Hour, she'd say, 'If you don't mind yourselves, Peg Powler will get you.'

Peg Powler, as Nana never tired of telling us, was a witch who lived in the river Tees and drowned boys and girls who didn't listen to their elders and betters.

'But we don't live on the river,' we'd say.

Nana was ready for that. 'Peg's in the <u>pipes</u>,' she'd say. 'She'll drag you down the netty (toilet to you, Stephan) by your bum.'

Usually, that was as far as the Peg stories went, but one day, when we must have been being particularly flippant, Nana said: 'Oh, so you think I'm having you on, do you? Did I ever tell you about how she almost got me?'

Mesmerised, Una plonked herself down at Nana's feet.

'I was about your age,' Nana said, her eyes turning to Una's drawing above the sea chest, 'a long, long time ago now. I lived in a place called Foulde, not far from Egglescliffe, right on the Tees. Back then there were none of these awful council estates. We weren't all squashed up like we are now.'

'Was it a farm?' Una asked.

'No, lass. Not a farm, but there was nature all around. Real dirt under our feet. We knew all the stars. I'll bet you girls don't know any stars.'

Which was true. Then as now, whenever I look up, all I see is orange. Missing stars were just one of the ways Nana complained about the Burn Estate. She often reminisced about how the good people of Foulde (and later St Esther, where she moved with Granddad) were told by the powers that be that their homes were in fact slums not fit for human purpose. It was an injustice, Nana said, made worse by those communities being split up and forced into 'these bloody cement chicken coops.' Whenever Mam and Dad were in earshot of this kind of talk, I'd catch them rolling their eyes at each other.

But back to the story. 'Anyway,' Nana went on, 'my Mam – that's your great Grandma – she used to warn us bairns against Peg Powler, just like I'm warning you lasses now. And just like you two, we paid her no mind. Peg Powler? Haway, that's <u>babby</u> stuff. So of course, one sunny day we all trotted off down to the river to play...'

Me and Una held each other on the hearth rug.

'If memory serves,' Nana said, 'it happened just past Egglescliffe, where the river bends towards Yarm. We were messing about, skimming flatties and catching sticklebacks in jam jars, when my brother Bill said we should play hide and seek. He counted while the rest of us scattered. I went the opposite way to everyone else, and found a willow tree growing out over the river. The dangly leaves came down and met the reeds to make a sort of veil around me. Its roots were just above the water, so I clambered down onto them and ducked. It was a good hiding place and soon, in the distance, I heard my friends screaming as Bill caught them. I remember thinking, "I'm going to win!"' Nana leaned forward in her chair. 'But then a cold feeling crept over me. I was being <u>watched</u>. I looked down and the river was going white. Mam had warned me about Powler's Cream. It meant she was close…' she glanced at the clock. 'Oh, I think its teatime girls.'

'NO!'

Nana flashed her dentures. 'Sure?'

'YES!'

We settled back down and Nana carried on.

'So,' she said, 'I was looking at the cream when Peg appeared. All I could see of her was her head above the water. She had a hand like this' – Nana splayed her hand over her face and glared at us through arthritic fingers – 'and she was looking <u>right at me</u>.'

Una dug her filthy nails into my arm.

'I couldn't move,' Nana said, 'couldn't speak. I was in some kind of trance. I could hear her in my head, calling my name, and the more I listened, the more I wanted to go to her.

'Then she took that bony claw away, and I'll tell you, girls, I never want to set eyes on another face like that as long as I live. Her skin was a sickly green stretched so tight you could see her skull. Black hair plastered down the sides of her head, and there were wriggly things in it. Worms and parasites, God knows. You could see her workings under what little flesh she had left – the bones, sinews, tendons. And the smell. Can you guess what she smelled of?'

We shook our heads.

'Mildew,' Nana said. 'She stank so bad I couldn't breathe. When she smiled her teeth were like broken bottles.' She shuddered at the memory. 'But do you know the worst thing, girls?'

Whisper: 'What?'

'She was beautiful.'

I didn't understand. How could someone so terrible looking be beautiful?

But before I could say anything, Una spoke. 'So what did she do?'

'Peg? She got closer and closer. I tried to move, scream, but I couldn't. I wet myself. My foot started slipping off the roots. It all happened so slowly, and her eyes – oh God girls, those eyes – they never left mine. When she was close enough, she reached out and her long slimy fingers closed round my ankle. They were so, so cold. Cold and dead. And that's when I heard Billy shouting my name from the top of the bank. Somehow his voice did something, broke the spell. I tried to scramble away, but Peg tightened her grip and started sinking. She wanted to take me down into the water with her.'

Una's leg jiggled against mine.

21

'I was in up to my knees, girls, I was <u>this close</u>,' Nana leaned forward in her chair, holding her thumb and index finger a centimetre apart, '<u>this close</u> to letting her have me. But then I thought of Billy and Mam and Dad, how I'd never see them again, and I yanked my leg as hard as I could and suddenly I was free. I staggered through muck and reeds and collapsed on the bank just down from Billy and the rest of my friends. Bill was white as a sheet, bless! My shoe was full of blood. She'd taken a chunk out of me.'

I glanced over at Una. Her fists were balled.

'I never played on the river again,' Nana said. 'I knew Peg had the taste for me.'

'Did you ever tell?' Una whispered, awed.

'I told everyone! Even Mam and Dad. I didn't want Peg getting anybody else, did I?'

'Did they believe you?'

'Why not likely. Me and Bill both took a hiding, and my friends thought I was soft in the head.' Nana worried a loose thread on her skirt. 'Anyway, shortly after, Bill got pneumonia and died…I didn't feel much like playing after that.'

'I'm sorry, Nana.' I said. I didn't know what I was supposed to say.

'It was a long time ago, hin.'

A silence. Then, me: 'Nana?'

'Aye?'

'None of that was real, was it? About Peg Powler?'

'What do you think?'

I shrugged.

'It was real,' Una said. 'How old was she?'

'I couldn't say,' Nana said. 'Old and young at the same time. It was queer.'

'What was she wearing?'

22

'I only saw her up to her chest, but it didn't look like she was wearing anything.'

Una clenched her fists. 'What do you think would've happened if she'd got you?'

'Una, lass, I don't know…'

Una turned to me. 'Don't you believe her?'

'I dunno…'

Nana wriggled her right foot. 'Slipper.'

Una pulled it off.

'Sock.'

Una gripped the toe of the sock and tugged it off inch by inch, revealing Nana's thin, splotchy shin. We gasped: there, just above the nub of her ankle, was a sickle of scar-tissue.

So I think that's the Green Girl in the painting, Stephan. Her name is Peg Powler and she quickly became more than just another spooky tale to Una. She kept pestering Nana to retell the story, demanding more information each time, and I think Nana was puzzled by her growing obsession. Worried, even.

One day not long after, Una didn't come to school, or appear round my house for tea the way she did most days. When she finally turned up in my backyard the next morning, her clothes were stiff with mud and she had sticky-jacks in her hair. She'd walked all the way to Egglescliffe, to where Nana had played hide and seek, and waited on the riverbank all night for Peg to come. She'd even splashed her feet in the water. I asked Una what she'd seen, and anyone in it simply to get swept up in some girlish nonsense would've gone, 'I saw her! I saw!' But Una just shook her head, ground filthy fists into her eyes.

*

I'm not sure I want to see this painting of Peg you tell me Una did. There's always been a cranny of my mind where that witch has festered (I never told Alan about her when he was a boy because I didn't want him carrying her around like I've carried her). I also worry that confronting Peg again would somehow <u>unleash</u> her…or more specifically, unleash the way I felt back then. It's ridiculous, but as Peg tightened her grip on Una's mind, I felt left out once more. Jealous even, because I wondered if Una, my only friend, heard Peg the same way Nana had done on the riverbank that day: a voice calling from a place I would never be brave enough to follow.

Jean.

Dear Stephan

My folks visited today, and it's the same old rigmarole each time Dad and Vincent get together. Nodding at each other like they're suffering whiplash.

Grunt: 'Vincent.'

Grunt: 'Ronnie.'

Men!

Today, after the usual warm salutations, Vincent had the good sense to make himself scarce and go over to his garage, or the Labour Club, or his allotment. Or wherever he really goes when he says he's going to those places. Once he was gone, Alan emerged from his room and made the tea. He gets on well with his Gran and Granddad, and I can't tell you how happy it makes me. Dad asks him the time-honoured question of whether he's courting. It makes the lad squirm, bless. I'd love it if Alan was courting, but he isn't. I know.

As always, Mam took me in, searching for signs of weight loss, bags under my eyes, new things of pills on the side. Her Avon foundation was the colour of a peach melba, and when she plonked herself down on my bedside chair, the cushions <u>whoomphed</u> exactly like the chip pan had when it went up last year and I, like a divvy, went to throw water on it. Vincent grabbed my arm at the last second, spinning me into the counter and bruising my hipbone, which lead to the X-rays that found the shadows on my ovaries. Lucky, really. Not that I could tell folk round here. When they saw me on my crutch, I knew what they <u>really</u> thought had gone on.

25

But that's all by-the-by. Mam told me about the family recently moved onto 1 Loom Street, Una's old house. More 2am slanging matches, more thudding 'techno' music. The parents looked barely out of school themselves, Mam said, yet had three bairns. I told her to look on the bright side. If they were anything like the last family, they'd be gone within the year.

'But pet,' she replied, 'what if the next lot's worse? At least these ones wear shirts most of the time.'

The estate is going to the dogs. Private landlords who've never once set foot in the place are snapping up the ex-council properties to rent back to the self-same council for silly money when they don't have enough homes to house the homeless. It's madness. Or they fill them with all kinds of trouble makers. Those who can are upping sticks. But not us. Vincent bought our house ten years ago, and he'll refuse to move no matter how bad it gets. And bad it's getting. There's less and less familiar faces around these days, and packs of kids roaming the streets. They hang around bus stops and corners until all hours. When I see them, I wonder: Where are your parents?

But then I think of George and Talitha, and I know.

To the north of the estate there is a patch of woodland through which the Cong Burn used to run, a little river which eventually fed into the Tees (well, I say river, but really it was more of a stream, and it's dried up now, or so I've heard. They blocked it to build the new houses somewhere between here and Yarm). On the bank of the burn was a large pipe above the water: an entrance to the underground labyrinth of old sewers connected to the derelict waterworks on the other side of the estate.

Mam had drummed it into me: <u>STAY AWAY FROM THE BURN PIPE.</u>

And, being a good girl, I always had. But then Una got her idea.

It was autumn and we must have been knocking on thirteen. The falling leaves were the red / gold of Mam's special New Year tablecloth and crunched like pork scratchings under our feet. I whined the whole way: 'We don't even know where it comes out.'

'Exactly,' Una said, clicking her torch on and off.

'But what if it doesn't come out anywhere?'

'What if it comes out in another world?'

'There'll be rats.'

'Rats schmats.'

We arrived at the bank opposite the pipe. The burn flowed on, towards the Tees, further than I had ever been. Without taking her shoes and socks off, Una sloshed into the water up to her bruised shins.

'Una, I don't want to…'

She pulled the spool of twine out of her knickers. 'It's like that minotaur story from school. We won't get lost.'

'We should go back.'

'Haway, Jean. Don't be a wimp.'

'I'm not <u>being</u> a wimp.'

She hoofed up a wing of water. 'We're always saying how boring everything round here is. Well <u>this</u> is adventure.'

'But I've got my new clothes on.' Which was true. A peach-coloured blouse and cotton skirt from Woolies.

Una's eyes narrowed to knife nicks. 'I'm going in with or without you.'

'Una, <u>please</u>.'

She tossed the spool into the pipe and clambered up after it.

'Please.' I had tears in my eyes.

She tied one end of the twine to a bolt on the pipe's rim and tugged it to make sure it held. The pipe sighed around her. Stooping, she shone the torch down its throat, wolf-howling – Awooooo – after it. Her face was all twisted when she looked back at me.

'Last chance,' she said.

'Una…' I said uselessly.

'Tell them I died a hero's death,' she said, and melted into the darkness.

I was frantic. I paced and blubbered along the bank. Once, twice, three times I took off my shoes and socks and tippy-toed into the freezing water, only to once, twice, three times turn back. I thought about running home and telling Mam, but I'd already been warned about being here. Plus, there was the unspoken rule every child knows – you NEVER told. Still, what if Una got lost? Became nothing but bones and a ghost story herself? I felt pulled in so many directions that the only thing for it was to sit on the bank and wait.

Una was right. I was a wimp.

Time passed. The light faded and cold crept on. To stave off panic, I started setting meaningless deadlines: 'One more minute and I'm leaving! One elephant, two elephant, **three** elephant…' But after sixty elephants had trooped past trunk-to-tail, I didn't budge. Then: 'Right, when that tree-shadow gets to that rock, I'm off!' Watching it inch towards its destination was torture because I knew I wasn't going anywhere once it did. I tried getting angry – this was all Una's fault! She had no right! But the gathering darkness chose to throw its weight behind Fear, not Rage, and my hissy fit quickly fizzled.

Finally, unable to hack it any longer, I got up to leave. I was just brushing the muck off when I heard a noise from deep within the pipe.

'Una?' I said, as loudly as I dared.

No answer. The noise got louder. What sounded like footsteps. Clanging footsteps getting closer.

'Una is that you?'

Clang…clang…clang…

'This isn't funny…'

Clang…clang…clang…

'Una, I'm leaving you!'

The string Una had tied to the bolt snapped and disappeared down the pipe like sucked spaghetti. It was sprinting now – Clang! Clang! Clang! – and just like Nana, my legs wouldn't work – **CLANG! CLANG! CLANG!** – The pipe opened wider, ready to swallow me, and a hideous voice wailed:

JJJJJJEEEEEAAANNNNNN!

I stumbled, tumbled into snarls of brambles, screaming.

Una's pale, laughing face appeared at the mouth of the pipe. 'Did you think it was Peg Powler come to get you?' She sploshed into the burn and waded up the bank to where I lay struggling in the thorns. I kicked at her hand when she held it out for me.

'Jean, I was just joking.'

With smears of scum under each eye, Una watched me

struggle free. My whole body felt slashed. Blood from my cut wrist stained my blouse, which was torn and twisted around me. I got shakily to my feet.

'God,' Una said, 'it was just a <u>joke.</u>'

'I hate you,' I said.

'I didn't mean to scare you.'

'I wasn't scared!'

She almost managed to supress her smile. Almost.

I stormed off through the dead leaf drifts before she could see me cry, my name following me through the trees as I did.

Oh, did I catch it when I got home! As punishment, I had to spend the whole half-term clearing out the cellar for the rag-and-bone man. Hauling stacks of mouldy old Gazettes and scuzzy lino offcuts in damp boxes that came apart in my hands. There were spiders, too. Big ones. But I never told on Una because, really, who was there to tell? She wasn't Mam's daughter. As young as I was, I still grasped the fact that getting my mother involved would have only rocked the uneasy reality of my family's relationship with hers. Una was allowed to keep me company while I worked, and she took care of the spiders for me because she felt bad. In the shadows of the cellar's single bare bulb, I was bedraggled and gaunt-looking. We looked like twins down there, I thought, me and Una. But only down there. That distinction being the real difference between us.

Now that I'm a mother, I look back differently on that day at the pipe. I wasn't a wimp. On the contrary, the reason I didn't follow Una was not because I was afraid of life, but because I <u>valued</u> life. It was Una who had no regard for it, because precious few people had ever had regard for her.

In your letter, you told me that the trail on Una had gone cold – 'dead' was the word I think you used – so it's impossible to know if she ever had children of her own. This may sound harsh, but I hope she never did. In a way, the Cruickshanks were a lot like this estate falling to pieces around me now. Just not up to supporting multiple generations.

Tired now. More soon.

Jean.

Dear Stephan,

What did you want to be when you grew up? Not what you became, I imagine. How many bairns dream of becoming art dealers? In my day, boys aspired to be train drivers and girls wanted to get married, or be air hostesses. Personally, my own future was always clouded, though I did do well enough at school to pass my 11+ and get into Thornaby Grammar. This was a real source of pride for my parents, as it was unusual for someone from my background to do that (my sister Agnes hadn't, much to my satisfaction). It also meant I no longer had to go to school with the likes of Elsie Stanger and my other bullies. I met new girls, started making friends.

Una bombed the 11+ and ended up at the secondary modern on the outskirts of the estate, 'Scunner Academy' as my Thornaby friends called it. Not that Una cared. You could have put her on the moon and she would have kept painting those riverbanks. She was focused in a way I would never be. For instance, I used to write. Just silly little stories and poems that I never showed anyone, and which I stopped once I got a bit older and boys came along. Maybe I shouldn't have done that, but giving up was easy because I didn't have the fire the way Una did.

In this respect, Alan is like me. He drifts. Vincent is always on at him to get a job, get a trade, and I try telling him our son just isn't cut out for that kind of thing. Besides, it's 1991. What 'trade' is there? Since I was a lass, the forges have been privatised, consolidated, chopped up, sold off. Why make steel here if it's cheaper to ship from China? Everybody is being made redundant – tens of thousands of people. Whole communities. Ironopolis is falling.

Even so, Vincent says: 'There's always work for a man what can use his hands.' (Vincent's hands are as hard as gravestones. I suspect he likes having parts of himself he can't feel.) He accuses me of mollycoddling our son. And maybe that's true, but I have my reasons.

It isn't motherly bias when I say Alan is one of the brightest people I've ever met. It's just that formal education never sat right with him. When he was fifteen, he had an accident and missed a lot of school. He tried catching up, but it would have been beyond anyone. He did badly in his CSEs, and the NVQs I encouraged him to do afterwards weren't a good fit either, so now he's in limbo like most folk around here. He did recently manage to get a part time job at the library in town, which at least gets him out of the house a few hours a week, but I still worry he'll shrivel up and lose his natural curiosity. I dread he forgets there are other ways to view the world, so thinks the world around him is the only one there is.

So I do my part to keep him engaged. For example, I have him bring home books from the library for him to read to me. Unfortunately for him, I have something of a weakness for the Danielle Steeles' and Jackie Collins' and, yes, the Mills and Boons' of this world, so we alternate those with books of his choosing. Alan hoovers up everything: astronomy, science, history, someone called Neecha (is that the spelling?). I'm not ashamed to admit most of it sends me cross-eyed. At the minute, we're learning about bridges. Did you know that in 1885, a woman threw herself off the Clifton Suspension Bridge (245ft) because she'd had a fight with her boyfriend, only for her big floaty Victorian dress and frilly underthings to slow her fall enough for her to survive? Tell me Stephan, does that count as being unlucky in love?

What am I on about? I'm trying to tell you about the library van.

Me and Una were bookworms, but while she liked reading about trapped riveters, I preferred more traditional stories. Enid Blyton was my thing: 'The Famous Five,' 'The Wishing Chair,' 'Naughty Amelia Jane,' and 'Mr Twiddle.' My favourite was 'The Magic Faraway Tree,' because of the helter-skelter down the centre of the trunk. Mam would climb into bed with me and read until I dropped off. Later, when I got older, I began reading along with her, until soon enough I was tearing through book after book on my own. By the time I got into my teens, I'd moved onto more 'mature' stories like the Marcy Rhodes series, which all my Thornaby friends were reading. They were full of squeaky-clean blondies, torn between two college-bound buzzcut boys – the Quarterback (whatever that was) or the Debate Team Champ (ditto) – as the Big Dance loomed. It was an alien American world that jarred with the one I knew, with the coal scuttles and cups of Bovril with cream crackers crumbled in. The way the back boiler never caught on mornings so nithering the first thing you saw when you opened your eyes was your own breath clouding above you. There were also books in Thornaby Grammar's library with titles like 'Air Hostess Ann,' and 'Emily in Electronics': about young lasses heading out into the World of Work. Usually they ended up leaving their male colleagues in the dust, doing so well that the boss' reward was to marry them and give them a big house full of bairns to look after. Daft, but we just accepted that kind of thing back then.

Every second Wednesday, the mobile library would come down Loom street, and I looked forward to that for two reasons. One, I wanted grown up books, and two, the man who drove that van. Henry. My first real crush.

If Teddy Boys had long since been out of style come the early 1960s, nobody had seen fit to tell Henry. He still booted around in his drape coat and brothel creepers, his hair pomaded into sleek liquorice. Swallow tattoos on his hands where his thumbs and index fingers met. Proper Geordie and proud, he said. Had grown up on Arthur's Hill, a stone's throw from St. James' Park. My name in his mouth did something to me that I still then didn't fully understand. He could make that 'ee' go on forever: Jeeeean…

I couldn't loan silly little girl books from Henry, so one second-Wednesday I put on my best skirt and sneaked a dab of Mam's perfume. I hung at the back of the van, browsing the shelves while Henry served the bairns. He was so good with children. Back then, remember, it was the era of speak-when-you're-spoken-to, of watch-your-Ps-and-Qs, but Henry let them say whatever they wanted. He crouched down to their level, looked them right in the eye, and didn't flinch from their sticky little hands. I didn't know why his being good like that was attractive to me, but it was.

Once most of the bairns were gone, I picked out the thickest book I could find and plonked it down for him to stamp.

He read the title. 'Finnegan's Wake. Its canny big, like.'

My thing at the time was Breakfast at Tiffany's, which me and my Thornaby friends had seen five thousand times at the Ritzy. I fixed him with the coquettish pout I'd perfected in the mirror, and in my best Audrey, said, 'I suppose you think I'm very brazen or tres fou or something?'

A blank look. I was mortified. He stamped the front page and handed the book back to me. Our transaction was complete.

Desperate to keep talking, I said, 'Have you read it?'

'I'm not a reader.'

'But you drive a library…'

He shrugged.

Someone else was behind me. Henry's eyes moved over my shoulder and I was forgotten.

Oh Jean! Stupid, stupid Jean! I scurried away with my book, on the lookout for the nearest hole to crawl into, but just as I was leaving I heard Henry say, 'I know this one! I saw a film of this.' I looked back.

Henry was turning the copy of 'Frankenstein' over in his hands. He said, 'They stuck a hunchback's brain in his body and he smashed up this posh dinner party.'

'I don't like films,' Una said, popping her elbow.

He looked at her strangely, a slow smile spreading. 'Who doesn't like films?'

'I don't want their pictures in my head.'

'You're a serious one, aren't you?' He stamped the book and held it out to her, but when she took it he didn't let go.

'And you,' Una said, 'are you serious?' Her voice was low and fluid in a way that unsettled me. Her eyes on his, the book trembling between them.

'Where it counts,' he said, letting go.

Neither of them seemed to be aware of my presence. I felt like a Peeping Tom, a creep.

'Tell me how it ends, eh?' he said.

I left the van and stalked home, my fingernails digging into the cover of my ridiculous book. What had just happened? Here was the one area I felt sure I had the better of Una, and yet everything I thought I knew about boys had somehow just been brushed aside by her flinty weirdness. She didn't even have a chest!

Which is, Stephan, all to say that I was out of my mind with jealousy.

I have to go. Alan's bringing the tea up now. Tonight, we're tackling some of the new Judith Krantz (Alan's birthday gift to me – I turned 45 a couple of weeks ago. Vincent got me the black dress from Selfridges I've had my eye on). Krantz-wise, I'll bring you up to speed: Eve was all set to become an opera singer before she defied her family and ran off with a music-hall crooner. But then he got pneumonia, and Eve was a smash when she started singing to pay the bills. Now this posh lad Paul de Lancel is sniffing about Eve. Not sure what his snooty family will make of it when he inevitably makes his move…

There's been a few racy bits. Alan gets a little flustered in places, bless him.

As always,

Jean.

Dear Stephan,

When we were about fourteen, Una's mother Talitha hit a rough patch and never quite recovered, although that we realised only in retrospect. Una had already told me what little she knew about her mother. When Talitha was about the same age we were then, she, along with her five brothers and sisters, were preparing to escape Poland to some distant Teesside relative, just as their country became a bloodbath. I've had Alan read me the history. In September 1939, the German armies advanced from the west, bombing and burning and slaughtering at random. Terrified Polish civilians fled east, only to run smack into the Red Army, who had signed a pact of non-aggression with the Nazis. Millions were lost: men, women, and children were massacred, raped, or worked to death in Siberian gulags. Twenty thousand souls per mass grave. Over three million Polish Jews alone erased in the Final Solution.

But what the books don't explain is how Talitha, a teenage girl who had previously never left her home town, could be swallowed up by such atrocity only to reappear on British shores three years later, clutching in a hand that was missing a ring finger a scrap of paper with her second-cousin's address on it. Those three years – where had she been? How had she survived where millions perished? What had happened to her parents? Her brothers and sisters? It was a mystery not even Una knew. Then, three months after her arrival on Teesside, the now eighteen-year-old Talitha met and married George Cruickshank, a young private. She fell pregnant just before he was shipped to

Sicily, where he lasted less than six months. When George came back he wasn't, as they say, the same.

Those were the facts as I knew them, but facts, as you know, aren't everything.

The last time I talked to Talitha was in the summer holidays a year after I'd started Thornaby, which would make it 1961. I wasn't seeing as much of Una by then, and my accumulated guilt eventually drove me to knock on her door one morning to see if she was in. Talitha answered, which was exactly what I hoped wouldn't happen.

The kitchen reeked. From the ceiling hung flypapers so loaded with bluebottles that they sagged like rank party streamers. Lino filthy. Sink clogged with dirty crockery. I declined tea, but she started making it anyway. Her loose-fitting dressing gown was Chinese in style, stitched all over with their funny writing. It kept falling open to reveal a stained chemise through which her large, dark nipples showed.

Kids always say the same laced-up things to their friend's parents, and I was no exception: 'How's Mr Cruickshank, Mrs Cruickshank?'

And any other friend's parent would have given a laced-up response, but this was Talitha: 'Oh, don't get me started on <u>him</u>. Laziest creature in all of Christendom, <u>him</u>. Promised me we'd live in a palace – sit, sit, <u>sit</u> – but is this a palace?' – she crouched to look in a cupboard for clean cups – 'This concrete coffin? This cement maze? People's googly eyes oogling through my windows, the nosey parkers!'

Was that directed at me? I liked a good look through a window.

Talitha put cups on the table. 'And that's not all,' she said. 'I <u>see</u> things.'

'What things, Mrs Cruickshank?'

She planted fists on the dirty tablecloth. The sleeves of her gown rose to reveal scarecrow arms laced with powder-blue veins. Stark black hairs against blanched skin.

'The dead,' she said.

'Is Una upstairs, Mrs Cruickshank?'

'The dead are everywhere round here,' she said. 'Trapped. Buried. Do you ever feel like that?'

'Like…what, Mrs Cruickshank?'

'Like we're all piled on top of each other? One mass grave?'

I was fourteen. What could I say?

Talitha shooed a fly from the sugar bowl. 'But all that idiot' – George, I guessed – 'does is moon about all day, staring into the aether.' The kettle jittered and whistled on the stove, but Talitha wasn't done. 'He's upstairs right now. Cosmonaut Cruickshank! And I think to myself, will I escape the Never-Never? Ever? Never! I take care of everything round here, it's true. George, I say, George – there's only so much I can hock, only so many times I can put the rent man off.' She looked sideways at me as she lifted her gown. 'Still,' she said, patting her crotch, 'a woman has her ways.'

Thank God she was wearing knickers.

Her hair was heaped high on her head, stabbed through with a knitting needle. She wrapped the handle of the shrieking kettle in a crusted tea towel and lifted it off the gas. 'War's over, I say. War's over! Hello! It's been over twenty bloody years! So what if all your pals are in bits? You think you're a special case?'

She slopped scalding water into the pot and sat down across from me, not caring how her gown gaped. An awful thought occurred – what if Una wasn't here? What if Talitha and I were all alone?

She stirred the pot with the handle of a butter knife. 'So I said to him, I said, what are you going to do about it, husband dear? How long are you going to weep? You have to think about the future because the future's <u>coming</u>. It's getting bigger every day. It might even be here already, not that you'd know. Time to get off your arse!' She smiled conspiratorially. 'But I'm wasting my time, Jean, really I am. I'd get more sense out of a maggoty old corpse than that man. Imagine!'

She was wearing makeup, but not that day's makeup. Cords stood out in her neck. She licked her lips and it was obscene.

'You're becoming a very pretty woman,' she said.

I blushed. 'Thank you.'

'No,' she said, 'I mean it. I was a beauty once too, so I know.' She snatched across the table and gripped my hands. Her nails were splintered, gnawed. The stump of her ring finger puckered at the end. She said, 'So don't let those fuckers take it from you.'

I fought panic. 'I won't, Mrs Cruickshank.'

'Call me Talitha. Una needn't worry, but <u>you</u>, I'm warning <u>you</u>. Because they'll try.'

'I'll remember that…Talitha.'

'They're pig ugly.' She loomed at me through the teapot steam. 'Ugly like <u>pigs</u>.'

'Thank you.' I pulled my hands from hers.

'<u>Oink</u>.'

And then, just like that, she was pouring tea and smiling and none of it had happened. The room spun. I heard the blessed sound of Una pounding down the stairs and into the kitchen. Mother and daughter fired flurries of Polish at each other, while I thanked Talitha for my untouched tea and made for the door.

Outside, warmth and reality were waiting. Una popped her elbows. 'What did she say?'

'Nothing. We were just chatting.'

'I hate her. Can I stay with you tonight? I can't take another one of her sprongs.'

Sprongs. Una's name for the times her mother acted strangely, as in: 'She sprong and tipped over a display of washing powder in the shop today.' Or, 'She sat in the yard all night in the rain, spronging out.' Talitha would get this look in her eyes, and you just knew. It was the look she'd had at our N.Y.E party. And they were getting worse, too, Talitha's sprongs.

Once I asked Una what she thought their root was.

'The war,' she'd said, as if those two tiny words stood for all the unfathomable madness in her house.

And who's to say they didn't?

Now please don't think I'm weird when I say that you, Stephan, might be the only friend I've got left. A person I've never even met. Leanne Dawson lives on Windhorst Avenue, and me and her have been friends ever since her boy Richard started playschool with my Alan. We'd go for a coffee every day after we dropped them off. I made the cake for her youngest Tori's christening. Then there's Rita from down the street, who I've known these past fifteen years. Michelle and Sally I've known since we were all bairns. I even went to Thornaby with Michelle, and I can count on one hand the amount of times they've all been round to visit me.

I thought, maybe I had some sort of massive personality flaw. One so big it was hiding in plain sight. I mean, you meet folk like that sometimes, don't you? Folk oblivious to their own awfulness. But no, I wasn't having it. I knew the real reason: Vincent. See, he's always tried hiding parts of himself from me, but I'm not daft. His 'late nights' at the garage, the shady men who slip in the back door when they think I'm asleep. I've heard all sorts of whispers about him (which, for your sake, I won't get into).

Earlier in our marriage, I used to invite couples round for dinner on Friday or Saturday night. Nice and neighbourly, nothing flash, but the excuses were knuckle-chewing. So many weddings of never-before-mentioned cousins that had to be attended, or bairns that suddenly came down with chickenpox for the second or third time. This, I'm sure, is also the reason Alan had such a hard time making friends growing up. The parents saw him as a proxy Vincent and warned their children to keep away.

I'll admit that this hurt, but I was able to console myself with the fact that it was Vincent they really wanted to avoid. Not me or Alan. They liked us. But then I remembered how Loom Street had treated the Cruickshanks. Nobody ever popped their head round Talitha's door for a cup of char and a natter. I recalled the cruel bets down the Labour Club as to the whether or not George wore a nappy to bed (we heard they'd found him in the burned-out cellar of some ruined Sicilian café. His whole squad had been wiped out, and he'd been down there for days, alone in the dark. Climbing the walls). You see, nobody was interested in the personal hardships experienced by George or Talitha, nor did they see Una as the tragic sum of both. No, to Loom Street, the

43

Cruickshanks were just that lot at Number 1. All of them lumped together.

Which makes me wonder, is that how people now see me? See us?

Later that night, after we'd escaped Talitha's kitchen, me and Una had a conversation. I think it will interest you, Stephan, considering how you discovered Una's work. The two of us lay squashed together in my single bed, and I was just drifting off when she whispered, 'We should be artists when we grow up.'

I thought about my art classes at Thornaby. My flat watercolour fruit and wonky charcoals, my kiln-fired deformities. 'We should?'

'Aye, and we can move to Paris and get rooms in the Le Bat-ee-uh La-voy-eer. That's where all the artists lived. That's where Modigliani lived.'

'Who's he?'

'A dead good painter. We'll paint masterpieces in the day, and drink red wine and smoke cigarettes and have affairs all night. We'll always have paint on our clothes.'

'Can we go up the Eiffel Tower?'

Una's breath tickled my neck. 'But the best thing is nobody'll know we paint these beautiful paintings. They'll think we're just scruffs, so they won't give us the time of day.'

'We're scruffy?'

'And then, then we'll die – because they all died young – and they'll find hundreds and hundreds of paintings in our room, and they're better than owt anyone's ever seen before. They put them in galleries all over the world, and the people who hated us before, they'll realise they wasted their chance to know us.'

'We'll have to speak French,' I said. 'We do French at my school. Do you do it at yours?'

'I'll learn when I'm there.'

'Oiseau, that means bird,' I said.

'Then our sculptor friends'll make a statue of us and put it in the town square so every day the people have to see it and be reminded of how boring and afraid of everything they are.'

'Dog is chien.'

At some point I slept and dreamed of the riverbank. The mist was so dense I lost my hand at the wrist when I reached into it. Cold black mud slipped between my toes, and I was naked. I shlurped my way down to the water, through reeds ghosting my goosebumpy skin. The world wrapped tightly around me, no boundary at all between river and fog. I stood in the water up to my ankles. Despite the cold, I wanted to swim, wanted to be inside this place. But I hesitated. Hadn't someone warned me about rivers? I climbed up through the reeds and walked into the mist, the river to my back. I'd never been naked outdoors before and it was exhilarating. I felt a strange churning inside me, an arousal. Blindly, I walked on until I heard the rustle of reeds and soon found myself at the riverbank again. Had I walked in a circle? I turned and went carefully back the way I'd come, reaching the reeds a third time. My crotch throbbed. It got harder to think. I sprinted aimlessly into the fog, ears roaring, hair streaming, mud splattering my back and bum, and I didn't stop until I was at the reeds once more. This made no sense. I caught my breath, worked my way down to the water and sat on a tangle of exposed willow root. Somewhere out in the fog, I was being

45

watched, but my sex was throbbing so monstrously I could no longer deny it. I touched myself. My ragged breath moved in and out with the river at my feet. A pressure began building, and I went with it until I cried out into the fog. Then, when I had myself back under control, I wrapped my arms around my shins, closed my eyes and slept.

I woke up with my back to Una, our curved spines touching. Early morning light strained through the curtains and I felt incredible. I'd always been a fitful sleeper, but that was the deepest I'd slept in my whole life. When I slipped fingers between my legs, I was wet.

I'm not trying to embarrass you here, Stephan. Only now I've started writing, I think it's important to include absolutely everything. That's what you wanted, wasn't it? This dream – this riverbank – I know you know it from the paintings she left behind, but I wonder if you've ever gone there like I did that night? And if so, did you feel that maybe, for the first time in your life, you were special? Chosen for something more?

Your friend,

Jean

Dear Stephan,

Sponge baths: all they do is make you aware of the bits you didn't sponge. About a week ago, I slipped getting out the bath and cracked my head on the toilet. I woke up bent on the bath mat as Vincent hoofed the door off its hinges. He didn't want me having any more baths, he said, unless he was there to wash me. When I refused, he brought me buckets of soapy water and waited outside my bedroom door. I tried it once, to humour him, but I felt like a Ford Cortina. So I put my foot down – I can be a twisty mare when I want to be. I asked him: when you want privacy, how many locked doors can you put between yourself and the world? Maybe the question touched a nerve because he gave in, but on the proviso I take a dinner bell in with me to ring if I feel a spell coming on. So long story short, this afternoon I had my first bath in days, and I can't tell you how good it felt. I even managed to snaffle my Kate Bush tapes back off Alan, and listened to 'Never for Ever' as the water turned grey.

When I stood to get out of the bath, I saw myself reflected in the mirror, what the cancer and the chemo had done. Nana's words: 'You could see her workings under what little flesh she had left – the bones, sinews, tendons.' I touched my pallid and thread-veined thigh. This body, somehow, was mine, but inside I was still me. The two truths superimposed and a wave of dizziness rushed over me, only the threat of Vincent's sponge bucket kept me upright. Still, I couldn't turn away, and suddenly I knew why Nana had said Peg was beautiful. Beauty and decay do not exist independently from each other. The one comes from the other, and it is us – people – who, out of ignorance or fear, insist on their separation. Peg collapsed all that. She was both what we want and fear most, and, like me in the bathroom mirror, we are powerless to look away.

I don't like false modesty, so let me say that I used to be a looker. By the time I was fourteen, I'd somehow emerged from my chub to sport a perfect hourglass figure and a 36C bust. Believe me, it was as much to my surprise as it was Mam and Agnes' when I started turning heads. I liked it when I caught men looking because who doesn't want to be wanted?

There was a handful of estate girls who'd got into Thornaby with me. We were girly girls and most of my money from my afterschool job at Woolies went on zippy-dresses, Maxi coats, Playtex girdles. There was a shop in the city centre that sold Ginger Group clothes, and we would have killed to afford those. My goal was to save up for one of their gabardine dresses. Some of the more well-off girls at Thornaby wore Ginger Group, and they made fun of us estate lasses, but that just made us closer. There were four of us – me, Michelle, Kerry, and Bernadette – and every weekend we went to the under 16s disco at Redcar Youth Club to Twist with boys and drop half aspirins into our cokes. I never asked Una to come. My friends called her Mr Tambourine Man, because of her hair. When they said it in front of me – laughing – I didn't correct them.

Another upshot of my transformation was that I was finally initiated into Mam and Agnes' beauty sessions. The three of us staying up nights, setting our hair, tweezing and bleaching and slathering our faces in Cold Cream. It was important to look your best, Mam said, because while true beauty <u>might</u> be on the inside, who'd hang round long enough to see it if the rest of you was a dog's dinner? So I smoothed down my sidelong figure in the mirror, tapped my chin ten times before bed with the back of each hand, just like Mam. She taught me all sorts: how to conceal spots, what colours made my eyes pop and, of course, periods. I think she was just relieved that I was, after all, turning into the kind of woman she understood.

Thornaby didn't allowed makeup, so we'd put it on at home in the mornings, to wear on the bus for the boys. You'd see us huddled together at the gates, peeling off our falsies and wiping our cheeks with spitty tissues. Daft, perhaps, but it worked. I remember sitting on my bed one Valentine's Day, reading Una all my cards from the Thornaby boys (it was a mixed Grammar, but we were kept on the other side of the grounds so were forced to arrange meetings through a complicated system of notes and whispers like in P.O.W. films). I read Una all the awful poetry, stuff that rhymed 'Jean' with 'queen' and 'most beautiful girl I ever seen' until she groaned and toppled to the floor like she was gutshot.

Despite the attention I was getting, I was sexually naïve. I knew where babies came from, of course, but the act itself was this far-off, abstract thing. Sex education at school consisted of medical-looking diagrams of reproductive systems that more resembled B-movie Martians than anything Down There. My own equipment certainly didn't look like that! And the gulf between the two confused me. About the act itself, I had a murky concept of skin on skin, an invasion of some kind. Something Mam and Dad had done, did. At night, I sometimes let my hands wander, but even in that not-too-distant past, masturbation was still very much entangled with blindness and madness. God Himself frowning as thunderclouds boiled up behind Him.

I was too embarrassed to speak to Mam, so in the end Una set me straight: 'His dick goes hard then he puts it up you. The first few times it hurts, then it doesn't. He moves it in and out 'til he shoots his spunk – this white stuff what comes out the end – and once he's done that, he won't want to know. And be careful with his spunk 'cause if he does it up you, you get pregnant. That's why you need johnnys. He'll want to put it in your gob, too.'

'The johnny?'

Una rolled her eyes.

Human beings weren't capable of that, were they? And if they were…<u>was I</u>? How did Una know all this?

'Just do,' she said.

Rumours circled Una. Folk shot her looks. Mothers whispered and tutted when we walked past. Lads nudged each other, and men my Dad's age followed her with their eyes (eyes that would usually be on me). I remember being in the newsagent's back when Mrs Connors still ran it, and the old crone slapping Una's change on the counter as if she was afraid of catching lurgy.

In the end, I got it out of Sally Peterson (the same Sally who doesn't visit me now). Sally went to Scunner Academy with Una: 'I heard she goes up the old waterworks with blokes. And not just one bloke, <u>loads</u> of blokes. She does <u>everything</u>.'

And me, doe-eyed Jean, still didn't cotton on. 'What do you mean?'

Sally sighed. 'Shagging, Jean. They take it in turns. She's worse than a dog.'

Did Una know what people were saying? I certainly never told her, though not because I was afraid of her reaction, but because of the pictures the rumours put in my head. I wasn't ready for a world where those things happened. Yes, I put my hair up in a French Twist and stuck my chest out in the mirror. Yes, I practised my Monroe pout, my Hepburn sashay, but for no other reason than that's what I thought girls did for their own sakes. The looks I got, the Valentine cards, to me they were simple confirmations that I was doing everything correctly. What's that chess word? The <u>endgame</u> was something I evidently still couldn't face, even if I did feel its weight pressing.

Oh, there's one more thing I want to tell you about. Mam's dresser, the place where me, Mam and Agnes pampered ourselves. It was <u>voluptuous</u>, Stephan, made with sections of varnished mahogany that slotted together like a Chinese puzzle. On it were rows and rows of creams and tonics and lacquers and oils. Tiny hinged boxes filled with scented powders. Perfumes in etched glass bottles. All kinds of secret compartments. Occasionally, during our beauty sessions, I'd glimpse the book Mam kept in one of the drawers, tucked away with her frillies. The bookworm inside me started wriggling, so one Saturday night while Mam and Dad were down the Labour Club, and Nana snored her head off downstairs, I snuck in and grabbed it. The book was called 'Beguiling Femininity.' Opening it at random, I read:

"A mother can become an artist, and an artist a mother; but a woman who is artist alone exhibits to an empty gallery."

51

I went through the whole thing cover to cover and had it back in the drawer before my folks got home. I showed it to Una once, too. You'll see what she thought of it next time.

Right. I know this is crackers, but I think I might have another bath. My fingers are un-pruning. Unacceptable!

Jean x

Dear Stephan,

Sorry this has taken so long, but I've been ill. I won't bore you with the details, but it boiled down to swapping white tablets for yellow capsules. I'm necking so many pills these days, most of them just to counteract the side effects of other pills again. It's a balancing act. It's Buckaroo! Me and Alan used to play that for hours when he was a bairn. I think it's still in the loft somewhere.

But staying positive is half the battle, so to that end I got Alan to bring home some brochures from the travel agents. I want to go somewhere while I still have the strength. There are so many places I'd love to see: the Taj Mahal, the Golden Gate Bridge, Machu Pichu, the Northern Lights…but deep down I know they're all too far away and too expensive. But somewhere closer to home could be possible. The Amalfi coast looks lovely, and I've never been to Paris. My only trip abroad was Majorca the week Elvis died. 'Love Me Tender' on every radio. Still the only Spanish I know: El Rey es muerto.

Back in the 1960s, Australia wanted British people to emigrate, and I always thought that sounded like an adventure. I'd seen Australia in books. Ayres Rock, maroon at sunset, looked magical.

Una didn't agree. 'I want to go to places that aren't in books,' she said.

'Like where?'

'Dunno. They aren't in the books.'

I was on the floor, painting my toenails. Una bent over my dresser, fingering my bottles and creams.

'But Australia's as far from England as you can go,' I said. 'It's tomorrow there already, and water goes down the plughole backwards.'

Una sniffed my bottle of Aqua Manda. 'All you'd be doing is swapping this grey drudgery for their sweaty one.' She grabbed 'Beguiling Femininity' from my bookcase (Mam had recently given it to me, obviously thinking me ready for its teachings), brandished it like a Bible and she a priest at an exorcism. 'They'll have this shite down there n'all. Her what wrote it's fucked in the head.'

I've never been a fan of the f-word. I said, 'What's wrong with keeping house and looking nice for your husband? He has his duties too, you know. Marriage is a partnership.'

Una flopped face down onto the bed. 'I'd rather top myself.'

'For a family to function, it's important that men and women know their duties.'

Blankets muffled her voice. 'Twice you've used that word.'

'Because if they don't, the children will–'

'Grow up rotten?'

'That's not what I was going to say.'

She rolled onto her back. 'People think I'm the weird one for seeing this place for what it is.'

'My parents like it here.'

'Do you?'

I thought about it. Or rather, I thought about what I'd already thought about: how I quietly approved of the way Loom Street sloped gently down to Stanhope Street. How it was Michelle's birthday in a couple of weeks, and how we Thornaby girls were going to have a pyjama party and play records and drink the bottle of peach brandy Kerry's big sister had slipped her on the sly. I had daydreams too, which I kept deep down, about having my own home one day. Sunflower wallpaper in the living room, bugger what the council said. I'd throw my own N.Y.E. parties with my own daughter taking the coats, clicking her heels like Dorothy in the Emerald City. I thought about how, when I imagined this future home, it always had the same dimensions as my home on Loom Street.

'This is a good place,' I said. 'And the people are nice. I've got friends here.'

'Your posh-school friends would just love me. They'll make me beautiful, just like <u>you</u>.'

'That's not fair. You don't know them.'

'And why's that, Jean?'

We let that hang in the air. Una lolled her head upside down off the edge of the bed. 'Your Nana's right, you know,' she said. 'People aren't supposed to live like this.'

'When Nana was our age she didn't have running water or central heating or inside toilets or nothing. No council to fix anything. At least now everyone has a nice home.'

Una popped her elbows.

'Will you stop that? It's horrible.'

Her upside-down eyes regarded me seriously. 'Do you remember when I went into that pipe?'

I still had the bramble scar on my wrist. 'Yes.'

'I never told you what I saw down there, did I?'

Feigning disinterest, I finished painting my right toes and moved onto the left.

'It was horrible, Jean.'

I started with the little one.

'Really awful.'

'OK, what?' I said.

'Seriously.'

'<u>WHAT</u>?'

Una closed her inky eyes, 'I saw…<u>nowt</u>, Jean. Absolutely <u>nowt</u>, and this whole estate is <u>built</u> on nowt. Is still being built.' That year, cranes had moved onto the north-western edge of the estate and begun erecting a horseshoe of steel grids that diced the sky as far back as you could tip your head. Soon to be some of the biggest tower blocks in the country, apparently: twenty-two storeys, God knew how many flats. The papers were full of the overcrowding, the ructions, the riots of such places. They weren't built properly, either, slotted together from pre-fabricated slabs. A gas explosion had collapsed a whole side of one in Glasgow, killing dozens. The estate was up in arms, of course – only scunners would be desperate enough to live in such places.

I said to Una, 'Just because you're unhappy here, doesn't mean everyone else is.'

'You think they're happy?'

'Just let me do my nails.'

She framed the air with fingers and thumbs. 'I can see it now, Mrs Jean Sadsack. You do a <u>smashing</u> suet pudding, and know how to get grass stains out. Mr Sadsack knocks you up a few times and your little Sadsacks are As Good As Gold. Well done Jean! Now, all that's left to do is kill time 'til you're a frumpy old biddy with shopping cutting into your fingers.' Upside down, Una's grimace was a grin. 'But the worst thing is, you teach your kids to reset the trap.'

I was so sick of her crassness. So sick of her. My toes doubled through my tears. 'I've got homework,' I said.

Una left without saying goodbye. There was pink nail

varnish all over my little toe: Wee wee wee, all the way home.

Are they happy, my folks? I don't know. They're people, and people aren't the same thing from one day to the next, though my belief now is that happiness is not virtue, but work. It's a constant fight to keep the darkness supressed. I'm pretty sure Una knew this even back then.

Will try not to take so long with next letter.

Jean x

Dear Stephan,

Remember I told you Alan had an accident when he was fifteen? Well, that was a fib. It wasn't an accident, it was attempted murder. Some bullies played a trick on him and he almost fell down a well. Thank God he didn't, but he damaged some important muscles in his leg and won't ever walk right again. The poor soul still has nightmares about it and wakes up screaming. Vincent thumps on the wall when he does and I want to go to him, but I can't. He's twenty-two. He'd be embarrassed.

Me and Alan don't talk about the future. It's just too big and, in some ways, boring. But the other day, as we were watching the telly, I could feel him struggling with something.

Then out it came: 'I'm a horrible son.'

'Why?'

'Because all I can think about is once you're gone, I'm going to be left with <u>him</u>.'

Stephan, what is a mother supposed to say to that?

It used to be different. Vincent didn't leave Alan's side when he was a boy. His firstborn son – nothing on Earth could have got between them, but as time passed they began to repel each other the way magnets do when you point their wrong ends together. It killed me to watch them both struggle with it: the more Alan tried to disappear, the more Vincent denied it and, at some point, his denial curdled. See, Vincent's relationship with his own father, Trevor, had been strained enough to come to blows more than once. Trevor was one of nine men killed in the Upton

Hill blast furnace explosion of 1972, and although he's never said, I know it's always pained Vincent that they never settled their differences. I think he worries about repeating the same mistakes with Alan, but there's anger there, too. He can't help but see his son's withdrawal as a personal slight. An F-you.

At least that's my take. Getting you men to talk about their feelings? Fat chance.

In Alan's eyes, me and Vincent represent two entirely different things, but in my heart of hearts I just don't know. When the police said they weren't going to do anything to the boys who tried to murder my son, I nearly lost my mind. I wanted to <u>kill</u>. Wanted to throttle someone until their eyes filled with blood. The dad of one of the boys actually brought his son round here to apologise, but Vincent...well, he took it out on the dad instead. It was ugly. I knew him, the dad. He's called Bernie, and we even courted for a while before Vincent came along. Bernie is a good man and I never thought I'd wish him harm, but that day I <u>hated</u> him. And as Vincent did that awful thing to him, all I remember thinking was: <u>THIS IS WHAT YOU GET</u>. I've since tried telling myself this bloodlust was just maternal instinct, but I'm not so sure.

When I told my parents that Vincent had asked me to the pictures, Dad put his foot down. 'That lad is headed for bad things.'

I was seventeen, thought I knew stuff. 'You don't even know him.'

'I know his Dad.'

'Vincent's not his Dad!'

'You're too young.'

Mam chipped in, 'She's the same age I was when we met. What would've happened to us if your dad had had his way?'

Checkmate. Dad was lacing up his boots for the nightshift at the steelworks. He'd been on nights for a while by then, and his skin was like rice paper. 'I don't have time for this,' he said, and huffed out.

When he was gone, Mam took me upstairs to do my hair.

Mam is an incredible stylist. Seriously – an artist, and self-taught. On some estates back then it wasn't considered 'respectable' for a woman to earn her own money. Can you imagine? But it was OK here, and she did most of Loom Street. Practical stuff mostly: short back and sides, trims, the odd Ringo or Peggy Moffitt, but for my date I really let her show her chops. We decided on a Mary Quant, who, alongside Audrey Hepburn, was a hero of mine.

While Mam worked, I asked her how she'd met Dad. Isn't it strange how most bairns don't know? It was during the war, she said. Dad worked on Smith Docks and couldn't fight on account of being nearly deaf in one ear. His family lived a few streets over from hers in St Esther, the old slums, and when Dad had leave he'd pal around with Mam's brother, my uncle Neville. That's how she got to know Dad and fall in love. Dad was nearly ten years older, which was apparently the least of the reasons why Mam's dad – my Granddad – was against it. Granddad died before I was born, but from what I can gather he was a hard man with a weakness for greyhounds and a hair-trigger temper. (Not long before Nana passed away, I'd asked her again how she'd got that scar on her ankle. She said he'd thrown a fire poker at her.) Between Granddad and the war, Mam and Dad didn't see much of each other – moonlit strolls weren't exactly advisable. Middlesbrough was one of the first places in England the Luftwaffe targeted, and at night bombs rained. It was scary, Mam said, but also exciting. She was living through something important. When the war ended, Dad was discharged and got a job at Redcar steelworks. They got married and I came along pretty soon after. When they heard about the plans to demolish St. Esther and build the Burn Estate, they put their names on the list.

Isn't it funny how the lives of others go from A to B in a way yours never quite can?

I asked Mam if she was happy.

The comb caught painfully in my hair. 'What makes you ask that?'

'No reason. Just something me and Una talked about once.'

She attacked my tangles with renewed passion. 'That girl…I've been putting off saying this, but I want you to stop seeing her.'

'Why?'

'Jean, love, I trust you. That's why I'm letting you go out with this Vincent boy. I've raised you right so I know you'll be sensible. But Una never had that, and now she's wild. Girls your age can get in trouble. You know what I'm talking about, don't you?'

By then I did.

But Mam needn't have worried. I barely saw Una at all. I had other friends, I was popular and boys liked me. I even had a boyfriend of sorts – Bernie, who I've mentioned. Una didn't fit into any of that. I had no idea what she did anymore, or where she did it, or who with, but that was

OK with me. Her slow fade from Loom Street suited my self-centredness down to the ground.

I say all this to my shame.

Alan has never asked how I met Vincent, so I'll tell you.

I'd just started in the typing pool at Littlefairs Confectionary when Cath Stoker's youngest Betty went missing. Betty was six or so, and my favourite of the Stoker bairns. She had curly red hair and freckles and a gap between her front teeth you could slide a ha'penny through. We used to pin her down and blow raspberries on her belly. A lovely girl. I remember how my heart stopped twenty years later when the film 'Annie' came out. It was like seeing her ghost.

She just didn't come in for tea one night. After the police searches and interviews and whatnot came to nothing, the whole estate turned out to look. Mr Johansson organised Loom Street into teams. He lived down the end and had been a captain on D-Day, or so Dad said. Everybody was there. Well, I say everybody – Talitha and George weren't. But Una was. She'd liked Betty too. It had been a while since I'd seen my friend and she looked thinner and paler than ever. We ignored each other.

My team was sent to search the derelict waterworks. I've mentioned the waterworks in passing a couple of times already, but they deserve more as they are important to this story – <u>my</u> story – in more ways than one. Before the war, the works used to supply the old slums like St Esther, but then the Nazis bombed it and the blackened shell was left to crumble on the eastern edge of the estate. A wide expanse of waste ground surrounded the ruins – piles of rubble and nettles and weeds – the kind of place mothers

62

warned their children to avoid, which of course made it all the more tempting. Alan was terrified of the place when he was a bairn, especially the cement water tower, because the top of it loomed over the houses from wherever you were on the estate. He'd seen 'War of the Worlds' and was convinced the tower was an alien tripod just biding its time, waiting to reactivate and start death-raying all and sundry. Bless him. There was also a well at the works – the same one those horrible boys almost murdered my Alan in, and he hasn't been the only one. For example, only a couple of years ago, some young people threw a party – a 'rave' I believe is the term – at the works, which ended in arson and violence, and one poor lad lying crippled at the bottom of that well. I hear the whole place is due to be knocked down and built over soon, and it's about bloody time.

Anyway, back to Betty Stoker. Our team spread out when we got to the waterworks, and I found myself on the wasteland, in a clearing of weeds. The well was there. In those days, it still had a metal safety grille over it. I hadn't been to the well in years, but as bairns me and Una had sometimes lain across it, our ears pushed between the bars, listening to the rising whispers from below. I thought I could still hear something, and I considered spreading myself across the drop once more but there were too many neighbours nearby, calling for Betty, so I moved on.

I'd never liked the waterworks itself. Secretly, I was half-convinced it was slowly coming <u>out of</u> the ground, like a tooth, rather than sinking into it. The sun had a hard time inside. Bombs had blackened the walls and left them ripe for collapsing on you, like in one of Una's ghost stories. Rusted water valves stuck out of the floor like the taps of giants. Inside the main hall, tumble-down inner walls and bird-crapped columns held up nothing. I saw a couple of old, shrivelled johnnys on the ground where two corners of a wall came together. I called out for Betty and the sound mushroomed horribly.

Vincent stepped from around a corner and made me jump.

'She's not here,' he said.

I knew who he was. Every year my parents dragged me and Agnes to church on Remembrance Sunday, where he'd be with his family. His oldest brother had been in the RAF and was lost somewhere over Germany. I always thought Vincent looked handsome in his suit.

'She's only six,' I said.

He smiled. 'When I was a bairn, I'd get up every tree, in every ditch. Bairns will be bairns. She'll turn up.'

He was tall and muscular with thick black hair – no beard as yet – broad shoulders, and a pair of eyes I've never seen the like of since. The unearthliest of blues. When he turned them on me, all thoughts of Bernie vanished. I felt myself colour. What did it say in 'Beguiling Femininity' about 'decorum'?

'You're Jean Healy from Loom Street,' he said, coming closer.

So he knew my name.

He said, 'You come up here much?'

'Not since I was a girl. Do you?'

He toed the condoms with the tip of his boot. 'Not really.'

A pigeon flapped in some high-up crack.

He said, 'Do you like films?'

'I love Audrey Hepburn,' I said.

There was a scraping behind us. I thought it was a rat,

but it wasn't – it was Una, stepping out from shadows so black they seemed solid. Maybe I imagined it, but just for a second her eyes met Vincent's and something passed between them. Then she walked outside, into the light.

Vincent watched her go, mouth set hard, but when he returned his attention to me, he was all smiles again. 'So what about Saturday?'

My Mary Quant was magnificent, Stephan. I have a photo somewhere I wish I could find to send you. Vincent took me to the Ritzy to see 'Paris When It Sizzles' and Audrey was perfect, as usual. Afterwards, we went to the Labour Club. I'd only ever been as child and had pop, but that night I drank two halves of lager and lime. I felt so grown up.

So that was the start of us, the beginning of this family. Me and Vincent fast became an item and nobody saw Betty Stoker ever again.

Jean x

30/10/1991

Dear Stephan,

Sorry this has taken so long. I've been in and out of hospital. Starting to feel a bit better now, but I couldn't write. Hope you understand.

My bowel ruptured. I woke up screaming the night it happened. They had to carry me out on a stretcher, the whole street gawking in their slippers and nighties. And despite the pain I was in, I was still reminded of the night twenty-five years ago, back on Loom Street, when they finally came for Talitha.

It was the blue lights that had drawn us into the street. Me and Mam watched from the front yard as they brought out Una's mother slumped in a wheelchair like a penny for the guy.

'Good riddance,' said Mary Eastbourne from Number 8.

They put her in the ambulance and drove away. Everyone went indoors. I looked over at Una's house. George and Talitha's bedroom light was on and George was at the window, staring up the street in the direction of the ambulance. I should go over, I thought. I should see if he is OK. Una too, wherever she was. But then George turned the light out and the house went dark and I didn't go over.

Can't write anymore now. But there isn't much left to tell. I hope I can finish. I hope you're still there.

Jean x

Dear Stephan,

I have donned my pinny once more. A Sunday roast: chicken with bacon across its back and a lemon up its jacksy. Yorkshires, stuffing, roasties, and proper gravy. Really push the boat out. Vincent fussed and buzzed: 'You're not up to it,' 'What if you scald yourself?' As if I couldn't do a roast in my sleep. I had to banish him from the kitchen, but he was right. I <u>didn't</u> feel up to it. It was, however, the only way I could think of breaking the tension that's been building for months now. And a stupid idea, as it turned out, because once the food was on the table, the tension was right there with it. Even worse than ever in fact, as we'd foolishly committed ourselves to at least an hour in close proximity in order to eat it. We scratched knives and forks around our plates in silence. I wasn't hungry in the slightest (I can't eat food like that anymore). Vincent held his cutlery in fists and watched Alan build a carrot dam to keep his gravy from his peas.

Vincent: 'Stop messing with your food.'

Alan: 'I don't like carrots.'

'Your Mam's slaved over this. <u>Eat</u>.'

Alan weakened the dam with the end of his fork. Gravy began oozing through.

Me: 'He doesn't have to eat them if he doesn't want to.'

Vincent threw his cutlery down and glared at Alan. 'Things are going to be different round here after, you mark me.'

Me: 'After what?'

I wonder if people round here would change their minds about Vincent if they could have seen his face then, the way realisation buckled into desolation. We finished the meal quickly, then Alan went upstairs and Vincent washed up. He closed the kitchen door behind him and banged the pots extra loud so I wouldn't hear him cry.

Vincent's love for me has always been unconflicted, unlike mine for him. Sometimes I can't shake the feeling that the main purpose of his love is to put my own discrepancies to shame. Whether this means I think too much or too little of myself, I can't say. Please keep this in mind as you read on.

Just after my eighteenth birthday, Vincent drove me in his brother's car to Guisborough forest for a picnic, where he got down on one knee. I said yes, of course, and for a while my view of the world became unfocused, like it was smeared with a layer of Vaseline.

About a month before the wedding, out of the blue, I got a phone call from Una. I was to meet her at the well, but she wouldn't say why. I almost didn't go but curiosity got the better of me. It was dusk when I arrived. On the other side of the estate the lights in the new high-rise blocks were going on. The buildings glowed like cruise ships and I thought about Una's trapped riveter, beating on the inside of that hull forever.

Una sat cross-legged over the well, smoking. 'I didn't think you'd come.'

'Where've you been?'

She blew smoke. 'Around.'

Crickets chirped in the nettles. Una looked down through the grille into the darkness. Was she whispering something? I didn't care, didn't have time for this. 'You called me, Una.'

'My mother's dead,' she said.

I'd almost forgotten about Talitha. 'How?'

'She did her wrists with a bit of mirror when they weren't watching.'

A sprong too far. I tried to go to Una but she waved me away. 'I just wanted to tell you I'm leaving.'

'Where to?'

She shrugged and dropped the glowing end of her cigarette down the well.

'You've been saying this for years, Una. Where to?'

'I've been telling you for years.'

A bat swooped. I shuddered to think how many there were in the waterworks, dangling from that water tower, unfurling their rawhide wings. I said, 'It's alright to live in dreamland when you're a lass, but we're not lasses anymore.'

'That's right,' she said. 'I hear congratulations are in order. When's the date?'

'Una, I'm sorry about your mam, but you don't have to go. Come back with me.' Even as I said the words, I wasn't sure I meant them.

'Don't marry him,' she said.

I tried and failed to keep my mouth shut. 'And why's that?'

Una popped her elbow.

'God, I haven't even seen you for about a year and now you creep out the woodwork and start with…no, I'm sorry, but you don't have the right.'

She looked up at the darkening mass of the waterworks. 'I know what people say I did in there.'

From a long way off, I could hear mothers calling their

children for tea. A recent thing. For a long time after Betty Stoker, children had been kept indoors.

'I need to know if you believe them,' she said.

'What does it matter?'

'Because if you do believe, you might be capable of understanding.'

'Stop playing games, Una. Understanding what?'

'Me.'

Images Sally Peterson had put in my head: the huddle of grunting, sighing men. The rasp of soles on raw cement. I said, 'I've known you all my life. It was just <u>gossip</u>.'

She nodded slowly. 'Right,' she said.

'I've got to get back.' I started walking away.

'It was me,' she said, climbing off the grille. 'I rang the hospital for them to take her away.'

I stopped. 'Talitha needed help.'

'Maybe,' she said, 'but what if that's not why I did it?'

The older we had got, the harder it had become for me to respond to the things Una said, and it finally happened: I had absolutely nothing to say.

Una's voice cracked. 'The same thing in her is in me. I can <u>feel</u> it. Growing.'

'What do you want me to do?'

'Come with me.'

'Una, I'm getting married.'

'You're my sister. You're the only family I have.' She was close enough now for me to see her tears. All those years and I'd never once seen her cry. She held something out to me, and in the dark I was slow to recognise it. A feather.

'I've already got a family,' I said.

The Earth turned from the last of the light. Una said, 'We saw you on the riverbank. We saw what you were doing.'

I walked away, 'I've got to get back, sorry.'

'Me and Peg, we saw.'

'I've got to go.'

I didn't turn back. It was a few days before I understood the feather.

And that, Stephan, was the last time I ever saw her. I think. Not long after I got married, they finally came for George, and a new family moved into 1 Loom Street. They were, according to Mam, very nice and respectable (unlike the family living there today). I never knew what became of Mr Cruickshank. It was easier not to think about him, so I didn't.

Before I go, I want to say thank you. I've always regretted giving up writing, so this has been important. All these years, I suppose I hadn't quite known how to say what I never quite knew I wanted to say. But I also want to apologise. The more I wrote, the more I realised the impossibility of helping you understand Una. But maybe that's the point. Maybe we aren't supposed to?

If you don't hear from me again, look after yourself.

Your friend,

Jean X

Stephan,

Something's been chewing at me since my last letter, and I can't rest until I've said one more thing.

Did I believe what Una was implying about herself and the waterworks? From the choice she offered me, did I choose correctly? Have the years proven me to be the cowardly fool I've always suspected she thought me to be?

I'd like to answer these questions by saying this: in a minute my son is coming in with the tea tray to read me the last of 'Zoya' by Danielle Steel, and at that moment all of the above – all of my letters to you, in fact – will mean absolutely nothing.

This time it really is goodbye.

X

Stephan,

I've been trying to find the strength to write. Not sure how long I've got left, so if I don't now I never will. Sorry my handwriting is a state. It's taken me all day to persuade Vincent to go over his brother's to see in the New Year. He didn't want to leave me, but as you know, I can be a twisty mare. Alan didn't go. He's in his room.

I know you only ever wanted to know about Una, and I ended up hijacking our letters more and more, but there's something else I need to say. I've got nobody else I can tell and the thought of being buried with it is unbearable.

Me and Vincent married in June 1967, and moved onto Vivienne Avenue. Back then it was almost unheard of to get a house on the estate without children, but Vincent said he knew someone at the council. It was my first inkling that perhaps things were not entirely kosher with my new husband, but the prospect of my own home meant I stifled curiosity. Then, not long after, Vincent was given twelve months for handling stolen vehicles. A fit up, he claimed, though the evidence seemed convincing enough.

Once he was in prison, his family swarmed me. His mother Doris would come round and sit night after night, playing endless games of Patience. Eddie and Curley, his two surviving brothers, dropped in almost every day to force greasy wads of money on me. I told them I was working full time at Littlefairs. I didn't need their money.

'But why slave away?' Curley would say. 'Maybe you should wrap in?'

Eddie: 'We saw you in town the other day, talking to some fella. Work pal, is he?'

They would nose around while they chatted, opening cupboards and drawers. Eddie would keep me talking while Curley 'nipped to the loo,' but I could tell from where the ceiling creaked that he wasn't spending a penny.

Vincent had put them up to it, of course.

Then, a couple of days before Vincent was due to be released, I was doing the washing up and found myself saying her name for the first time in years: 'Una.' What if I'd gone with her that night at the well? Would I now be smoking little French cigarettes in some Parisian loft? Would I be in the arms of some dark-eyed lover? Would oiseaus one day have nested on my bronze crown?

I lay on the settee, dozed off, and found myself in fog. The riverbank was the same as when I was a girl. The reeds, the thick black mud between my toes, all the same. Only my naked body had changed. I worked my way down to the softly lapping river and waded in as far as my knees. I couldn't see a thing.

Something moved out in the water.

'Una?' I said.

Nothing. I listened – Splash.

'…Peg?'

I had just enough time to see her shape – whoever <u>she</u> was – break the river's surface before I woke up.

I was aroused. I ran my hands over my body and static crackled. Something was strange. According to the carriage clock on the mantelpiece, it wasn't even noon, yet the room was dim. I looked out of the window at the greenish-black clouds piling up in the sky, and it crossed my mind I'd somehow brought the riverbank with me back into reality.

The library van drove past my window and parked at the end of the street. I didn't make a conscious decision, I just left the house. In the van, I browsed the shelves like the girl with a crush I'd once been. Henry's eyes followed me the whole time as he joked with the children and stamped their books. The swallows on his hands flexed as if beating their wings. His hair was still ducks-arsed, but greying at the temples.

He leaned out of the door as the first drops of rain rattled across the roof. 'Come on kids. Best you be off afore it really comes down.'

When the last child had left, I handed him 'Finnegan's Wake.'

'I never finished this,' I said.

He smiled slowly.

Thunder cracked open the sky as Henry closed the doors, burying us alive in books.

The Day of the Dark: the worst storm in living memory. I don't how long it raged, but when I finally emerged, bins and trees and debris lay scattered across the road. Windows shattered, entire rooftops ripped off. Fist-sized hailstones bobbed in the gutters. Henry's van looked as if it had been machine-gunned. I went home and we never spoke again.

Vincent got out of prison two days later. Nine months after that, Alan was born.

I've never told anyone this.

*

It's later than I thought. I can hear voices in the street. This time it really is goodbye, Stephan. I'm going to call Alan now and see out the year with him. I think there's still time. Like I said at the start, the last moments are always the most exciting.

Happy New Year,

X

THIS
ACID
LIFE

Jim Clarke of Hessle Rise

I

If you're from around here, he won't require introduction. But for the rest of you, a vignette: watch as he pitches through the darkening street – his right hand throttling his crutch, the dead spider of his left swinging in the wind; that gurgle in his chest like a clogged sink. Peek through your fingers as his momentum takes him too-fast around the corner and – *whallop* – into the girl.

She's barely three years old, gawps up at him with whatever blue, E-numbered glop she's been eating smeared around her mouth. For one febrile moment neither party moves but then, around his smashed head, the wind whips the straggles of his remaining hair into a mindless swarm and the girl *howls*. He staggers into a nearby lamppost, almost pole-axing the poor child with his tumbling crutch.

Mother scoops up child. By the looks of her, she's only in her early twenties.

He closes his eyes.

'*Freak*,' she hisses, pushing her mewling daughter into her breasts as she kicks his crutch further away. She steps into the road to give him the widest of berths. 'You're fucking *cracked*.'

The lamppost smells like urine, and only when he's sure they're gone does he open his eyes. His useless left hand dangles hopelessly in the wind. His crutch in the gutter a long, long way away.

So perhaps you know of him, but what is his name? While you may be aware of the many cruel sobriquets that followed like carrion birds in his wake – *The Freak* was one; *Rocky* another (a reference not to the Stallone franchise, but rather Eric Stoltz in the film *Mask*) – what of the name bestowed upon him by his mother? You don't know? Well, today this wrong will be righted. Today his true name shall be known, and that name is Jim.

His name was Jim.

Jim passes the building site that was once Loom Street, then onto Stanhope Street, then Mill Road, the stink from his pulled-up Parka collar rising. Teenagers mooch around the phoneless phone box, but it's too late for Jim to volte-face. They've spotted him.

The first stone strikes the wall ahead, the second clips the pavement at his heel, the third bullseyes his elbow, right on the hinge of bone. *Move!* He tangles feet in crutch as more stones arc against the lowering sky, only just swerving onto Bathurst Drive to escape.

A brick wall frosted with shards of pitted glass protects the electricity transformer. It looks like a contraption a demented scientist might tear a dustsheet from in the B-movies he used to obsess over, its concentric coils of steel sprouting into a late November sky. The *Missing* poster is pasted to the wall. Someone has torn it so only the top half of Lily Butler's head survives, but her photocopied eyes glower at him. Knowing eyes.

Jim catches his breath. His elbow throbs, but there's no time to lick wounds.

Sticks and stones, etc.

Full dark by the time he drags himself to his flat on Hessle Rise, and his top lip is crusted with snot. He jitters the key into the lock just as a voice says his name. The only person left to say his name.

Corina, his sister.

'Where the hell've you been?' she says. 'I've been ringing.' Wearing only a denim jacket, she hugs herself against the night like that schoolyard game where, from behind, it looks like you're Frenching.

'Fat Gary's,' he says. 'I needed batteries.'

He sees her see the damage to his front door. Red paint splatters, the zigzagging cracks across the glass.

'What this?' she asks.

'Nowt. Kids. Twats.'

'Are you going to let me in? I'm *brass*.'

He hobbles past the toilet and the closed living room door, towards the kitchen, praying she'll follow. Corina has a habit of poking her head through doors just to see what's what, but if she tried that now, questions such as *Why's your living room locked? What've you got in there?* would be raised. Bad questions. Very bad questions. But she doesn't even glance at it. In his kitchen, she opens cupboards.

'There's nowt in,' she says. 'What do you eat?'

'Soup.'

'You're thinner every time I see you.'

He sheds his coat to reveal a grey, sweat-stained T-shirt beneath which his bones and humps and gnarls are visible. His head a baroque pearl gleaming under the strip light. He feels his sister's eyes on him as he starts making tea; his reduced hand shoving cups around the counter top.

'Let me,' Corina says, but when he doesn't respond she doesn't offer again.

They watch the kettle boil in silence. There's milk in the fridge but it's separated. Corina, at the small kitchen table, takes her cup in both hands. 'Black's fine,' she says.

He lowers himself into the chair opposite.

'Radio reckons there's thousands of sheep up in Scotland suffocating under snow drifts,' she says. 'They say it's the coldest winter since 1960-something.'

'I hate the cold.'

'Is your heating on?'

He doesn't answer. The hot cup in his chapped hands sends skewers of pain through cold bones. Corina hunches over her own drink, blowing steam. 'You heard any more about your incapacity review?' she asks.

He shakes his head.

'Fucking DWP. Do you want me to get onto them?'

'I can do it.'

'What about finding a new place? Have you started looking yet?'

'I'm going to.'

Corina starts to say something, stops, takes a breath. 'Jim, you need to get a move on. It's no picnic – just ask my clients. You need to be on the computer every single day.'

'I don't have a computer.'

'Talk to the council, they'll register you. Do you want me to–'

'I can *do* it.'

'Fine,' Corina snaps. 'But there's less places going if you live on your own. Loads less. From what I hear, they're shifting people miles away.'

'Shame I can't come and live with you guys.'

Corina's clear, green eyes find his. 'What's that supposed to mean?'

'Nowt.'

The wind moans in the window.

Finally, he says, 'Blonde?'

She touches her hair self-consciously. 'Thought I'd try it. What do you think?'

'Suits you.'

'You reckon? I wasn't sure.' She tucks a stray strand behind her ear. The gesture reminds him wonderfully, appallingly, of JJ.

They drink their tea in silence. Or rather, Corina drinks hers. Drinking – like eating – in front of people fills Jim with dread.

She asks, 'So how are you for money?'

'How are *you* for money?'

'Jim, I'm just asking.'

'And I'm just telling.'

All kinds of darkness waves around outside.

'The salon's probably going to close,' she says quietly.

'Why?'

'Like I said, my clients are being rehoused all over, and they won't be coming back. There'll be nowhere for most of them to come back *to*. Not that I can even blame that, really…' She rolls her cup between her palms. 'Besides, it's only a matter of time before they knock everything down.'

'I'm sorry,' he says.

She pushes her drink forward, clasps her hands together as if in prayer. 'Maybe someone's trying to tell me something?'

'What's Max say?'

She looks at him from between raised forearms. 'I wouldn't know. He moved out.'

'When?'

'A while back.'

'Why?'

'It doesn't matter.' There's a fissure in the table's plastic coating. She picks at it with her thumbnail. 'Anyway, I've been thinking about moving on.'

Something colourless and cold spreads its wings in his chest. 'Where to?'

'I don't know.'

'What about Mam?'

'What *about* Mam? Why don't you see her yourself?'

'You know why.'

'Haway Jim, that was half a fucking lifetime ago. You're not a bairn anymore. Every day she drifts further away. Soon she'll not remember us at all.'

'Is she still knitting that thing?'

Corina nods.

'How big is it now?'

'I don't know. Big. Look, just go, OK? They miss you.'

'*They?*'

'Dad, too.'

His bent mouth twitches.

Corina rubs her pink eyes. 'Look, I'm not here to get into this again.'

'Then why are you here?'

She searches his face for something she doesn't seem to find. 'You do know what they're saying about you, don't you?'

'Who? What who are saying?'

'People. *Rumours.*' From her large, overfilled handbag she removes a sheet of paper folded almost into a cube. Fear furs the chambers of Jim's heart as she unfolds it and, suddenly, Lily's eyes are in his kitchen. Stark red text burning like molten steel:

MISSING

LILY BUTLER.

**LAST SEEN 28TH OCTOBER 2015, NEAR CONG BURN.
IF YOU HAVE ANY INFORMATION REGARDING
HER WHEREABOUTS THEN CONTACT
CLEVELAND POLICE ON:
0164 226 0800**

In the accompanying photograph, Lily is no more than ten years old and her skin is smooth and blameless. Hair dark, eyes persecuting. A crudely drawn speech bubble emanates from her mouth:

JIM THE FREEKS GOT ME

The cold, colourless thing in his chest beats its wings. 'Where did you get this?'

'Off the side of the chippy, but there's more. I've been pulling down as many as I can.'

'I've got nowt to do with her.'

'I know, but Jim…people round here don't understand you. Sometimes, frankly, neither do I.'

'You think I'm a freak?'

She touches the back of her hand to her forehead. 'You know I don't, but you're not doing yourself any favours. The way you go on, man, you *scare* people.'

He turns his clawed hand in his lap. 'I wonder why.'

'You know what happens once enough people start gabbing. Who did that to your door? What's going to happen when the likes of Vincent Barr get wind?'

'I didn't do nowt.'

She smokes too much, you can see it in the lines around her mouth. She goes around the table, rests her head on his. He smells, he knows he does, and he's embarrassed, but the sensation of being touched is too precious to forgo.

'I have to get on,' she says. 'Just let me use your loo.'

When Corina clicks shut the toilet door, he snags her bag with the tip of his crutch. The chances of her still having Alive's number – and of Alive still plying the same trade – aren't great, but if they both *did* it would be the final kink straightened in a plan that might very well have no precedent in human history. With his good hand, he rummages to find her old Nokia, scrolls through her contacts and there, there he is! There's no time to scribble down the number, he just barely manages to prod the bag back under the chair before the toilet flushes and Corina returns, drying her hands on her denim buttocks.

She picks up her bag. She seems troubled. 'I'll see you, love,' she says.

He holds his breath to see whether she'll try the living room door, but she doesn't. Once she's gone, he can speak aloud the numbers in his head, '…91 7176, 291 7176, 291 7176, 29…'

Between himself and the blocks stand the empty streets earmarked for regeneration. He passes what was once The Avenues – First, Second, Third, Fourth – now desolate expanses of muck and rubble. A steel fence jangles against the night; signs attached at intervals to its diamond links:

ROWAN-TREE HOMES:
IT'S WHERE YOUR HEART IS.

Beyond that, the blocks burden the sky; huge high-rises with only a scattering of tiny windows glinting amid floors of darkness. Each step toward them increases his anxiety. How many years since he was last there?

His parents live in Asquith House, the block at the apex of a horseshoe of six. He can see them now: Dad steeped in irradiated TV-glow, stubbing out his rollies into his spiralled orange peel. And Mam – Corina had told him about the thing she was knitting; how it collected in folds at her swollen feet. How monstrous it was, how without end.

Alive lives six floors up in Palmerston House, and the lift is kaput. In nuclear orange across its metal doors, someone has tagged: **MONGSTEPA**.

The funk of the place slaps him from across two decades: cold, old piss haunting the stairwells as he climbs. There's another *Missing* poster somewhere in the middle of his ascent, but he dodges Lily's eyes, stopping only to shake a mummified condom from the tip of his crutch. Somehow, he ends up overshooting the sixth floor and is half way along the seventh-floor walkway before he realises. This high up the wind is pitiless. He leans over the side and sees the circle of black earth in the centre of the communal green. A climbing frame had stood there once: the Thunderdome. Lethal, it was. What had happened to it? Doesn't matter. He hobbles back to the stairwell, past dozens of abandoned flats. The urge to step inside one of them, to slide the deadbolt behind him, is overpowering.

He stops. Light and music is coming from a flat. The beat is one he recognises: 'Spinach Power' by MTS! A classic from '89, back when he was young. Back when his heart was still a weightless ball of white light.

87

In the dark and cold – though for that fleeting moment he is unaware of either – he listens.

The walkway halogens on the sixth floor cut and splutter. Jim locates Alive's door and regulates his breathing. The smell of himself rising up out of his Parka is atrocious. He smells like an old man.

'You *are* an old man,' he whispers, and buzzes the doorbell.

The door jolts open on two inches of chain: 'Yeah?'

Jim's voice is saliva-thick, slurred. 'Alive, it's Dave. I rang before, remember? Corina gave me your number.'

The door closes and stays closed. Panic descends, and he's either about to buzz again or flee – he's not quite sure which – when locks revolve and the door opens.

Alive's reaction upon seeing Jim is, unfortunately, textbook: his shoulders jerk back while his head snaps to the side and away, his nose hauling up top lip as it wrinkles: imagine someone taking a whiff of badly gone-off milk. Jim's resolve wobbles. Coming here was a mistake.

But Alive gathers himself quickly. 'Sound. Dave, yeah,' he says, though a little cautiously, pressing himself to the wall to allow Jim entry.

Alive's living room is *exactly* as he remembers it: settees draped in resin-burned ethnic throws, strings of fairy lights drooping against mauve walls heavy with pictures, posters, and photographs. The twin-deck setup in the corner and one entire wall of breezeblock shelves bowing under the weight of three-plus decades of wax. The large, low coffee table is still the same frenzy of ashtrays, stems, rolled-empty B&Hs, and methodically-roached pizza flyers. Even the same cactus on the subwoofer.

Jim centres himself on his crutch. He isn't expecting this. Too much. Too much to take. He'd once been seventeen and beautiful in this room.

'So how d'you know Corina?' Alive says from the doorway, still on his guard.

Struggling to haul himself back into the present, Jim repeats the line he's been practising all the way over. 'Oh, you know, Krissy Mackenzie and that lot. Years ago now.'

Alive seems to relax upon hearing this. Absently, he shows his eyeteeth and scratches his belly. Make no mistake, Alive used to be ripped – did sit ups, pull ups, press ups all day every day. People used to poke at his abdomen, not quite believing he didn't have an oven tray under his vest. Now he is doughier, his kinky black curtains replaced by close-cropped stubble betraying a receding hairline. And yet, there also survived aspects of the man Jim had once known: the same wide-set brown eyes and Roman nose, the same needle-and-bic-ink butterfly tattooed on his left bicep. He was still Alive; still the same man Jim occasionally summons to mind the rare times he masturbates these days.

Alive sits, nods at Jim to do the same, who perches on the arm of the settee.

Alive skins up. His hands move autonomously, perfectly. He says, 'Me and Cor used to kick it quite a bit. She'd come round for a smoke. Is she still doing hair? Last I heard she was doing hair.'

'She's got the salon on the precinct,' Jim says.

'Yeah. Right, yeah.'

'I heard she's moving away, though.'

Alive lights the joint and drags. 'Ah, no way. Where to?'

'I don't know. Just what I heard.'

Smoke leaks from between the gaps in Alive's teeth. 'She was sound, Cor. I knew her little bro, too. He was a proper little raver.'

'I don't think I met him.'

'Didn't Vincent Barr throw him down a fucking well or something? At that rave? Remember that waterworks rave?'

'I don't know,' Jim says.

He offers the joint to Jim, who refuses. Alive exhales slowly and when he speaks, he's speaking mostly to himself. 'Me and Cor drifted apart. I guess that was always on the cards back in them days. You'd just be off on one all the time, you know?'

'I was at Sunrise,' Jim says.

Alive's face lights up. 'No fucking way. Which one?'

'The June one. Midsummer Nights.'

'Mental. I never made it down, but a few mates did. What was it like?'

Jim finds himself smiling. 'We were just…*gone*.'

From within laurels of blue-grey smoke, Alive shakes his head in admiration.

Jim fingers the adjustment holes drilled along his crutch. 'Best days of my life.'

'Tell me to fuck off if you want,' Alive says, 'but can I ask…?' He motions up and down Jim's body with the orange ember of the joint.

'I had a car accident about twenty year ago now. Totally my fault.'

'Shit…' A moment goes by, after which Alive says, 'I'll just go get your stuff.' He leaves in a whorl of smoke while Jim – ignoring the pain in his hip and leg – thuds across the dirty shag carpet to take a closer look at the walls. There's more pictures now, a lifetime: photographs of people Jim doesn't know; posters and flyers for club nights long gone. One such poster in a simple wooden frame catches his eye. A woman's face rises from a cerulean matrix, floating in the void, her features melting into the gridded neon lines.

Alive comes back. 'I fell in love with her that night. Couldn't take my eyes off her.'

'It's beautiful.'

'Dreamscape at Denbigh Leisure Centre, December '91. Mental. Were you there?'

'I'd had my accident by then, so no.'

Alive rubs his shorn head and gazes at the woman's face in the frame. 'Everything was breaking up by that point. You had your Hardcore, Jungle on the way…but we were all too deep into it to stop. There was no going back.' He walks over to the window. Across the courtyard is Peel House; Alive juts his chin in its direction. 'I was part of that crew from the start. Everyone was up for it. Everyone sound-as.'

Jim limps to join Alive at the window. Peel House is Blitz-black, not a single light on anywhere. A few bedsheets hang forlornly from windows, the slogans written on them too washed out and far away to read. They are the only indications that life ever dwelled within.

'I never went to any Peel House parties,' Jim says.

'No? The cunts condemned it six months ago. Last year we ran a No Transfer campaign like before, when we stopped them taking over back in the early nineties. It was magic, man, like old times. There was this *energy* about us again…' His voice softens. 'But it wasn't enough. We fought 'til the end but….aye.'

Jim looks across the courtyard, tries to see what Alive

sees, but all he glimpses is his own ruined reflection. He gives Alive the money and Alive gives him the tiny plastic baggie containing two hexagonal-shaped pills.

'Where will you go when they knock this place down?' Jim asks.

Alive shrugs. 'Wherever they put me, I suppose. Mickey's still upstairs, but pretty much everyone else's gone. Nobody tells you nowt.' His eyes drift once more to Peel House. 'But there's still time.'

'I should get off.'

Alive walks him out. 'Dave, next time you see Cor, tell her I said hello, yeah?'

'Sure,' Jim says as Alive closes the door on him, shutting him off from light and warmth and human contact. 'No worries.'

Lily Butler's poster is still in his kitchen. He bins it and boils the kettle. The clock on the oven says 22:22. Time enough.

He has a cup with a special lid, designed for geriatrics who are no longer liquid-credible. He fills it with tea and takes it into the hall, removes the tarnished key from the string around his neck, and unlocks the living room door.

Inside, a solitary lamp does little to shore up the dark. An obsolete computer and printer on the fold-out dinner table (next to a volume of *Internet for Dummies*) throw monolithic shapes across the pictures on the walls, pictures printed from the internet. They are of women – *woman*, singular – the same woman interpreted a dozen ways. Nor is the term 'woman' entirely accurate. With its gaunt face and hobgoblin arms, the entity depicted isn't strictly human. Until recently, crude hundred-year-old illustrations were the only evidence he'd managed to uncover, but that had all changed when, logging on one day, he'd stumbled across the print now taking pride of place above the bar fire. He'd ordered it direct from the London gallery displaying the original work: a glossy 27 x 40 poster. *The Green Girl* by Una Cruickshank. The same painting he'd blundered upon that night all those years ago.

Jim pops his cup and looks up at the print, looks up at her. She holds a skeletal hand over her beautifully cadaverous face, and between her parted fingers are eyes that have haunted him forever.

The tape rack is beside the fire. The tape he wants is in a green case near the bottom. He feels its weight – both physical and psychic – as he slides it into the stereo. Farley 'Jackmaster' Funk – 'The Acid Life'. Though he's listened to this track thousands of times, each time is new. Each time the 303s kicks in over the deep-space beat, his bones realign and grow solid. His organs unpuncture and his spine cracks straight. His jaw unshatters.

A large map comprising three layers lies in the centre of the room. The bottom layer is a 1928 civic plan of the local water supply from the then still-operational waterworks, which had supplied the St. Esther slums to the east, and High Leven and Maltby to the west; its mains and channels running beneath land on which the Burn Estate would be built a decade after the war. This was the second layer: the original 1954 estate plans, including a 1965 addendum to the north-western edge when the blocks were built. The final layer was Moorside, the first Rowan-Tree homes, completed in late 1994. Moorside now occupies the site of the waterworks and long-demolished St Esther slums, the resulting homes a stones-throw from the eastern-most boundary of the Burn Estate. He had found all the plans in the Teesside Municipal Online Archives, and painstakingly rescaled them onto sheets of tracing paper.

Jim lowers himself stiffly to the floor and smooths the layers of his map. A hundred years of superimposed history, each as ephemeral and brittle as the paper on which they were printed.

Beneath the traced layers of Moorside and the Burn Estate, he has, with coloured pens, highlighted every subterranean water channel into and out of the area. For months now, across dual carriageways and ice-stubbled fields and copses of rotting trees filled with fly-tipped TVs, he'd been tracking them, ensuring none let out above ground. That there was nowhere she could *escape*. But each pipe had stopped, blocked and forgotten, below ground. Now only one channel remains. Marked in dark green, it ends at the Cong Burn, out in the woods to the north. It's a place he knows well. As a youth, from his bedroom window on the fourteenth floor, he'd stared nightly at that dark crosshatch of trees.

Jim finishes his tea. He puts new batteries in his torch and turns off the music. He takes a last look at the map before folding it into his rucksack. In his mind, he follows the glimmering dark green line as it curves back beneath the estate, beneath Vivienne Avenue, beneath Stanhope Street, and beneath his own flat on Hessle Rise; beneath street after street, towards its source: the ghost of the waterworks and the tightly drawn circle of the well.

Towards a monster.

He takes a final look around the room, turns off the lights, and heads into the night.

But monsters don't scare him. He's a monster himself.

II

(

...gone...

...Where are we? It's proper misty. Is this where you're from?

Tonight, I went back to where *I'm* from. The blocks. For the first time in twenty-odd year, and I was bricking it. I mean, I see them every day when I go out – you can't miss them – but I do this trick where I keep them in the peripheral. Like the moon, like clouds. They're there, but you sort of don't see them. Tonight, though, I found that only works at a distance. Get close enough and you run out of space to kid yourself.

Living there used to be so...like have you heard The Smiths? Consider yourself lucky if you haven't because the singer's such a moaning twat. See, to me, music should lift you up, yeah? It should tell you things can be better than what they are, but bang The Smiths on and here's this fucker telling you to stick a bag over your head and go to sleep? Haway, man – not for me. All my mates back then were into them though, and at the time I guess I pretended I liked it too because I didn't know any other kinds of music existed. Like I'd make myself sit down with a Cure record, or a Cocteau Twins record, a Beatles or Bob Dylan record – and really study it like homework, trying to find a way in. Only I never could. It was the guitars, man. Guitars, guitars, guitars. Nobody cared about *the beat*. The drums on those records were all shite. My sister Corina used to be into hip hop – real pioneer stuff like MC Shan and Ultramagnetic MCs – and that was better, but there were too many words. I don't like lyrics neither. I mean, when has anything what truly mattered to you ever rhymed?

Anyway, the point is, there's this one Smiths' song – or was it his solo stuff? – anyway, this song called 'Every Day is Like Sunday', which was the blocks to a T: grey. Miserable. Suffocating. I'd look out my bedroom window, up on the fourteenth floor, see concrete to the horizon, and wonder if maybe The Smiths guy had the flat below.

There were six blocks in a kind of half circle. I lived in Asquith House, Macca was in Chamberlin, Tracey and Kim were in Lloyd George, and Dano was in Attlee. We were all mates from school, but after we left there was nowt to do. Macca stayed on for some pointless NVQs, but I wanted to start earning. Fuck knows why. I think Mam was sad, but I'd be lying if that didn't spur me on to some extent. Me and Dano started labouring, and Trace pulled pints down the Labour Club until the landlord tried to get her to do a 'private show' at a lock-in for the regulars, so she wrapped in.

Dad got laid off at the end of 1988, I think, and that's when shite got bad because there's nowt worse than someone who believes that guff about an honest day's work not having an honest day's work. Nightmare. He drove everyone crackers, and took it out on me especially – *no son of mine's going to be a dosser* blah-blah-blah, even though technically, *he* was just as much of a dosser as me. Worse, even. At least I never dropped half my dole on the greyhounds. Only a proper mug does that – everyone knows they're rigged. Me and Cor kept out the flat as much as possible in them days, and I think the main reason Mam joined the Tenants' Association was just so's to get out his way for a few hours at a time.

Like, the only peace I got was after everyone went to bed and I could watch horror films. *Frankenstein, Dracula, The Wolfman* – they're your mainstays, but there was all kinds of other naff crap nobody even remembers anymore. I loved this one from the 70s called *The Stone Tape*. It was about this old house which acted like a kind of supernatural tape recorder, the walls recording ghosts and playing them back on loop. I reckon whoever wrote that one must've done a stint in a council high-rise. So I'd sit watching this stuff in the dark, taping them for nights when the telly was shite. Sometimes Cor'd watch with me, but that was alright.

Frankenstein was my favourite. And, aye, I know the monster's just the monster and Victor Frankenstein's the guy what made him, but it's easier to call the monster Frankenstein, and besides, everyone deserves a name. There was something about Frankenstein I really got off on, the Boris Karloff ones especially. Like there's this bit in the first Karloff one where Victor's got Frankenstein in this chair in a dark room just after he's made him. Frankenstein looks wrecked, man. Proper miserable. Victor pulls a chain to open a hatch in the roof, sunlight falls across Frankenstein's face for the first time, and you can *see* something happening inside him. He stands up, staggering and wobbling, reaching – fingers moving in the light, like this – like he's trying to hold onto a warmth he's never known. Then Victor shuts the hatch. He's like, *No.* No more for you. Then this close up of Frankenstein's face. He's utterly crushed, holding his stitched hands out like, *Why are you doing this to me?* That bit kills me. It's no wonder he starts mashing everybody. I mean, wouldn't you? At the end he always dies, too. Either he burns to death, or gets electrocuted, or gets chucked off the fucking roof, and the people – these scunner villagers – think, aye, everything's back to normal. Sound. Nowt more to see here.

If you ask me, Frankenstein's tragedy, not horror.

Anyhow, so that was pretty much my life back then. There used to be this climbing frame on the communal green – we called it the Thunderdome – and when you climbed it, the blocks panorama-ed around you and it was like you'd never escape. At the time, I thought it was *bleak*, but now we've got cunts ploughing trucks into crowds, cunts strapping bombs to kids, and I don't know if bleak's the right word. Maybe the word doesn't exist. It was Teesside in the late 1980s, if that means owt to anyone. And I was seventeen.

Were you ever seventeen, Peg?

So the thing that led me to Adam and JJ, and then to acid music and everything I'm about to tell you, was us coming into possession of like three hundred vibrators, dildos, and sex toys of various shapes and sizes. There used to be this industrial estate south of the estate, on the other side of Peelaw Bank, about as far from the blocks as we'd get in those days. Just non-descript warehouses and lock ups and stuff, but there was this one with a flat roof that was easy to get on, so we'd knock about on it, drinking cider or whatever. One night me, Macca, and Dano were up on it, playing footie with stones, and one spooned off Dano's foot and put this little skylight window out. Of course we legged it, but when we went back a few weeks later, it was still broken. Nobody had noticed, so we stuck our heads in to have a look. There were loads of crates inside, and it looked easy to get down the gangway thing. There didn't seem to be any alarm or security bloke, so we had an idea. We'd leave it another week, and if there was no change we'd take it as a sign to go on the rob. At the time it was just a joke, but you know what lads are like – nobody wants to chicken out first – so that's how we ended up back on the roof a week later, decked out in black Joy Division t-shirts, carrying two holdalls each, bricking it.

We didn't know what we were doing. Just thought, aye, there's bound to be *something* worth pinching. Easy-to-carry, top-end gear like VHS players or Nintendos. I think I can safely say that none of us were expecting dildos. Dano prised open about ten crates and they were all the same – hundreds of them packed in polystyrene bits. Then Macca swore he heard sirens, so we shovelled as many as we could into our bags and legged it.

We went to Dano's because it was only him and his mam, and most nights she was passed out blotto in front of the telly by 8 o'clock. We tipped the bags onto his bed and tried to make sense of them. It was my first dildo experience. Some had two shafts, like big weird tuning forks. Some were double-ended and as long as my arm. There were strings of rubber balls I didn't even want to guess at. This was before the internet, remember.

Macca held up a big glittery black one with veins along the sides. He was like, What the fuck are we going to do with these?

Dano was freaking out. He wanted to dump them, but I was like, Haway, we took the risk, we should at least try and get something. And Dano was like, Oh, you're going to go door to door? Avon calling? So we decided what we needed was to find someone to take them all off our hands in one

99

go and pay a lump sum. But who? Plus we didn't even know how much they went for. We didn't want to look like amateurs and get ripped off, did we? The only people we thought might know were Trace and Kim. They were girls at least. Nonchalantly, we were like, Would you ladies happen to know how much a decent *dildo* goes for these days? They looked at us like we were fucked in the head. Then about three days later, Cor came in my room. She was like, Anywhere from £5-£20. Then she said, Jim, Mam's birthday's coming up, and I'm a bit worried what you've got in mind. Cor knew Kim, see, and Kim must have said something. I feigned ignorance, but Cor knows me. Knew me. She sat on my bed with this little smile on her face and waited for me to crack, and I lasted about thirty seconds before I spilled my guts. She pissed herself laughing as I told her. Proper tears, rolling on the bed trying to breathe – the kind of pure-as laughter you might only get a handful of times in your life. Anyway, a few days later, she took me to see Clive Alive. Alive's not his real name of course, it just suits him. He lived on the blocks – still does actually. I saw him earlier tonight, to get those pills.

Speaking of which, are you feeling it yet? I think I am. I can feel it…

Back then, Alive was Cor's mate and weed dealer. He was also proper into his music. Before Acid, he was a hip hop-head, which is how Cor first got into it. Alive had hundreds of records, like loads of white labels and imports and shite what was solid to get hold of. They weren't cheap, hence the dealing, but Cor told me he only sold to mates because sooner or later you had to butt heads with a psycho, and he was too nice for that. To be honest, I always thought she was a bit sweet on him.

He was older than her, and looked like a dude from a muscle mag. I liked him straight away, but not just because of that. It was the way he shook my hand when Cor introduced me. Like he *wanted* to, right? Not like he was just humouring his mate's kid brother. He lit a spliff and passed it to me and I'd never smoked before – I mean, I'd smoked cigs – so I was a bit wary, but Cor was like, whatever. I didn't want to look clueless, so I took a proper harsh drag while Alive told me the plan.

He knew this guy Adam, who lived on the estate, who had a cousin who ran a sex shop in Soho, London. Soho, apparently, was a place where people looked at you funny if you *weren't* in the market for a big rubber dick. This cousin wanted to give us £1,500 for the dildos! Even split three ways, it was the most money possible in the world. All we had to do was get them over to Adam, who'd take them down to his cousin. Alive wrote Adam's address and telephone number down for me.

When I rang Adam the next day – from the phone box – he said he couldn't pick them up because his car was knackered, so we'd have to take them over to him. I reckon Dano would've carried them all the way to London himself he was so desperate to have them out of his flat. See, he'd hidden them all over his room and was shitting himself in case his mam went on one of her sporadic cleaning binges, which she did whenever she sobered up enough. Would've been bad if she had. Sex toys tumbling out of every available storage space in your teenage son's room would drive anyone back to drink.

Right, this next bit's going to sound dramatic, but it's true: when Adam opened his door and I saw this lanky, freckled lad with neon-blue hair twisting out of the top of his head like a Bunsen burner flame, my whole life changed. Just like that, I was in love – couldn't take my eyes off him. The first words I heard him say, in his weirdly deep voice, were, *My cocks have arrived!* which didn't impress Macca and Dano, but I was grinning like a moron. I mean, it'd been there all along, of course. I'm not going to pretend I hadn't, like, snuck glances at Macca when he took his shirt off on hot days, but I'd been able to deal with it up to that point in the same way I deal with seeing the blocks now – that peripheral trick. Adam, though, he blasted all that apart.

In the living room, he unzipped the bags and took a closer look. This serious face on, hefting the dildos like they were ripe fruit. I couldn't get enough of him. He was like, These are quality items, gents, and such an *array*. He worked the shaft of a big black one, winking at Macca, and Macca looked like he was about to dive through the window.

That was when I became aware of the music, and for a second everything else – even Adam – vanished. *That beat!* Hissing hi-hats that sent my balls crawling back up inside me, the evil stabs of bass – three notes only – and then a sound I'd never heard before in my life, this completely inhuman squelching that shook my *guts*.

I was like, I need to know what this is.

'The Acid Life', Adam said. Farley Jackmaster Funk.

Aye, but what *music*?

His smile ruptured me. Acid, he said.

I was floored. Felt the bolts burning in my neck, my eyes opening for the first time, a voice screaming: *It's Alive! It's Alive!...*

...So Adam gave us his cousin's money – more money

than I'd ever seen – and Macca and Dano couldn't get out fast enough. It was only me and Adam in the room.

Your mates are leaving, he said. Even then I think he knew. He got the tape out the stereo. It was a mix he'd made for the trip down to London, but he was giving it to me. If I liked what was on it, he said, then I could come over another time and listen to more. My hands were probably dripping with sweat when I took it.

On the way home, despite the deal going well, Macca and Dano were pissed off. They were like, I bet he's keeping them dildos for himself. And they hated his music, too. Shitty computer noise, they said. It wasn't real. But it felt real to me. I kept touching the tape in my pocket to make sure I hadn't dreamed it.

I've still got that tape. I listened to it tonight before I came here. It hurts to listen to it, but it's still the realest thing anyone's ever given me.

After Adam gave it to me, I listened to it for like two solid days, then rang him from the phone box. I kept hanging up after pressing the last number, pacing up and down, calling myself chickenshit. I only managed to call him in the end by pretending I wasn't myself, and letting that person – whoever he was – take over. Adam picked up after half a ring. He sounded happy to hear from me, asked if I'd dug the tape. I said it was the best music I'd ever heard and he chuckled down the phone like a cartoon bear. In that case, he said, would I like to come down to London with him and his housemate JJ that Friday, to deliver the dildos? There might also be a party happening which would be up my street. I said yes before he'd even finished speaking, would've went with him to an asbestos disposal centre if he'd asked.

He was like, Sound, meet us outside the blocks Friday morning. And bring some of your ill-gotten gains.

I hung up and danced in that pissy phone box. I was ecstatic, but not entirely sure why. What did I want out of him then? Just a desire to be near him, I think. Have you ever felt that? To just, like, *bask* in a person? Like a lizard on a rock? The rest, whatever it was, I thought, would follow.

Friday morning, I told Mam I was staying at Dano's. There was a double bill of Hammer Horrors on the telly and we were going to make a night of it. Innocent fun. I think she smelled a rat, but let it slide. We were all looking for chances to get out of the flat in them days.

They were waiting for me in Adam's old Austin Metro. Adam driving, JJ in the passenger seat. It was my first time meeting her. When I'd been round the first time she'd been at work, and I didn't know if she'd take to me, but she got out and jumped on me like I'd just come back from the war. She was like, Hi handsome, and sunk her teeth into my earlobe.

So there we were, the three of us, caning it down the A1, talking and laughing and listening to music the whole way, and I'm dead serious when I say they were already my best friends. I know what people think of me these days, what they say I'm capable of. But it's not true. Adam and JJ – *that's* what I'm capable of.

I'd never been to London before. Never thought a place could be so big. It didn't seem to end – mile after mile of pent-up oomph. Like, take a bus, a train, a tube – rattle through the spark flashing dark – come back up, and London's *still* there. It was hard to wrap my head around after a lifetime on the blocks.

Adam's cousin was this fat bloke called Randall who wore clothes like my dad's. His sex shop was through a beaded curtain, down steps so steep you needed the walls for balance. He sold tapes with bored women on the fronts, and loads of weird, black plastic gear. Catsuits, crotch-less keks, gasmask-things with balls that went in your gob. I remember this massive rubber arm-thing. *Das Fist*, it was called. I mean…who would – *could* – be into that? These things were simply not part of my world or vocabulary. Greasy-as blokes drifted about, studying merchandise and not looking at each other.

Randall started sorting through the dildos right there at the counter, and his eyes lit up when he saw that double-shafted one. Then he slipped Adam something: a tiny plastic bag that went straight into Adam's pocket. I saw, but they didn't see me see. But JJ, she did. She caught my eye from across the shop, where she was cruising the aisles and unnerving the creeps, and did that train-whistle thing with her arm. You know: *Woo Woo*.

When we left, Adam rang a number on a flier he'd picked up a few streets over from Randall's sex pit. That was how you kept ahead of the police in them days, you rang a number what gave you a recorded message telling you the place to meet to *get told* where to go. Only I didn't know that then. Then we lined our stomachs – hard for me to eat, I remember – got in the car, and headed for the orbital.

And you know when people say it's not the destination, but the journey? Well that, like pretty much everything else people said to me in them days, didn't used to make much sense. I'd never been on a journey before, but that night I finally got it. The motorway was rammed – a chain of red lights circling the city – and there we were, right there, part of it. People had their windows down to have a bit craic between cars, passing spliffs and cans. I felt like a traveller. England was just some other place that didn't matter, different rules applied. Cars stopped at service stations and blasted music right on the forecourt. I remember one time we'd been at a rave somewhere out of St. Albans, where the generators had blown early, so on the way back everyone pulled into this multi-storey in Brent Cross and went mental until the sun came up. Adam liked to quote this thing Thatcher said – *there is no such thing as society* – and he'd be like, Fine by me, who fucking needs it? We're going *deeper*. And at the time, I thought he was onto something.

But I'm getting ahead of myself. All that was later. That first night, when we were in the car, I was so nervous and excited. JJ leaned round to me in the back. She had a scar here, through her right eyebrow, where the hair wouldn't grow.

You're going to love this, Jim, she said. Then she kissed me gently on the lips. She tasted of fake strawberries and, of course, I got a hard on. I don't know if she realised or not. She just laughed.

A long time later we got to the meeting place and word got round we had to go to some airstrip out by Maidenhead, and it was nearly midnight before we pulled into a field and I saw it for the first time. We parked at the top of a long hill rolling down into the dark landscape, and at the bottom was this hanger fifty times bigger than the warehouse we'd robbed the dildos from. Strobes lit the windows along the sides and coloured fog seeped across the ground. There were even fairground rides blazing away, but it was the music that was calling me, man – I could feel the low end even from where we were standing, and there were thousands of people just like me being drawn to it.

Adam gave me my ticket. He was like, Are you ready for this? And I totally, totally was. Once we got into the hanger, I flipped my wig. Like, I'd only ever heard acid on walkmans and crappy stereos, so I wasn't prepared for that sound system. It *broke* me. Seriously, *nowt* had ever been that loud. People everywhere just going for it, and I was like, this is it – the pure strain of what I hadn't known even belonged to me. Adam put a pill in my hand. He swallowed one with a sip of water, JJ too. I didn't understand, but necked it anyway. Forgot about it instantly.

Later on – I don't know when, I didn't care about time – I started feeling it. This lightness in my stomach, sort of wings brushing my insides. Everything ratcheting up inside me, around me. My vision going at the edges and a feeling of love expanding outwards. This love and beauty that was entirely new to me, that mixed with the music and became the music. All these people I didn't know, but did know, you know? I wanted to tell them all I loved them, and that I knew they loved me too. And I thought, *Where's this come from?* But the question didn't matter either. All that mattered was I wanted to dance. I'd been shot into the eye of the universe. Gone. *Poof.* I'd lost Adam and JJ but I didn't care. Problems melted away. Faces came and went, and I kept dancing. Then we found each other in a crowd of thousands, just like I knew we would, because the universe knew we were connected. We were young and free and *part of this*, and it was never going to end. Adam had more pills, and we did them.

At some point, the sun came up and mist rolled over the

fields. This heaviness starting to slink up, and I could feel myself dipping into the reality of who's and where's. I couldn't control my jaw and I needed to sit. JJ sat next to me, wrapped arms around me. I told her I loved her and she squeezed my neck. We stumbled to the car. Being out in the cool morning brought us all down and made talking difficult. The car was freezing. Adam drove hunched over the wheel, gurning and silent in the slow-crawl back to the road. Every cell of my body vibrated and, like, I felt something monumental had just happened, but it was too big – I was too close – for it to make sense.

It took yonks to get back to London. We pulled up next to this tower block that vaguely reminded me of some other place I knew. Adam had a key to Randall's flat and we took the lift up, let ourselves in, nobody saying nowt. We took our clothes off in the spare room and all three of us got into bed, shivering in our keks. I lay there, breathing. My hard on was pressed against Adam's leg but he didn't move. Nobody moved and slowly, whatever passed for my mind drifted away…

We drove back up to Teesside the next day and when I saw Asquith House rising out of the grey, I felt like I was being driven to the noose. It was real now, the hatred I felt for the place, now I knew what else was out there. It wasn't just a comedown I was experiencing, it was the reorganisation of my world.

I started spending more and more time round Adam and JJ's. We'd get pissed and listen to music, but we didn't drop that much. Back then, pills were well expensive, a tenner or more – a 1989 tenner – and we were all pretty skint. I was eking out my dildo money, using it for our London trips, clubs and raves. I started wearing baggy, florescent clothes. Mam used to knit these proper day-glow mind-bending jumpers that were *perfect*. I even got her to do Adam and JJ some. Stuff like that felt good to wear, like my uniform – the first time in my life I'd ever wanted to wear one, though it didn't go down well in the blocks. Like, some scunner sees you in your Global Hypercolour or whatever, and that was all it took for them to start. You had to not take the bait, though, because once you did you were on their terms. Still, I got brayed a few times and I started thinking, How can this place even *exist?* These blocks, this estate – they were cancer. Soul rot, man. Why didn't people see? Why weren't they picking up sledgehammers and bringing it all down? What was *wrong* with the world?

Then Dad started reading about it in the papers. Acid Monsters. Evil drug pushers beastifying kids with their tablets and powders. Inhuman, repetitive music brutalising the senses. Mass orgies of teenage flesh in abandoned fertilizer factories. Fucking *ecstasy wrappers* littering hard concrete floors. Twitching youth left for dead with foam on their lips. Torn, bloody underwear. Sodomised. He'd slap the headlines with the back of his hairy hand: *Crazed Acid Mob Attacks Police*, and he'd be like, Where are the parents, eh? What's *wrong* with the world?

Druggy scum. Aye, that's what he'd say – *druggy scum*. Blah blah blah, druggy scum. Blah blah blah, no discipline. Blah blah blah, bring back conscription, send them over to Ireland, let the IRA sort them out. When he went off like that, I'd go to my room and chew the duvet.

Another thing was, it was getting harder and harder to think up excuses for my weekends away, why I shambled home Sunday nights like something out of a George A.

Romero film. I told my parents I was pulling nightshifts at the post office depot over in Cannon Park, sorting out the week's backlog. Told them it was easier to crash at a mate's who lived nearby, rather than drag myself all the way home for a few hours kip between shifts. They seemed to buy it. Mam would even do me some bait on the Friday, which we'd eat on the drive down to London.

But Cor was too sharp. She collared me one night and said she knew what I was up to. I was like, So what? What's your point? She didn't like it, she said, any of it – the music, the people, the drugs. Alive had got into Acid in a big way, she said. Now whenever she went round all he did was mix acid records and bang on about the parties he'd been to, how battered he'd got. It was boring-as, she said. He'd dragged her to Peel House and everyone was battered. Big, black, possessed eyes. She hadn't been able to breathe. Alive tried getting her to drop an E, but she was like, Fuck that. Said it made her puke to see him turn from the kind, sweet person she knew into a clammy zombie. He was on E all the time now. She was like, I just want you to be safe. But secretly, her worry pleased me. This was *my* thing. The first thing of mine she didn't understand and hadn't beaten me to.

Man, I'm definitely coming up now…

So anyway, one night me, Mam, and Dad were sitting watching the telly, when there was a knock at the door. It was Adam. He'd dyed his hair spaceman silver. He was like, Hey, I was just in the neighbourhood and thought I'd pop up to say hello.

Mam invited him in, and as soon as I saw his eyes I knew he was battered.

Dad eyed him suspiciously. He wanted to know who he

was, and Adam was like, Oh I'm sorry, so rude of me. I'm Adam, I'm a friend of your son's. We work together at the depot sorting through all that mail. He's a great lad. You've done a smashing job raising that one.

Mam asked if he wanted a cup of tea, but I was already guiding him into my room.

He collapsed on my bed, laughing, and there was no point getting pissed off because it wouldn't have got through to him, and, in truth, I was ecstatic he wanted to see me. He said, I'm hurt – I've dropped you off so many times and you've never once invited me up. He lay on my bed with a spaced-out smile on his face, and I was embarrassed because I still had posters on my walls, stuff like the Middlesbrough team, and the Pixies, what Trace had ripped out of an *NME* for me after I'd pretended I liked them.

There was a stack of videos on the dresser next to my bed. Taped off TV mostly, but a few from Oxfam. Adam read the spines.

You like spooky films? he said.

I shrugged. I guess.

You don't have to be like that with me, Jim. I like them too. What's your favourite?

Frankenstein, probably.

Adam stuck his arms in the air and groaned, *Urrrrrr*. Me and JJ just watched one on the telly the other night. Fuck, what was it called?

I'd watched it too. *The Revenge of Frankenstein*, I said. A Hammer Horror.

Yeah! *The Revenge of Frankenstein*. Fuck me, man.

I told him I wasn't so keen on the Hammer Frankensteins because they focused too much on the creator, Victor. I liked

111

the old Universal ones best, the early ones. They were about the monster – I told him I called the monster Frankenstein – this poor fucker who's been created and rejected and hated and doesn't know why. All he wants is a home, someone what loves him.

Adam's eyes on mine. Frankenstein, he said. See, he's proof.

Of what?

That we're all part of the same consciousness. Victor made a vessel to receive it, and the universe obliged – poured it right in. The way I see it, Victor and Frankenstein were both part of the same life force, right? But Victor's closed himself off from that knowledge and Frankenstein, see, Frankenstein the monster, he doesn't know either, only for a different reason. He's not in denial like Victor, he's just been born and got nobody to show him how things really are. And that's when the world starts fucking with his head.

He ran a fingernail gently down my tapes. Frankenstein should've given them all some pills, he said. Things would've have worked out a lot differently.

He patted my single bed for me to lie with him. I did, though not without difficulty. Up close his eyes were like well holes. He whispered, I just want to say that I'm so fucking glad we met. I love you, Jim Jams. But you knew that already, didn't you?

I was flat on my back and Adam was on his side, facing me. His hand moved down my chest and I can still feel that hand, still cold from the outside. It moved down my belly, both of us taking shallow silvery breaths. He brushed my dick through my jeans and I didn't move, couldn't move. I'd never wanted anybody so badly, even though I

112

knew that once I had him, things would never be the same, and that that was maybe what I wanted most of all. He kissed me…his lips were as cold as his hands, but warming, and it's always a shock to me how soft other people are. You forget. I inhaled him, tried to make him part of me as he undid my jeans. I didn't know what to do. I went to touch him but he said, Don't, this is for you. He slipped down to the bottom of the bed, pulling my jeans and boxers off in one fluid move. The bed springs were proper creaking and I was worried people could hear. I closed my eyes as I felt his lips on my ankle – quick pecks that made tiny smacking sounds as they moved up the inside of my leg. I was falling in all directions at once. Then he stopped. I looked down and he was staring up at me, my twitching dick an inch from his lips…and then I felt his tongue…

Sorry, I'll stop there. I've got a habit of oversharing when I'm coming up. But do you know what that's like? To be with someone like that? It's been twenty-five year and I haven't forgotten a second, not of *anything* that happened that year, though the further away I drift from the person Adam kissed on that bed, the harder it is to tell myself it really happened at all. But then, that's normal, isn't it? Isn't that everyone?

After that night, I wanted more. More of him, more everything. I wasn't thinking about jobs, or the blocks, or the estate. I didn't care, I'd escaped. Word got round, though, and one day as I was heading over to Adam and JJ's, I bumped into Macca and them. They were drinking cider round the rec. centre, sitting lined up against the wall like derelicts.

Trace was like, Why'd you ditch us, eh?

I said I hadn't, but I suppose I had.

Dano said, We heard you're off partying down London with them weirdos.

I was like, What would you know about it?

That Adam's bent-as, he said.

So what if he is?

He'll end up bumming you.

Fuck off.

Kim was like, And that music's shite. It's not real music.

So I said, What's real music, eh? It feels realer than all your dreary guitar shite. In fact, I said, what's real anything?

Macca span a finger in the air. He was like, *this* – meaning the blocks – *this* is real. Only you don't see it because you're too busy jumping about like a twat, off your face on drugs. It's pathetic, mate. You think you're onto something, but you're not.

I told them they didn't know what they were on about. Told them if they thought listening to The Smiths and scratching round for cider money was reality, then they were fucking welcome to it.

Didn't see any of them after that.

But Dad was another one. Ever since Adam's visit, he'd been worse than usual. Started coming back late from the Labour Club, or the dogs, grumbling and knocking stuff over in the dark. Mam said to pay him no mind, he just didn't like being out of work, didn't know what to do with himself. I remember thinking how depressing that statement was. Like, take away a person's job and the person crumbles. I stopped out of his way, but the thing was, because I was master at avoiding *him*, I didn't realise he was actually avoiding *me*. Say if it was just me and him in the room, he'd leave. Just me and him in the flat, he'd go out. It dawned on me gradually, but once it had, I

114

started haunting him. I'd follow him round, like, How's the job hunt going, *Dad*? Got any tips for the dogs, *Dad*? I hadn't seen it coming, the anger I felt. It hit like a brick.

One night it was just me in – Mam must've been at a tenants' meeting, Cor at her apprenticeship or something – and he came back stinking of drink. He stood in my bedroom doorway.

Pack your bags, he said. He had the family suitcases, the same ones we'd taken on holiday to Scarborough and Mablethorpe. He was like, Haway, James, I mean it. Pack your clothes, whatever else you need, and get out. His eyes all unfocused and red.

I asked him why. I mean, I knew already, I just wanted to hear him say it.

But he couldn't even look at me.

I said, I'm staying put.

He said nowt. I said nowt.

Then he said, It's *him*. And *you*. *Together*. Turns my stomach.

I don't know what you're on about.

He made himself look at me, something which I knew was hard for him to do.

What's Mam say about this? I said.

Never mind your mother.

Because what you say goes, right?

Just get packed.

This anger blooming in my head. I said, Because Morris is the man of the house? What would your Labour Club mates say if they knew your son was a *puff*, eh?

He stumbled into the hall and I followed. I was like, What's it say about you, if your boy loves *cock*?

He went into his room and shut the door. I pressed my

ear to it, couldn't hear anything. I was shaking. I spoke into the crack. I said, And seeing as we're being honest with each other, Dad, I may as well tell that I'm also *druggy scum*. I don't work at the post depot at weekends. I drive down to London and take *ecstasy*.

I braced myself for him to come out swinging, I *wanted* him to, but there was nowt but silence. I tried the handle but he'd slid the bolt, so I went into my room and threw some stuff into a case. He'd left me three, but everything fit easily into one. I only took one tape – the Universal *Frankenstein* – got the last of my dildo money from an old biscuit tin on top of the wardrobe. I put my ear to his door again before I went. I wanted to shout something. *Fuck you* or something. But I didn't have the strength.

So that's how I ended up at Adam and JJ's. I just walked straight round, didn't even have to ask. They welcomed me with open arms. I got the box room with the bare mattress on the floor, and that first night I curled up and cried myself to sleep. I was a month shy of eighteen.

Adam and JJ became my new family, and I did stuff with them I'd never done with my real family. And I don't mean drugs – I mean little things, like sitting down to eat together. We took it in turns with the cooking, and I was awful, but JJ taught me. I can still make an amazing lasagne from scratch, no jars or nowt, even the white sauce.

We went out most nights. Not always to London – that was pricey – or even the places springing up locally, like Club Havana in town, or Philmores in Saltburn. Mostly we went over to Peel House. The blocks had been dropping to bits for ages and those who could were getting out, which meant there were loads of empty flats for people to move into for dead cheap or just, like, squat there. It all centred round Peel House for whatever reason, and they started calling themselves The Residual Collective. This bloke called Mickey was the leader, and they turned it into this amazing space, covered the stairs in murals and even knocked through walls to make art spaces and dance floors and shite. Always a party happening, everyone was sound-as, and it didn't matter who you were. See, I'd grown up in this sackless world where, for reasons nobody remembered, Asquith House was supposed to hate Attlee House, right? People from one side of Stanhope Street were supposed to be against them from the other. And woe betide if you were from Peelaw Bank and got caught on the Crescent after the sun went down. Now, think about that for second. Here were people what should've been sticking together, hard-grind people whose fingers were being systematically prised off the ledge by unemployment and shite housing and a government what couldn't give two fucks about them, but still, *still*, they'd kick each other's heads in because they lived on different sides of the same estate. I mean, what *is* that? Human nature? Class politics? Whatever it was, it wasn't us. We were different. Like, I could be anywhere, man – I could be in Peel House, just over the green from the flat I grew up in, or three hundred miles down the motorway, under some grimy East End railway arches – and *know* if a certain kind of music was playing, I was loved. Seven-foot Rastas, posh lasses from Buckinghamshire – it didn't matter. Even the lairy footy scunners in their tracky tops – blokes who a year earlier would've bounced your head off the kerb, here they were hugging each other and saying I love you. I started thinking Adam was right, that deep down we *were* all part of a whole, single energy, and that all we had to do was be ready to sink down together.

And the irony was, because we'd be out three, four times a week, it meant I did actually have to get a job. Adam and JJ both worked crap shop jobs at the Rumbelows in town, and I got shifts in a factory that powdered glass. Like, you know when you see kitchen tiles or, like, jelly sandals – come to think of it, some of them dildos were the same – and they're all glittery? Well that's because powdered glass has been mixed in. It got ground up in this machine and it was my job to shovel it into sacks. I had to wear goggles and a resp. mask because you didn't want that shite on your lungs. It was fine like dust, and it got on your skin, so when the light hit me I was transformed. Sparkling like I was made of diamond. Adam and JJ would bow down, waving their arms in worship like, Oh, Mighty Sun God of Ironopolis! Take pity on we feeble mortals and put the kettle on, two sugars, forever and ever, amen. But I didn't care. The bottom line was I could pay my way and do what I really loved, which was being with them.

Adam would come in my room at night and we'd have sex. He was patient with me because I didn't have experience with another guy. I didn't have much experience with anyone, really, and I know it's a total cliché, but he was as much of a drug to me as the drugs. I could've fucked him forever, and I think I gave it a good go. Afterwards, we'd lie tangled together and plan huge, amazing raves with smoke machines and lasers and Nitrous Oxide canisters in the chill-out zones. The best soundsystem and DJs, the bangingest set lists. Venue was key, and we came to the conclusion that the old waterworks near the estate would be perfect. And we'd do it, too, we said. One day. Swear down. We spent hours like that, whispering and giggling in the dark. It was…the best.

Then one night, I came back late from the glass factory and crashed straight out. I was just dropping off when I heard my door creak and Adam slip inside. I kept my eyes shut, rolled onto my back, ready. He lifted the duvet and crawled inside, up between my legs, running his tongue up my erection as he did. His head came out inches above mine. I felt hair tickling my face and when I opened my eyes it was JJ, arching her split eyebrow at me. She was like, Bet you weren't expecting this? She guided my hand between her legs and she had nowt on.

I mean, I loved Adam, I really did…but you've got to understand, this was before the world crushed me. Here's another bullshit saying: youth is wasted on the young. Aye? Well it was never wasted on me, and it's weird, but I felt like because of my appreciation of it, life was prepared to cut me some slack. It made me special. Or maybe it just made me eighteen and horny. Either way, she tasted of fake strawberries when I kissed her back.

But afterwards, man. *The guilt.* I started dodging them both, Adam especially. I stayed longer at work, went to bed early, feigned belly aches to get out of Peel House raves. It was torture. Then, after a couple of weeks of that, Adam came into my room as I pretended to sleep. He was like, You're fooling no one. So I took a deep breath and told him everything. When I was done, he hugged me.

Ah Jim Jams, he said. What are we going to do with you?

You're not angry?

Why would I be angry?

The first thing I felt was relief, but then I was like, *Why* wasn't he angry?

And maybe you can guess what happened next. We came back from Peel House one morning and were just

119

getting ready to crash. I was brushing my teeth when I heard Adam ask JJ if he could come in her bed with her, and she was like, You don't even have to ask. Then she stuck her head round the door and said to me, What about you? Now, on one hand, I didn't know if I was ready for something like that – I was still trying to figure out the dynamic between the three of us – but on the other, like a bairn, I didn't want to be left out…

…Are you feeling anything? Man, it's been so long since I've done this…

Right, anyway. Get to the point, Jim. Shanks. We first met Armitage Shanks at some London club night later that summer. He'd got talking to JJ and she'd brought him over. He said he was a promoter that did warehouses and outdoor raves. Said he'd done the one on the South Downs that we'd gone to a few weeks before. Peg, you should've seen this guy. So tanned it was like he'd rubbed himself with gravy powder, slicked-back waiter hair, and his teeth were amazing – totally straight, no stains or chips or dead ones, and when he laughed they glowed green in the UV lights. He said we were all welcome back to his place after, and I was like, Aye, nice one, thinking in a minute he'd do one, but come the end of the night he was still hanging around. Sweet on JJ, obviously.

Oh, and this little detail should tell you all you need to know about the man. As we were heading towards the exit, there was this bloke slumped on his tod with drool hanging off his face and eyes like this, fluttering.

Poor dear's cabbaged, Shanks said. Then he told us about these pills coming in from Eastern Europe that were full of all kinds of evil shite. Said he'd heard about someone who'd dropped one and spent the next ten hours carving his own face off with a broken plate.

I was like, Shouldn't we help him? But Shanks was like, *Sweetie* – I can't do his accent, sorry – he was like, *Sweetie*, I don't think he'll fit in the cab.

He took us to the West End, to this house off a wide street lined with palm trees. The place was a palace, seriously. High ceilings and French windows that opened onto a private square. Expensive looking oil-paintings in expensive looking frames, white walls, no wallpaper or dado rails. Red leather settees with bronze lion feet. And he had coke, too. Lots of it on a black glass coffee table.

I did a line and an electric ball burst behind my eyes.

JJ was sitting on the floor next to him. Nice place, she said. Promoting must pay well.

Shanks laughed. Not this well, sweetie. This is one of Daddy's pads. Perhaps you've heard of him? Stephan Santerre? He's in the arts. Let's just say he has more than two shekels to rub together. He mostly uses this place to keep his treasures. I don't think he even knows I have a key.

What does he reckon about what you do? JJ said.

He sneered. Daddy? Oh, he's *far* too busy and important to care about the likes of me.

Adam asked Shanks how he'd came to promoting.

Shanks chopped out three more lines and said, All my circle, they're in the city – hedge funds, futures and the like. They're making a mint but it's so *dull*, sweetie. I'm a people person, I like being out and about.

Yeah, Adam said, fuck money.

Oh, sweetie, Shanks said, never say that.

JJ asked, How much? To do a big outdoor thing?

Shanks did that tippy-hand gesture. Mucho moolah – ten, fifteen grand or more. The sound rigs aren't cheap, then you've got to power the place, refreshments and decorations. Then there's all the behind the scenes factors people never consider – printing costs, security. It adds up. Still, if all goes to plan, an enterprising anarchocapitalist can expect a healthy return.

Put that towards the next one? Adam said.

Shanks winked. You catch on quick. But then he was like, It's changing though. Gangsters are muscling in now, real villains. They want their security on the gates, want their cut of the doors. And if they turned round and demand half – demand it all – what can you do? Go to the police?

Cunts, JJ said, sniffing.

Pills, Shanks said. That's what it's about. He who controls the pills, rakes it in. Say you've come to an arrangement with someone to supply an event – your own man, so to speak – but then along comes some diamond geezer who says, Nah, that's not happening. You're selling *our* pills, right? And if we see any others in there, well, we know where you live.

What would they do to you? Adam asked.

Shanks was like, What would they *do*? Sweetie, they'd kibosh you.

Things were getting hardcore, he said. People were getting out of the game, *and* that was all assuming the police didn't raid you. Think about it – you sink twenty grand into a major event, then plod rolls up an hour before and shuts you down. All that cash down the commode.

They're putting their thinking caps on, too, the boys in blue, Shanks said. There was this special division – the Rave-Squad or whatever – that used dirty tactics. Spreading phoney rave rumours over pirate radio, flooding clubs with undercovers. Roadblocks on the B-roads. That kind of thing. Hardly fair, really.

Shanks passed the rolled up twenty to me over the thick lines of cocaine. Sweetie, he said, it's getting harder and harder to make ends meet.

That's when Adam told him about the old waterworks, the fantasy rave the two of us had dreamed up in the dark. He was like, It's the perfect place – out of the way enough so as not to draw too much attention, but not so far that it'd be a ballache to supply.

Go on, Shanks said, I'm listening.

So he did. He was like, Where we live, nobody's done owt like it. It'd take everybody by surprise, which'd be good for you because there'll be nobody to extort you. The cops wouldn't have any idea how to handle it either. By the time they've got their heads round it, it'll be too late.

Most people round there hate the police anyway, JJ said. They'd rather put up with the noise than call them fuckers.

And best of all, Adam said, there are thousands of us. We're starving. Put this on, *everyone* will come. Guaranteed.

We'd help you, JJ said, putting her hand on his leg.

The coke had got to Shanks, you could see the cogs turning in his head. He banged the table. He was like, *Fuck*, my lovelies! *Fuck!*

I said I needed a slash. Shanks gave me directions, but I just wandered around, looking into random rooms and trying to sort my head out. What had just happened? I was still too battered to know for sure, but I felt like I'd just lost something important.

Shanks' place was massive. Literally about thirty times bigger than Mam and Dads entire flat in Asquith, and he said his dad never used it! Rich people, man. Most of the rooms gave off dead vibes with sheets over the furniture, but one was different. It was full of paintings of, well, at the time I didn't *know* what. These grey, watery worlds. But now, standing here in this mist, I think I get it. And you were there, Peg. A painting of you.

By the way, for years I didn't even know your name was Peg Powler. I didn't know your history either, until the internet came along. People have been afraid of you round here for a long, long time. There's old drawings of you, sketches and that, though none of them did you justice – they made you out to be a ghoul, a bogey. There's only one that comes close to the truth of you, and it's the painting I saw that morning in that room. *The Green Girl.* It's in some famous gallery in London now, someone called Una Cruickshank did it. I've researched her too. She used to live round here. Who is she to you? Is she still around?

Anyway, from that point on, Shanks was all over us. He came up the next week and stuck out like a sore thumb, strutting about the estate in a white suit like the man from Del Monte, a clear foot taller than everybody. Diet, I reckon. No chips or boil-in-the-bags. Once, this boy racer went past and chucked a can of Lilt at him and Shanks just giggled. He didn't think the place was real. Thought he was just doing us all a favour by using the light he was born with to illuminate our urchin existence. He didn't think any harm could come to him.

He flipped his wig when he saw the waterworks. Adam was right, he said, it *was* perfect, and with our help he could make it work. From then on, our days were spent plotting and organising and making phone calls. I tried to enjoy it, but something was clenched up inside me. Now the focus was on Shanks, I was jealous. When he was up – which was a lot – Adam always insisted that he take his bed, because Shanks didn't look like someone who'd crashed on a settee in his life. Somehow, that broke the spell between the three of us. Adam would be on the settee, JJ stayed in her room, and neither of them came into mine.

Even our little dinner routine was wrecked. Shanks could *cook*, man. He'd make stuff with coriander and *cooz cooz* – shite I'd never even heard of, all brought up from London. Can't get it in the outposts, he'd say, waggling a fucking *plantain* at me. As I choked it down, he'd be all like, Oh, the spices are *Moroccan*, or, Just a little Persian dish I threw together. I remember him and JJ were in the kitchen once, and he was teaching her how to do something with a mango or something, and when he moved past her he slid his hand across the small of her back, like this, and kept it there a second longer than he needed to. I had to stop myself from taking a bite out of his fucking neck.

Even once he'd gone back to London, all Adam and JJ wanted to talk about was the rave, and, by association, Shanks. They were mesmerised by his – what? – his *aura*, or whatever. What in their minds he represented. How he could waltz into our world and do the things we ourselves couldn't.

Nights, I'd lie awake on my mattress with my door open, but neither of them came. Then I woke up in the night once, needing a slash, and when I passed JJ's room I heard low voices. My stomach sank. They were in there together, Adam and JJ. Just the two of them. I went back to my mattress and lay there until morning.

I started being a proper dick. Stomping about and boozing and that. Like, we'd be going over some ideas for visuals, you know, like what if we hung sheets on the walls and looped NASA footage? Stuff like that. And they'd ask me what I thought and I'd just pout.

Cor got Adam's number off Alive and rang the house. Mam was upset, she said, and wanted to see me. I said I was busy and Cor was like, Shut your fucking hole, she's your *mam*. Told me to meet them both at Yvette's – this café on the precinct – but I was like, I'm going to London tomorrow. Cor was like, Be there, dickhead, and hung up. I said to Adam, Can you believe her? But he said I should go because they were my family and not everyone had that. See, Adam had been taken into care when he was just a bairn, and JJ'd been living on her own in council flats since she was like fifteen. Dark stuff in her family, you know. Her stepdad, she told me once, was going to be flayed in Hell.

So the next morning I got up and threw a few things in my bag for the London trip, but as soon as I got downstairs I knew the house was empty. And sure enough, there on the kitchen counter, a note: *Decided to head down early. Me and JJ can handle everything. We'll say hi to A.S. for you. Don't get the hump but you need to talk to your mam. See you when we get back, kiss kiss.*

I thought, *Fuckers!* They *wanted* to go without me! *Wanted* time alone with Shanks. Cuddling up to that posh bastard in his king size bed and stocked bar and piles of coke they never paid for. They'd been looking for an excuse to ditch me. I stomped upstairs and started packing the rest of my glittery possessions. I'd be gone when they got back! Aye, that'd teach them! But after a minute, I stopped. I was putting on a show for no one. There was nowhere else for me to go.

So I went to meet Mam.

Yvette's café has been there as long as the estate, and it's where all the biddies go for a fried slice. Mam used to take us on Saturday mornings for a quote-unquote *treat*, before we went food shopping in town. I hated the place. It was always full of crones puffing on Superkings and Berkley Reds – them really long ones only old women buy – and you couldn't see for the smoke. Mam and Cor were at the back table as per, and Mam gave me a hug that was almost a choke, launching into the standard Mam questions: Are you eating properly? Why are you so thin?

Cor didn't get up. She was like, So, Jim, what's the craic?

Ask *him*, I said.

Your dad didn't mean it, Mam said.

He chucked suitcases at me and told me to get out.

You know what he's like. He's under a lot of stress.

What does that even mean? You're telling me *you're* not under stress?

He's a worker, that's his life.

Not anymore it's not. And you're married to that miserable twat for the rest of yours.

Cor was like, Jim, what the *fuck*?

And Mam was like, Corina! Language!

Under different circumstances, Cor's outraged face then would've cracked me up.

Mam said to me, He loves you.

He threw me out.

Pet, he was drunk.

He still meant it. Everybody rejects you in time.

Oh, son, that's not true.

Cor kicked my shin under the table.

Mam started to cry. It was the first time ever I'd seen her cry, and it twisted me up inside, but in the end my anger outweighed my guilt. Cor put her arms around her, glaring at me. She mouthed the words *You dick*.

Mam was like, I don't care if you're gay.

Jesus, Mam.

Then she said, are you...*addicted?*

Aye that's it, Mam, I said, I'm addicted. Can't get enough of them *ecstasy tablets*. I'm howling at the moon most nights. See, that's him, that's Dad talking.

But we're a family, she said.

There *is* no such thing as family, I said. It's everybody for themselves. You think someone loves you, but they'll chuck you like *that*. At least Dad's honest about it.

When I got up Mam grabbed me, but I shrugged her off. I left with tears in my eyes for the second time that day...

Cor was right, though. I *was* a dick. Maybe everyone is at eighteen, but if that's true, what's my excuse now? I live fifteen minutes' walk away and I haven't seen them in more than twenty year. After I moved out of Cor's place, Mam used to knock on my flat all the time. She'd talk through the letter box – *Son, if you're in there, please just open the door* – and I'd be in the living room with the curtains drawn. Thing is, I wanted to let her in, but I never did... and I don't know why I didn't. She's ill now, Cor says. She might have even forgotten who I am and, well, that's the least of what I deserve, but what haunts me is what if she hasn't forgotten all the pain I've caused her? What if it's still there, unattached and swirling around inside her, only now she doesn't know why?

And while we're on the subject, were you ever anybody's daughter? Who *are* you? You know, when me and Cor were bairns, Mam used to tell us stories about you. *Peg Powler's in the pipes*, she'd say. You'd come up through the toilet to snatch us. Back then, because we didn't really believe you were real, it was alright to make you a monster, but now I know different. Now I've got to believe you're not. I've got to believe you didn't take that girl, Lily. I *need* to believe. People have seen me as a monster for so long I'm starting to believe it myself…

So, anyway, after a few more weeks, we were set for the rave. And I've got to hand it to him, Shanks was good. He'd thought of everything – he'd even forged some documents to flash under the noses of any authority figures who came sniffing, saying the rave had been signed off by the council and corresponded to all fire and safety codes. Adam and JJ had been doing the rounds in Peel House and the local club nights, building a buzz. Tickets flew. We were charging fifteen quid each – steep for some people we knew – but it was Shank's money and he was adamant it was a steal for what would be the best night of their lives.

Nowt else mattered for Adam and JJ, and they started getting ideas. If the rave went well, they said, they'd put on another, bigger one. They'd bring London to the North and be big time promoters like Shanks! Go into business together, even! Get out of the estate and never come back!

The night before the rave, Shanks' mates came up – half a dozen fuckers who looked like they'd slid out of a Dolce and Gabanna advert. They towered over us, too stunning to be real, picking at the wallpaper in the hall where it was coming away. They were staying at ours, and the house was bursting. Adam and JJ were the centre of attention and though they pretended otherwise, they lapped it up. These angels! Shanks'd say, These angels that dropped into my life! Me, I skulked in the kitchen, necking drinks. I just wanted it all to be over. I was so sick of everything, and I swear the next bit happened exactly like this: Shanks had just cracked some joke in the living room and everyone was laughing, and I thought, *I hope it's a fucking disaster* – them exact words – and at that very second someone banged on the door.

Silence. That kind of knock was never good. Adam stuck his head into the hall and whispered, *Who's that?*

I was like, How should I know?

Answer it, he said. Chicken.

So I did.

There was this massive bloke on the doorstep, hands tucked into his waistcoat.

He said, And you are?

I'm Jim, I said. Who are you?

Vincent, he said. Where's your Mammy and Daddy? He saw Adam over my shoulder.

You, Vincent said.

Adam shit a brick. *Me?*

Vincent walked through me; I bounced off his hip like I didn't exist. He herded Adam into the living room. I peeped round the door from the hall.

By the way, in case you don't know, Vincent Barr was – *is* – Scunner-in-Chief round the estate. The one bloke you hope doesn't know your name. You heard crazy as stories about him, like he'd once got banged up for rolling an armoured truck in Manchester, or how his dog ripped off some poor fucker's ballsack. Crazy shite. And now he was in our house.

Everyone went mute. Shanks was sat on the floor like one of them Tibetan monks, flummoxed.

Vincent said to Adam, A little birdy tells me something's going off at the waterworks tomorrow night.

No, Adam said.

Think carefully before you tell me any porkies, Vincent said.

Shanks spoke. And just who the perfect fuck might you be?

Vincent ignored him, kept his creepy blue eyes on Adam.

Adam looked at JJ, who was rocking back and forth on the floor.

Don't look at her, Vincent said. Look at me. So, my little birdy is right?

Adam nodded.

Vincent wanted to know how many people. When Adam said about six thousand, Vincent whistled. And these people are…?

Just local people, Adam said. From around.

Just local people, Vincent said. From around. You know, my wife is very ill at the minute and needs her rest. I'm not having six thousand scunners tearing up the place.

It's not like that, Adam said. We don't want any trouble.

I've read the papers, Vincent said. Acid Nutters Gang Rape Old Dear and whatnot.

That's all bollocks, JJ said.

Vincent chuckled. You're telling me people who go round wearing gear a fucking Downs kid wouldn't be caught dead in don't have a few screws loose?

Shanks stood up. He was almost as tall as Vincent, almost. He was like, Listen here! I don't know who the hell you think you are, but I'm running the show and this is happening!

What's your name? Vincent said, taking a step into Shanks. Shanks lost his bottle.

Aiden, he said. Aiden Santerre. Can you believe that? What a name! Aiden Santerre!

And where do you hail from, Aiden Santerre?

London.

Long way from home, aren't you?

Shanks said nowt.

Vincent looked around the room. Nowt happens on this estate without my say so, right? So this rave, it's off.

You can't do that, Shanks said.

Vincent drilled holes through him. I can do whatever I want, sunshine. I catch any of you cunts up here again, they'll never find the bodies, right?

No one spoke.

RIGHT!?

Mumble mumble went the room.

Then Vincent cocked his head, like a dog watching telly. He said, But six thousand druggy little fucks at fifteen quid a pop? That's not to be sniffed at, is it?

This is *mine*, Shanks said. You should have seen the look on his face. At that moment, I could totally see him as some snotty brat, his nanny taking his toys off him because he hadn't done his Latin verbs or something.

Thirty percent, Vincent said. Now that's fair.

No, Shanks snarled.

I could take it all if I wanted. Not like you can ring the pigs. These things are illegal, aren't they?

Shanks' gob was a white slit in his tanned face.

It's either that, Vincent said, or me and the boys go in tomorrow night and fuck the place right up. How's that sound?

Fine, thirty percent, Adam said, but Shanks was like, *No!* I'm sick of you haggard bastards thinking you can just

132

sweep in and take what you want! Your time is *done*, old man! Finito! You're not getting a penny, you hear! Not a penny! There, what do you say to that?

His face inches from Vincent's. Shanks' friends clung to each other. Adam and JJ tried to melt into the corner, while I ran into the kitchen and hid round the side of the fridge, ready to bolt out the back door. I'm telling you, I thought Shanks was literally dead.

But I heard Vincent say calmly, Well, enjoy your party. Then he left.

In the living room, nobody spoke. Shanks' mates looked green-as. JJ had her head on Adam's shoulder, Adam had his head in his hands. Only Shanks was on his feet, staring into space, lips moving. Fuck him, he said.

You don't understand who that was, Adam said.

I don't care. We've got security. They can handle it.

We should've given him the money.

Shanks pointed at him, livid. That was *my* money you wanted to give away! Remember that!

And Adam actually apologised!

Needless to say, Shanks got his way and, despite everything – *ahh*, I'm really feeling it now – despite everything, the waterworks looked class. Ever since I was a kid, it'd been a wreck – graffiti as high as the spray cans could go, reeking of piss, but that night it was transformed. Everyone was drilled and knew their jobs, and within a few hours we had sound, power, toilets. A security team from Middlesbrough came in on a coach and Shanks put a guy every hundred yards around the perimeter of knotweed surrounding the place, telling them a local wannabe tough-guy had made threats. Inside, everything was decked out to Adam and JJ's designs –

mirror balls and projectors with NASA-launch loops of rocket boosters flaming in the stratosphere. We even scored a crate of glow sticks from someone Shanks knew in the army and, aye, I know, glow sticks are proper clichéd nowadays, but back then they were pure sci-fi. Shanks showed me how to do it – crack the middle, shake – and slipped a couple in my pocket.

Everything was ready. All we had to do was wait and I'll admit, little bitch that I was, I was excited.

The first people started showing up. Ravers – Acid Teds and proud. Shanks was dressed like a yacht captain – his normal getup – and had a walkie talkie on his belt. He said a few words into it and over on the platform, the DJ dropped a million decibels of Phuture's *Acid Trax* across the wasteland.

I felt in my pocket for my bag of pills. I'd done extra shifts at the glass factory to afford them and I felt like getting purely battered. Like burying my jealousy and sadness under an avalanche of love. I necked one, so did Adam and JJ. Shanks, too, who usually abstained, but since it was a special occasion and all that. Then we went inside.

The place was filling up. On the ticket, we'd put no cars because there was nowhere to park except on the estate, and that would've riled people. So they came pouring through the streets and I hoped whoever saw them – like Macca, Trace, Dad – I hoped the sight would jolt them out of their pinhole worlds.

The E got to work, and I started to lose myself in the music. Started thinking, haway, life's not so bad. Expecting everything to stay the same forever is childish, isn't it? The trick is to change with change, embrace it. That was how love grew – over time, through experience and adversity. Love locked up dies. I wanted to find Adam and JJ, say

134

sorry for how I'd been acting, but first I'd do another pill. You do that for some reason – do another pill – right when you're coming up on the first and need it the least. So in the middle of the dancing crowd, I went to fiddle one out of my bag, but I got knocked and they flew out my hand. I dropped to my knees but it was no good, they were gone. My goodwill, though, was solid. I was like, Fuck it – easy come, easy go. I could always get more. Everybody in there was battered. I went looking for Adam and JJ.

And before everything went to shite that night, it was beautiful. So many people all having a good time, all these walks of life, from acid kids to scunners and everyone in between. I thought we'd finally cracked it, you know? Here we were – we'd finally sank down to the secret where all our individual selves had become one. I bumped into Alive and his mate Mickey. Alive had his shirt off, proper gurning. He stuck a fat wet kiss on me. They hadn't seen Adam or JJ, so I wandered around for a bit and started thinking about pills again. I should've asked Alive while I'd had the chance, but when I got back to where I thought they were, I couldn't see them. I started asking randoms, and after a couple of tries this guy said he'd do me two for a tenner, which was a proper bargain. They looked weird, though. They were bigger than normal and had gnarly flecks in them that glowed under the lights. Still, I paid him and necked one.

Now, anyone who's done pills'll tell you one of the first things to go is time. Like, you can light a cigarette and somehow you're still smoking it an hour later. Or you reckon it's *got* to be five or six in the morning, but your watch says not even midnight. Shite like that. What I'm trying to say is the next part is hard to sequence.

At some point, I found Adam, JJ, and Shanks. They were all proper loved up and I hugged everyone, including Shanks, and for a bit all the grooves of the universe dovetailed. But then Shanks looked over the top of the crowd at something we weren't tall enough to see, and all of a sudden he was gone. We followed him outside and found Vincent leaning against a segment of old concrete pipe.

Just thought I'd see what all the fuss was about, he said.

Shanks was like, How'd you get in here? He was trying to be tough, and if you've never seen someone try to act the hard man on pills, you should.

Vincent swigged from a can of lager. He said, This music sounds like a tumble dryer what needs its bearings changed.

I'm getting security, Shanks said.

I wouldn't do that if I were you. What I said would happen, happened. I had hundreds of shitheads pouring down my street.

We're just having fun, Shanks said. Why can't you people understand?

What I understand, Vincent said, is that my wife has barely slept in three days, but tonight, miracle of miracles, she manages to drift off, only to be woken up by these mongs blowing fucking whistles outside her window.

Sorry, Shanks said.

Vincent was like, So I'm here to give you one last chance, only now the rates have gone up. Give me half the door or – and here he pointed out into the knotweed, all around the clock face – or my boys come in and we have an altercation.

I'm getting security, Shanks slurred. He fumbled around his belt for the walkie talkie, but it had gone. That's another thing – when you're on pills, stuff just vanishes.

Vincent put his can down on the pipe, went over to

Shanks and gripped his shoulders. He stared into Shanks' twitching face. You're a fucking mess, son, he said. What would *mama* and *papa* say if they could see you now? Cut your inheritance, I'd bet. And this shite – he nods over at the rave – people will be *laughing* at this shite in five years' time. Mark me, I've seen it happen. Teddy Boys, Mods, Rockers, Skinheads, Punks…you think you're all onto something, but you wait. Now, do we have a deal?

Shanks squirmed free. You get nothing, he said. Nada. Zip.

Vincent went back to the pipe and picked up his beer. Have it your way, he said, and disappeared into the dark.

I just spiked that cunt's can, JJ said.

Shanks scanned the night. Nobody's out there, he said. He thinks he can scare me.

We went back in and put it out of our minds, pretty easy to do considering the contents of our bloodstreams. But then I started feeling wrong – I was coming up again, only this time it was different. Too hard and fast. I retched, but nowt came up. I staggered to the wall, but it kept coming. Waves of it. Then my head filled with blue-grey. I can't explain it better than that, just blue-grey, like this mist we're standing in now, and I looked up at this lass and she started melting, her face running off her skull, lard globbing off her jawbone. A bloke's ear slid off in a dollop. I'd forgotten about that second pill, hadn't I? I started freaking out and the music got louder, got crushing. I pressed my face against the wall, wet with breath and sweat, and closed my eyes, and that's when the screaming started. I tried looking, but if I focused on any one spot for more than a few seconds, it melted, so I used the wall for support and kind of groped my way towards the entrance.

A man with a shaved head was beating the shite out of some poor fucker in dungarees, the impacts making lumps of his face fly. Another guy swung a length of pipe at some terrified kids who, in my eyes, collapsed like waxworks in the sun. Someone pulled the plug on the music and the crowd stampeded – people coming at me with eyes, noses, mouths splattering. Gristle and bone beneath. These blokes lashing out at anyone trying to escape, three of them around a security guard, kicking the shite out of him. I grabbed hold of someone's leg and begged him for help, but his face came apart. I got slammed into the floor and the lights went out, so I crawled. Somehow I made it outside and the coach the security guards had come in on was burning. The flames threw crazy shapes over everything, greasy smoke pumping into the night. People fighting everywhere, people senseless, people screaming, people running. I stumbled away from the fire, into the darkness, and I was *still* coming up – monstrous waves of it, like it was never going to end.

Adam and JJ were huddled not far from the concrete pipe where JJ had spiked Vincent's can. Shadows swooped, hiding them one second, exposing them the next. I forced myself to watch as they melted together, their faces and bodies liquefying into one, and I hated them. Hated the oozing thing that had once been my friends. It turned what was left of its head in my direction, staring with its one remaining eye. A dripping stump that might've once been part of JJ reached out to me, and I think I heard it say my name, but I was already running for the knotweed...

Peg, don't worry. That's not going to happen to us. Our pills are from Alive. You can trust him.

How long was I out there? Like I said, time bends on

you. There's holes in my memory, and that knotweed was no joke, man. It was taller than I was, and thick like in a Vietnam film. Proper slashed my hands pushing through it. I'd lost my jacket and I was freezing. I started coming down, and sometimes the weeds parted just enough so I could see there was no moon or stars. Threads of smoke and sounds drifted over my head – sirens, chaos – but I couldn't figure out where they were coming from, or why.

I came out into the clearing. I'd only been there once or twice, when I was growing up. Being from the blocks meant you couldn't just go and hang around there without some kind of comeback from the more local estate kids. In the centre of the clearing, sticking a few feet out of the ground, was the well. I didn't want to get closer, but I did anyway. It was like I wasn't in control, like it wasn't me stepping up onto the edge and leaning over. There was a sound from the bottom, this watery breathing. I still had the glow sticks Shanks had given me, so I cracked one and dropped it. It fell so far I didn't even hear it land.

Then a voice said, Careful. And I was *this close* to falling in.

There was a shape at the edge of the clearing, almost invisible. I tried focusing on it, but my vision was all pixelly. I cracked the other glow stick and chucked it over. Vincent's face lit up in deep skull-socket shadow.

Haway over here, he said. He was sitting with his legs out in front of him.

Again, I knew I shouldn't, but I went.

It's you, he said, when I got close. How the fuck are *you*? His eyes took up half his gently melting face. He was trying to light a little cigar, but he couldn't figure out which way round it went. Finally, he got it going and inhaled. He was like, I've just been sitting here thinking about how fucking amazing everything is. Don't you think? All these people having fun…it should be like that, shouldn't it? People having fun. There isn't enough fun round here sometimes.

But you killed it, I said.

It took him a minute to process that. Under his beard, his jaw was going hard. He was like, Aye, but I *had* to do that. Business is business. Was that what all that noise was before? I wasn't there. I'd started feeling a bit queer, so I came out here for a breather.

Exhaustion hit me. Sometimes the fatigue clouts you all at once. I sat down on the other side of the glow stick.

Vincent looked over to the well. He said, My boy nearly died down that. Some local lads did it. Left him to die.

I'd heard about that. When Vincent stories came to us, we savoured them because we weren't involved. His kid was called Evan, or Alan, or something. A couple of years above us in school, this weird lad. Nowt like his dad.

Vincent's eyes rolled in his head. I feel *really* fucking good. How do you feel?

Cabbaged, I said.

He kept talking about his kid. He was like, I'm hard on him, I know I am, but he needs it because it's a hard world. That's how my dad raised me, that's how I'm raising him. Only he's…different. I don't understand him.

My dad doesn't understand me either, I said.

We both wrestled with our sinking heads for a bit. Then Vincent said, But whose fault is that? If he doesn't understand you? Kids change too quickly these days.

You closed the hatch on us, I said. What did you expect?

I don't know if he understood that. I think he just wanted to talk. He said, Jean treats him like he's made of glass, and it only got worse after what them bastards done to him. It makes me look like the bad guy…and maybe I am…but it's because I love him. He's my only kid. We tried to have another one, you know, but it just didn't happen.

His cigar had gone out, so he flicked it.

He said, I should tell him that, shouldn't I? That I love him? And tell Jean too. She's the light of my life. I should tell her, shouldn't I?

Uh, I said.

You know, he said, I've done things. Bad, bad fucking things she's none the wiser about. But when I'm with her, it's like I've still got a chance. We'll have been married twenty-two year next year.

S'nice, I said.

Then, in the slushy voice of someone rushing on pills, he said, She's got ovarian cancer. Doctors say she might have another year or two if she's lucky. Cunts actually used that word. *Lucky*.

His face was dripping, but nowhere near as badly, and if I looked away for a moment, his features reset. He lay flat on his back. I even tried praying, he said. Got down on my knees and offered myself up to God, but there was nobody there. Nobody anywhere. Just emptiness.

I couldn't think of owt to say.

Then he was like, I used to think me and her were part of each other. She's a part of me, at least. But I catch her looking through me sometimes, like I'm not even there, and it makes me feel like maybe I've been alone all along.

He lay for a while in silence. Then he said, I can't see the moon.

Me either, I said.

He got up. You know, you're alright. Come on, givuz a hug. And he scooped me into his arms like I weighed nowt, and I was this close to his face, looking right into his eyes, and I don't know why, but I kissed him. Proper smooched him – Vincent Barr! – right on the lips. He didn't kiss me back, but he didn't pull away neither. Then he put me down, walked into knotweed, and left me alone.

That's when you spoke, Peg. At first, I was like, chill out Jim, it's just the drugs, but then you said, *Down. Here.* And I realised it was coming from the well.

So I stepped onto the edge and leaned over. The glow stick at the bottom was less than a speck, and the last thing I remember thinking was maybe I had imagined it, maybe Vincent was right – when it came down to it, we were all alone – and then something moved in the weeds behind me and I turned and fell. There was wind, darkness, then nowt. How long was I unconscious? All I know is that I woke up twisted in a puddle of water. I didn't feel any pain yet. Over to one side there was a kind of, I don't know what, a kind of shrine made of beer cans and cider bottles. Some of the cans had been beaten flat and bent into weird patterns. Cigarette ends were arranged in neat rows around it, like years scratched into a prison wall. And in the middle, the weirdest thing of all – a trainer with a feather sticking out of it. I was trying to work out what it all meant when I glimpsed you, crouched and swaying, just beyond the glow stick's light. I tried to speak but my jaw was smashed. You came closer and you were naked, like you are now – skin and bones, hair over your face. You weren't a hallucination, I knew that much. You were *real*. Real and beautiful. What did you think of me? There was no time to find out because then you were gone, and I woke up in the hospital two weeks later.

The people I'd heard behind me in the weeds had been police, rounding people up. Apparently, they'd bumped into Vincent after he'd left me, and in his agreeable state, he'd told them I was in the clearing. When they got there, one of them thought to shine a torch down the well and that's how I was found. I'd caved the left side of my ribcage, collapsed my left lung, shattered my left hip and left side of my jaw. Left hand smashed to smithereens. The police wanted to pin it on Vincent and wouldn't believe it was just an accident. They were like, When it comes to him, there *are* no accidents. Cor went mental when I told her I wasn't pressing charges. She actually went round and called him out in his own house. The fucking balls on her.

I was in hospital for a month. Mam and Cor visited a lot. Even Auntie Bea flew back from Spain. The only person who didn't come was Dad. Adam and JJ came, too. They said Shanks was due up in court and was looking at a heavy fine, maybe even jail. Adam had dyed his hair Dracula-black. He was like, Shanks swears he's never crossing the Watford Gap for the rest of his life.

Long pause.

We're moving down there, JJ said.

Adam almost put his hand on my good hand, but chickened out. Come down when you're better, he said.

Sure, JJ echoed.

And I said, Try and stop me. I blamed my tears on needing more morphine.

So long story short, I moved back to Asquith. My old room with the Middlesbrough FC and Pixies posters. Mam haunted me morning, noon, and night with bowls of soup and rice pudding. Waiting outside the bog while I had a shit, in case I couldn't pull my keks back up. And Dad…

well, if he despised me before, it was nowt compared to his revulsion once I was back. I wasn't just a freak on the inside anymore. Now it was there for all to see.

The tension in the flat all got too much for Cor. She put her name down for a place on the estate, and who can blame her? Getting a house was still pretty easy back then, as it wasn't exactly a desirable area. I started physiotherapy, and when I was well enough she invited me to live with her. I'll never be able to repay her for that. We lived together for a while and…well, maybe I could have coped with things better than how I did before we fell out…but I don't want to get into that now.

Time passed. I healed bent. My scars turned pink, then white. My hair dropped out and I stopped going out in daylight. People avoided me in the street. Bairns cried at the sight of me. Teenagers chucked stones. And then it hit me, what I was…

>   …what I…

…Man…I feel…Hey, hey – it's OK, this is normal. Just let it come. I'm right here with you…Hey, did you know…

…did you know…

…I started *dreaming* of you? We're down the well again.
>   You come out of the darkness.
>   Rest your cold fingers on

my broken face and

>   I trace your bones through your skin as the glow

144

stick dies. Then I wake up alone, my lips
brackish…

…and…

…For a while I thought

that we – me, Adam, JJ, everyone – I thought
we were sinking down to the place where we wouldn't
need each other,

anymore

because we *were* each other…But look at me now.

Here I am,
talking to you,

and I haven't seen those people in half a lifetime…

…

…But for years I thought Adam was right. Like
Thatcher said…

…*There is no such thing as society*…

…and that I was alone…

…but…

…do you know what she

145

said after that?

Thatcher...?

...I didn't, until recently...I found it on the...

...Internet...
...She said...

...I memorised it, she said...

...There is no such thing as society...

...There is a living tapestry

of men and women and people...and the...

...beauty of that tapestry and the quality of our lives...

...will depend...

...will depend on how much each of us is prepared

to take responsibility for ourselves and each of us prepared

to turn around and help...

...by our own efforts those who

are…

…*unfortunate…*

…Which is why I'm here,

…

Like I said…we'll start small, just the two of us…

…

…take it from there…

…I haven't felt like this in *years*…look at my

hand! I can move it!

Look…

…!…

…Hey…

…It's OK…we've got all th

                              e
                         t
                            i
                            m
                              e
                                i

n
t
h
e…

.

..

....c'mere…

....*oh*…

…givuz a…
…givu
z…

…a…

…hug
)

III

Moorside: apricot-coloured residences with Georgian-barred windows, double garages, *drapes*. Children's bicycles lie unswiped from front lawns as uniform and verdant as butcher's grass. And now, reeling through it like a bronchial Nosferatu, comes Jim. Up ahead, a late-night dog walker pre-emptively crosses the road.

Best as he can figure, the well itself once stood where he stands now, at the junction of Chestnut Close and Pine Street, two streets so hushed it's as if their audio tracks have been muted. He imagines the drop directly below his feet, though knows it isn't. In 1993, while Rowan-Tree were razing the waterworks in preparation for the final phase of Moorside's construction, an uncovered World War Two bomb exploded and collapsed the shaft forever. The well exists now only in Jim's mind, something any victim of that void knows is still more than enough.

He shines his torch on the map, checks his compass. From here, the pipe heads north east, so that's the way he goes, pushing through snarls of knotweed that only he can see.

His shoes are too old for these woods and the black treacle of autumn soaks his soles. Occasionally, his torch illuminates shreds of police tape still tied around the trunks of trees, the low-hanging fretwork of branches reminiscent of stripped nervous systems. He uses his crutch like an insectoid feeler, sweeping and tapping. The pain in his hip and back harmonise and there is no moon that he can see. Things vanish. No explanation.

The burn, when he finally reaches it, is no longer a burn

but a pool – barely – of stagnant water, obscured by thorns and roots.

But the pipe is still there, jutting from the bank. The flimsy-looking and badly rusted grille across its mouth lattices the darkness therein. He turns his ear towards it and listens, his breath coming in white bursts. Corroded beer cans bob in the pool. Shining his torch there, he sees a thin scrim of white liquid on the surface.

'Hello?' he says.

The top of her head emerges; black hair against white water.

'It's Jim,' he says. 'It's me.'

Slowly, out of less than two feet of water, she rises: rivulets of scum contour her bones, her skin a ghastly green pall, her stomach a concaved twist. Black nipples erect on small breasts and a shadowy patch of pubic hair between wasted, ossified legs. She stands fully upright.

'Hi Peg,' he says.

Peg doesn't answer. Her chest rises and falls, rises and falls.

He takes a shambling step into the pool. 'I'm sorry I took so long.'

Peg is taller than he is. She lets him come.

'You've been dreaming of me,' he says.

She rests her numbing hand on his scarred jaw.

He brings out the ecstasy Alive sold him, and swallows one with a palmful of white water. He puts the other on Peg's black tongue. She lets him tilt back her head and dribble water into her mouth. Sinew shifts in her throat as the drug goes down.

'We'll start small,' he says. 'Just the two of us.'

The pool begins to bubble and a thick fog creeps

through the trees. Peg takes Jim's clawed hand in her clawed hand as the world dissolves, until it's impossible to see where she ends and he begins, until they're…

…going…

…going…

MIDNIGHT

Frank and Scott Hulme
of Second Avenue

Scott skulks five, six steps behind Frank, toe-ending pebbles and milky cubes of safety glass from the kicked-in bus stop. He's in a huff, but alright – let him stew. After the stunt he's pulled, Frank's not exactly itching to talk either.

They keep their distance until the downturned mouth of Hollis Road, which splits the estate in two. Traffic sounds like grey waves on a slag shore, a torrent of vehicles using the road as thoroughfare to places, perhaps, where things like this mess now unfolding don't happen. Frank shields his eyes. Should've gone a bit further up, he thinks, crossed at the zebra by the Labour Club, but then Scott's beside him, eyeballing his feet, chewing his lip.

'Son,' Frank says, 'screw your head on while you're crossing.'

Scott hoiks a gob of something nasty onto the grass verge and, for the first time since the phone call earlier that day, looks at his father.

'I'm sorry, right?' he says. 'Can we just go home? I don't want to go there. I *really* don't want to go there.'

Join the club, Frank thinks, but before he can say this, a gap appears in the traffic and the two of them dart like assassins between the headlights.

From Hollis Road, you go along Stanhope Street then cut across Emery Street onto the Crescent. Two options then present themselves: either head up to Vivienne Avenue via Ashworth Road, or across the Green and through the alley onto Tan Row – skirting the bins behind the precinct – and up to the house that way. Frank chooses Tan Row because it takes longer. The streetlights emit clouds of flat orange light that falls like dust. On the north-western edge of the estate, the six Brutalist high-rises crowd the sky;

155

beyond them, the slow-fingered spotlights of the greyhound track on the dual carriageway crisscross as if warding off hoodoo. The *Missing* poster slapped to the bricks in the alley: Lily Butler. Vanished weeks ago. Appeal for witnesses, etc. Neither father nor son acknowledge it.

'Tell me again what you're going to say,' Frank says.

Scott shrugs.

'You can't just shrug at this man.'

Scott shrugs.

'Be respectful, say it was an accident. You got carried away, but you've learned your lesson. *Sound like you mean it.*'

When Scott shrugs again, Frank grabs him by the shoulders, thrusts his face into his son's close enough to smell his menthol gum. Not quite fifteen, and already his boy is a shade taller than he is. 'I mean it, Scott. This isn't just about you.'

'What's it matter?' Scott says. 'In a month's time we won't even *be* here.'

'It matters because when we come back – and we will – who's to say we won't end up even nearer him? *Neighbours?*'

'*When* we come back? You act like it's going to be next week or something.'

'Christ, not this again.'

'It's easy for you,' Scott says. 'You don't have mates.' He struggles out of his father's grasp and for an instant Frank thinks he's going to run. But he doesn't.

'That doesn't change this,' Frank says. 'You know who he is, don't you?'

Scott pulls up his hood. 'I know.'

He lives at the end of Vivienne Avenue, by the garages. The biggest house on the estate because it's actually two terraces knocked through. There's an ancient Peugeot 505 in the front yard, *Barr Autos & MOTs* on the side, a pair of steel-toed boots lie where they've been kicked off beside a badly listing bird table. Crushed rollies everywhere. Light from the front windows brush all with an eerie deep-sea glow. They slow to a shuffle at the front gate.

'This'll take five minutes,' Frank says. He puts an arm around Scott; a small gesture which ordinarily his son would shirk but this time does not, and for that moment Frank forgets about the blood-red door on which he's about to knock. About the man who waits behind.

Paint flakes off in his hand when he opens the gate. There's no movement in the windows, but from somewhere inside Frank hears the short, sharp bursts of a power drill.

'Haway, Scott.'

The drill gets louder, rising in pitch.

'Five minutes…

(He thinks about the last time he was here, at this door. That horrific day.)

…five minutes and we're out of here.'

There's a lull in the drilling. Frank takes a deep breath and bangs on the door. The sound is monstrous. He can hear voices – more than one, he's sure – coming from inside. Scott moves instinctively behind his father, but Frank says no, that won't look good.

'And get your hood down,' he says. 'Ready?'

Ambient estate noise swallows his son's one-syllable reply.

Footsteps, and then Vincent throws the door wide, stands before them in a blaze of light.

He hates how fast he's speaking. 'Mr Barr – Vincent – I'm Frank Hulme, and this is my son Scott. You rang before. You're expecting us.'

Beside his father, Scott shrinks.

'That I am,' Vincent says.

—

Way back when, a derelict waterworks stood where the spacious detached and semi-detached homes of Moorside now stand. Bombed by the Nazis, it was left to rot, along with a monstrous concrete water tower terrifyingly reminiscent of a tripod from *War of the Worlds*. Surrounding both was what was generally referred to in those days as The Field, a tract of wasteland where the Japanese knotweed was six feet high. You could miss your tea trying to escape.

All of which, of course, magnetised children. Rolling games of Hide-and-Seek, Manhunt, Armies – games at which youths these days with their Playstations and their Benson & Hedges would scoff – took place there, though caution was advisable. Jagged bricks, rusty cans, and broken glass lay half-buried in the undergrowth, glinting with tetanus. There was a well, too. Or rather, a maintenance shaft that had once granted engineers access to the now-dry and defunct water channels below. The well stood in a clearing of knotweed and might have once been covered by a safety grille, though by the mid-1980s it had vanished, leaving nothing between you and a sheer drop into pitch black zilch. How far down it went was a mystery. Rocks were dropped but never heard to land. Children dared each other to step up onto the edge – an edge rimmed with corroded steel and rusted bolts – to lean out over the darkness, and spit. Doing so was a show of bravado, a substratum in the complex hierarchy of prepubescence, and commanded respect not only by dint of the obvious perils, but due also to that which remained unspoken: that a child craning his or her neck over the void might get the distinct sense something was down there, looking up at them. *Watching.* Some even heard a whisper, like a seashell at the ear. Their own blood – something that lived.

Naturally, mothers warned their offspring to steer clear, and teenage Frank's mother was no exception: *Don't mess on round that well!*

And Frank, sprinting from the house to meet his friends, already half-blinded by dazzling hexagons of summer sun, shouted back, *I won't!*

But he would.

And keep away from that Alan Barr!

Alan Barr was Vincent's son.

Frank: *I will!*

But he didn't. And here's the rub: if he had, you wouldn't be reading this.

—

Vincent's house smells like meat. Not frying sirloin or roast chicken, but *meat* – dripping claret.

'Shut that door,' he says, 'you're letting the heat out.' It's impossible to believe Vincent is in his seventies. The same age as Frank's own father, or would have been had the strokes not claimed him a decade ago.

Frank manages what he hopes is a comforting look at his boy. There's a nest of spots on Scott's forehead, vivid like spackled blood. He has his mother's jaw but his skin, and that's a shame because acne is an awful thing. Whenever Franks thinks of his teenage self – attempts to tap into the youth he once was – the memories are opaque, thought and deed best-guessed and second hand; but the visceral misery of acne…even nowadays, tracing fingertips across his own flesh, he can almost feel the raw boils, the hot pus pulse. Scott, it seemed, was to be similarly cursed, and lately Frank has sensed his son resenting him for it. Felt it added to the list of mounting grievances against his name.

They follow Vincent down a hallway lit by unshaded, high watt bulbs. The wallpaper is the spongey stuff everyone had back in the 80s. Framed photographs: a long-haired Vincent with his wife, a peroxide-curled woman so tiny it's hard to imagine how Vincent hadn't simply crushed her like a starling egg. Next, a black and white portrait of an unsmiling young man in an RAF uniform, a crease in the photo slicing neatly across his throat. Beside that, a picture of a giant, grizzled man clamping onto his knee what appears to be Vincent as a toddler. Child Vincent's face is set hard, as if attempting to ignite something with his mind. Alan's photograph is the last one. In it, he looks much like he did that day at the well: young and scraggly and grinning that doomed grin of his. Not much older than Scott is now. Frank looks away.

Vincent is waiting for them in the living room. His antifreeze-blue eyes crawl over Frank's face. 'It's been a long time,' he says. He shifts his gaze to Scott. 'And this is your boy.'

Scott nods.

Frank says, 'We won't take up too much of your time. Scott here has something he wants to say, don't you Scott?'

For a moment, Frank thinks his son's going to flub his lines but then, in a voice that holds a knife to his heart,

Scott says, 'Mr Barr, I'm sorry for what I did. It was –'

'One sec,' Vincent says. His white beard is stained yellow at the corners. He smoothes it down with his free hand. 'Before we get into that, I need a favour.'

Father and son exchange looks.

'Relax,' Vincent says. 'It's a simple job. I just need a hand with something in the back room.'

Frank knows he should be balling his fists, planting his feet. But he says, 'What job?'

'Easier if I just show you.'

Frank glances at his boy. Scott could be in Madame Tussaudes. 'OK,' he says.

Vincent smiles. He still has all his own teeth, and they are black, pin-like things.

'Champion,' he says, like he and Frank are old pals. Like he doesn't recall what happened between them in this very house all those years ago. 'Champion.'

—

Alan was in the year above Frank and his friends at school, and just one of those kids. Just *off*. In P.E., the rare times anybody passed him the ball, Alan was like some mouse-startled woman in a cartoon, up on her stool, twisting her petticoats. And forget trying to speak to him because as soon as you opened your mouth he'd literally cringe, this God-awful grin leaking across his spastic face, like he didn't understand a word you were saying. Like you were conversing in Moonspeak. That he was the son of a man like Vincent made little sense to Frank.

Until, that is, the day Frank was on his way to Fat Gary's for football stickers and saw the two of them leaving the chip shop. The buttons on Vincent's waistcoat flashed heliographs in the sun as he strode ahead to the car, though they lived only five minutes away. Alan trailed behind with the bags of food. Chip shop carrier bags are perennially flimsy affairs, and one started to droop and tear, disgorging wrapped packets and cans of pop. Alan dropped to his knees, desperate to salvage what he could, and foolishly picked up a portion by its greasy corner, unravelling chips all over the pavement.

Vincent went ape. He stomped back to his boy and even from the other side of the road, where he was now peeking from behind a parked car, Frank heard: '*You're not even fit to carry fucking chips now?*' He reached down and Alan skittered backwards through the mess, but all Vincent wanted was to yank the rest of the bags off his son's wrist. Then he got in the car and screeched off.

Surrounded by battered sausages, Alan stayed on his knees while the gulls moved in. He looked like someone kneeling by the side of a pit, awaiting the bullet to the base of the skull. Then he got to his feet, wiped his nose on his sleeve, and started home.

Once he'd gone, Frank broke cover. There was a can of Tizer in the gutter and he opened it at arm's length, wary of fizz. It was warm, but he sipped it anyway and began for the first time to question the supposed anomaly that was Alan Barr. Maybe it did, after all, make some sense that Alan was Vincent's son.

Maybe it made perfect sense.

—

There's something maritime about Vincent, some aura of brine. White shirtsleeves rolled up over densely tattooed forearms – skulls, sirens, krakens, scimitars – the black ink long since gone a queasy myrtle green. The buttons on his waistcoat strain against the man's sheer bulk; braces almost as wide as gurney straps hanging down the backs of his pinstripe trousers. He whistles in a delicate, soaring register as Frank and Scott follow him to the backroom.

They reach a closed door. Vincent scratches his shaved head, the action kicking up flakes. 'Just in here,' he says.

Vincent extends a hand, palm out, inviting them to step inside, and it occurs to Frank that at the front door, he'd sworn there had been not one but two voices coming from the house.

'It's your gaff,' Frank says, feigning nonchalance, 'so after you.'

Vincent's pleasant smile does not change. His open palm, fissured like a salt plain, does not close.

'Dad,' Scott says.

So Frank makes a decision. He opens the door and steps inside.

—

It happened during the summer holidays of 1986. Frank was as old as Scott is now – fourteen going on fifteen – part of a listless pack of boys murdering the long days by kicking balls off the sides of houses, and making single cigarettes go around five sets of lungs. It was late afternoon on one such indolent day when they saw Alan coming up the other side of the road, jumping from paving slab to paving slab to avoid stepping on cracks. He hadn't seen them.

'Hey Al!' Tommy Greener shouted.

Alan froze. He pushed his glasses up his nose and peered over, grinning that terrible, trembling grin.

Tommy was their leader. A thick-necked boy with moles and a mean streak. 'Al, we're heading up the field if you fancy?'

Alan didn't respond.

Some boys stared up a chant – '*Aaaa-lan, Aaaa-lan*' – but some vague sense of self-preservation appeared to be holding Alan back.

'Haway, Al,' Tommy said. 'It'll be a laugh.'

Alan took a step towards them, stopped, looked up the street in the direction of home. What was he weighing up at that moment? Surely he had to have sensed something malevolent afoot? But if so, why did he go with them? What those boys did to him in that field, was it still better to risk *that*, than continue home to Vivienne Avenue and his father?

And if it was then…well.

At the field, Tommy hoofed the ball into the knotweed and Alan plunged eagerly in after it. Tommy had this look on his face, all his moles coming together in a smirk. Tommy's best friend Brian Simm sniggered.

Tommy had kicked the ball in the direction of the well. The rest of the boys followed Alan's path, melting into the knotweed like beings from another world.

—

The first thing Frank sees when he steps into the room is the disembodied head of a St. Bernard. It rests on the table, its large glassy eyes pondering the aertex ceiling. Scott sees it a second later and clamps his hands over his mouth. Vincent closes the door behind them.

'That's Ludwig,' he says. 'The greatest beast I ever knew.' He puts one blunt-trauma hand on each of their shoulders.

'Where's the rest of him?' Frank asks.

Vincent's breath is an underground coal blaze. 'The rest of him's *fucked*.' He goes over to the table and swivels the head so as to be able to look into the thing's eyes. 'Had him since he was a pup,' he says. 'He used to be able to fit here, in the palm of my hand…a gentle giant, he was.' He laughs softly, fondly.

Frank forces a facsimile of a smile.

'Aye,' Vincent says, 'but get on the wrong side of him and say goodbye to your knackers. Some cunt tried getting in here about five year back, and he didn't get ten steps inside the yard before Ludwig was on him. I heard the screams from upstairs and when I got down all I found was a trail of gore going back over the wall and a ripped-off ballsack, still in its trackies. Ludwig was chewing one knacker, but he left the other for, like, *elevenses*, you might say. I was there when he ate it. It burst like a fucking *goooozeberry*.' He pops his lips deep inside his beard. 'You lads believe that?'

Scott nods violently.

Vincent sets the head with a thump to face them. The thing is attached to a dark mahogany shield of the sort deer and elk are traditionally mounted. The head itself is a distended horrorshow that reminds Frank of a news report he'd once seen about a botched drug trial, where the heads of the participants had swelled into hellacious blackberries. Between his eternally parted jaws, Ludwig's yellow fangs are visible. A pink tongue cradled in dead meat and bone. Ears all over the place.

Vincent's voice roughens. 'I backed over him in the van last week. I'd had a few, you know…His guts were hanging out his arse.' He traces a thick thumb sensually down the thing's muzzle. 'I couldn't bear to be parted, so I stuffed him. Done it myself.'

Frank gazes into the glass of Ludwig's dumb, dark eyes. The left one is set significantly lower than the right.

'Point is,' Vincent continues, 'his head was the only thing I could save, and it's a bugger to hang. I'm doing it wonky, and I keep changing my mind about where he'll look best. See.' He points to dozens of holes drilled around the room. 'I need to take it in with my own eye. Get a bead on it. This is where you lads come in.'

'Isn't there anybody else in to help out?' Frank asks.

Vincent eyes crawling again. 'No, Frank, I'm all alone.'

'It's just that, well, Pam wants Scott back for his tea. His exams are coming up and you know what kids are like these days, what with their computer games and that. I was thinking, maybe he could say what you invited him round to say, then let him be on his way. I'll stay, of course, and help you with…with Ludwig. How about that?'

Vincent strokes Ludwig gently between its offset ears. 'We'll get to my business with your boy after. This is a three-man job. One to hold Ludwig, one to see if he's in the right place, and one for a second opinion. Because mistakes are so easy to make, aren't they, Frank?'

He paws the head and waits for Frank to reply, but it's Scott who speaks.

'Alright, Mr Barr,' he says. 'What do you want us to do?'

—

166

In the clearing of knotweed, Tommy explained *Clocks*. A simple game: 'Right, everybody stands in a circle with the well in the middle and then someone – me – is three o'clock, right? So I run and jump over and tag nine o'clock – that's my opposite – then *he's* got to jump, right? That's one round. Then nine o'clock says another time and it starts again, only you've got to get faster and faster. Get it?'

They got it. Frank, light-headed with trepidation, was six o'clock and, over the well, facing him, was Alan. Midnight. The sun sank behind the water tower and the first bats came out. In the centre of the circle of boys, the well seemed to expand with each passing second.

Tommy went first. Stocky but athletic, he sailed over the hole with ease to tag Brian Simm, who cleared it in similar fashion. More boys followed. The pace cranked up, the boys dragging heels through the dust like *toros* before a matador, fake-screaming to throw off jumpers on the final steps of their approach. Frank looked over at Alan. He was rocking on his heels, transfixed. Then it was Rob's turn. Rob was Frank's friend and a little on the heavy side. He lolloped towards the well and for the heart-freezing second he was airborne, Frank thought he wasn't going to make it, but then he clipped the far side of the rim and sprawled into the dirt. The boys whooped. Rob looked green, hollowed-out, his croaked '*six*' barely audible above the frenzy. But Frank heard, and on legs that felt like draft-excluding snakes, he sprinted at the well. They'd done long-jump at school – success lay in counting the steps of your run-up, but how many steps had he taken? Ten? Fifteen? Too late anyway – he was already up on the rim, the wind howling in his ears – so he threw a mental prayer into the void and jumped…

167

…and to this day he can't explain it. A psychic break, maybe, brought on by acute terror, but as he flew through space his nostrils filled with the dank, undeniable stench of mildew and he blacked out. Only that wasn't right, because far off in the darkness there was a tiny, dusky circle of light which, peering closer, contained a mote-like speck floating across the centre. It was *him*, Frank, seeing himself through someone else's eyes. *Someone at the bottom of the well!* But before he could understand more, he landed on the other side of the well and snapped back to himself, crackling volts. Alan was ahead, grinning, awed. He held out his hand for Frank to slap – *go Alan! Fucking go!* – and then he – Alan – took off as fast as he could, his arms and legs pumping like an engine of steam-powered Victoriana. The loudest cheer of all went up, but Frank was still too buzzed – still too confused – after his own jump to see what was about to happen, until it was too late.

Brian had teed the ball up at the nine o'clock position and Tommy, who'd had trials for Hartlepool FC, stood poised a few steps behind. When Alan jumped Tommy booted the ball so hard it went egg-shaped. It hit him square in the temple, blasting his glasses twenty feet off his face. Alan came apart in mid-air. He was almost beautiful, like a ballet dancer, like art…

But then he was falling into the well and the boys were screaming for real.

—

The TV in the corner is muted, the sound replaced by multi-coloured, error strewn Ceefax subtitles. A gardening show. The host hefts a long weed from the earth, silent soil

168

tumbling from roots. She thrusts it at the camera, and Frank clings to these seconds of normalcy. On the arm of the settee is an old power drill that sends a ripple of unease through him.

Turquoise lettering:

You must showno mrcy with these terrors.
Or they will come backw ith avengnence.

'You hold Ludwig,' Vincent dumps the head into his arms. It's dismayingly heavy.

'He didn't feel right before. Too light,' Vincent says. 'So I filled him with sand.' He points Scott over to the far end of the room. 'Go over there. You're my adviser.'

Frank clasps the head to his chest. His arms ache already. 'Where do you want it?'

'Well…' Vincent says, 'let's try over the mantelpiece first. Scotty?'

Scott shrugs. Frank walks stiffly to the mantelpiece and heaves the head onto it.

There's a framed picture there: Vincent, a lifetime younger, with his arm around his wife. Beside that is what appears to be a small trophy no bigger than an egg cup, but which on closer inspection turns out to be a tiny urn. JEAN PENELOPE ANNE BARR engraved on a brass plaque two-inches long.

'I said *over* the mantelpiece,' Vincent's tone is chummy. A tone Frank has heard before, in a different time.

Frank takes a deep breath and hoists Ludwig up against the wall.

'Not bad,' Vincent says.

Sweat runs down Frank's back. Shoulders quivering.

'Scott?'

'Good,' Scott mumbles. 'Yeah.'

'You don't mince your words, do you? I think we need a comparison. Hey Frank, try over there, the opposite wall.'

Frank rests the head on the mantelpiece, summoning strength. An overpowering bouquet of decay emanates from Ludwig's core as he bundles the thing into his criss-crossed arms and waddles across the room.

'Next to the window, aye,' Vincent says. 'Between the window and the picture of Jean doing the Timewarp. Aye, right there.'

There is no mantelpiece for support this time. Frank presses the back of the wooden shield against the wall and slides it upwards.

'Watch the fucking wallpaper.' Vincent says. '*Lift* the cunt.'

'But there's holes drilled all over already,' Scott says.

'Holes you can fix, scrapes you can't.'

Frank's seen weightlifters do this. He dips at the knees and uses the resulting momentum to launch Ludwig into the air, snapping his legs and arms straight in unison.

'Left a bit,' Vincent says.

Frank goes left.

'Down. Just a touch.'

Frank goes down. Just a touch. Grimacing.

'There. Scott?'

The hollow enthusiasm in his son's voice is touching. 'It looks great! So much better than the mantelpiece. This is definitely the best place, definitely.'

Vincent sucks his teeth. 'It's top of the list for now, I'll give you that. But let's experiment.'

Frank imagines the chaos inside his own body –

ligaments tearing free of bone, a tsunami of ruptured blood and lactic acid scouring crosshatched musculature. His shirt is drenched.

They try Ludwig near the TV, but it's deemed too off-putting. Next, by the door to the kitchen, but the light switch is an encumbrance. Frank's exhaustion is beyond concealment. Sweat burning in his eyes, he lumbers about the room with the dog's head sagging lower and lower in his arms. He catches Scott's eye. Scott is scared.

Vincent leans against the wall, one hand tucked into his waistcoat. 'You know,' he says, 'I think Scott was right. Next to the window was the winner all along. Frank, your boy's got a future in – whatsit? – interior design.' Suddenly there are three long, evil screws jutting from his fist. He transfers the screws to his mouth and claws become fangs. He picks up the power drill and speaks from around the screws, 'Go on, Frank. Next to the window it is. Think you've got one more in you?'

All Frank can do is nod. His thoughts are sparks in the dark, confused and sporadic. Autopilot guides him back to the window. The framed picture of Vincent's wife swims before his eyes. She must have died in the early 90s, around the time he'd started seeing Pam. He could remember watching the funeral procession as it cinched a slow noose around the estate, JEAN spelled out in neat yellow blossoms on the coffin. She had asked him a question the last time he had been in this house: *What kind of human being does what you did?* It is a question for which he still has no decent answer.

One more lift. But can he? It's all growing dim, his consciousness dissipating, but then, from some unknowable distance, he hears his father's loose change clattering onto floorboards; sees him as he was then: still young, wobbling on one leg to free his foot from his trouser cuff.

Frank feels Ludwig in his hands, feels the acid in his jugular, and lifts.

Vincent speaks from directly behind him, pinning him to the wall. He no longer sounds friendly. 'Left a bit,' he says.

Frank goes left a bit, arms shaking freely. Vincent inserts the first brutal screw into the plaque, brushing the barrel of the drill against Frank's right cheek and, without warning, pumps the trigger. The noise is deafening. Frank's eyes and nose fill with brick dust.

The drill bit is hot when it caresses Frank's left cheek. Vincent's beard tickling his sweaty neck. *'Big man, aren't you?'* he whispers. *'Bigger than your da.'*

This time Frank is braced for the sound. When both screws are in and Ludwig is secure, he slides out from between Vincent and the wall and staggers over to the settee with all the dignity remaining to him. Scott, who's been watching from the corner, sits with him. They don't look at each other. Frank's mouth is too full of saliva to speak. His ears ring.

Vincent secures the final screw and tosses the drill aside without admiring his handiwork. The gardening show is still on. The host strokes a cluster of small, fragile flowers:

**They are delicate things. Too delicate to
fend fot Themselve s.**

—

All he could do – all any of them could do – was watch him fall. *He's dead*, Frank thought, even as Alan's momentum carried his unconscious frame across the drop and smashed his solar plexus into the rim's inside edge; his body snapping – *crack* – into an L, chest slamming into the raised steel ledge, legs dangling puppet-like in space.

Around the clock face, time stood still. Nobody moved. Nobody breathed. And then two things happened almost simultaneously:

Alan came to.

And Alan began slipping into the hole.

(Now take a moment here. Put yourself in Alan's shoes: head pounding, you regain consciousness and blink myopically into the dusk as a crushing but as-yet indistinct humiliation settles over you. Your legs don't feel right. You hear your Dunlop Green-Flashed feet clang against the vertical shaft and then, in your first true moment of comprehension, you look behind yourself only to confront the widening abyss staring back…

Can you imagine that?

Well?)

The boys watched, stunned, as Alan slid into the hole. Hands clawing at the rusted rim, whining like AM-radio. And still none of them moved.

'*Frank*,' Alan whimpered, and Frank jolted awake. He wasn't aware Alan even knew his name. He sprinted round the well, grabbed Alan's wrists, but the boy's terror weighed tonnes. He was slipping rapidly through his grip, but then Rob was there and, with a wrist each, they hauled him out, all three of them tumbling into the dirt. Alan was missing a Dunlop and his right trouser leg was sheered haberdasher-like from knee to groin. He gripped the leg tightly, curling the rest of himself around it. In the twilight, the blood slipping through his fingers was crude oil.

The boys, who had been clustering around, backed off.

The jagged rim of the well. They may as well have dragged him over a giant, rusted cheese grater.

When Tommy ran, the others followed. Only Frank, Rob, and Alan remained.

'Mate, this is bad,' Rob said.

Black blood soaked the ground. Frank turned to say something to Rob, but Rob, too, was disappearing into the knotweed. Frank didn't blame him.

He rocked Alan's shoulder gently. 'Hey? Alan, hey?'

Alan didn't move. Not even a moan escaped him.

Overhead, bats stitched the night into place.

And while he may still have been a teenage boy in possession of only the dimmest sense of the world outside himself, exactly how oblivious was Frank to the fact that his life was about to hurtle down one of two paths? Was he aware on some metaphysical level that one path in particular would set in motion a sequence of events whose consequences would reverberate across three entire generations? Or was he, to put it crudely, *s-h-i-t-t-i-n-g* himself?

Again, put yourself in his shoes. What would you have done?

—

Frank is scooped out. He puts a hand on Scott's knee – *I'm alright* – but the urge to close his eyes is immense.

'He's gone in the kitchen,' Scott says.

Ludwig's huge, deformed head stares benignly down on them.

'Why can't we go?' Scott asks.

The thought has crossed his mind, too, but he says, 'No, and you know why.' He holds out his arms so Scott can help him up.

In the kitchen, Vincent leans against the counter and drinks from a dark bottle. He raises it in sombre greeting. 'Got the thirst,' he says.

The kitchen is large. Scuffed counters, tarnished sink, a fridge which, judging by the *Italia'90* magnet, must still chug CFCs. The oven hob is spattered with brittle, black grease. A chip pan similarly caked. The bin overflowing with silver trays, pizza boxes, ale bottles. Dirty boot prints crisscross lino so worn in places it's as if the kitchen has been floored with medieval parchment. Most of the room is taken up by a massive table. There's a leash and collar on it. Ludwig's, no doubt.

Vincent says, 'I've been getting sentimental lately. *Me*. What the fuck's that about?'

Frank says, 'If Scott could just say what he came here to say, we'll leave you be.'

Vincent tips the bottle this way and that, watching the final inches of liquid roll. 'In a second, in a second…So, this sentimentality, it got me thinking why. You know? Why now?'

Frank notices how both collar and leash are stained with something dark.

Vincent finishes the bottle. There's another on the counter, which he opens with his teeth, spitting the cap across the room. 'Is this what happens when you get to my age? Am I supposed to *take stock*?' he says, 'Most people I know are dead. My folks. My brothers – Kit, Eddie… Curley died this year. Most of my mates, too. Jean…' He takes a long pull on the bottle. 'Everyone's going, or gone…and now there's that Butler girl, too. You mark me, she won't be back. She's not the first to go missing round here.'

'She's not?' Frank says.

'Nah. People have been going missing as far back as I can remember. Young lasses, mostly. They're never found.'

'I didn't know.'

Vincent isn't listening. 'And it's not just people, now it's the estate. The other week some cunt from that Rowan-Tree housing association come round wanting to buy this place. I says, to do what with? He says, to *regenerate*. So I told him to fuck off, only not as politely.' He *tink-tinks* the lip of the bottle against his rotten teeth. 'They been round yours yet, these cunts?'

'We don't have a mortgage, so no.'

'Oh aye? So you would've had a vote?'

Frank steadies his voice. 'Yes.'

'So?'

'So what?'

'So how did you vote? Yes or no?'

Vincent's big, Frank thinks, but he's also in his seventies. If he took a swing, surely that had to count for *something*?

'I voted yes,' Frank says.

'For regeneration?'

'For regeneration.'

'*Regeneration*,' Vincent says. 'They mean *knock it down*.'

'We get one of the new houses when they're done,' Frank says. 'You can too, with the money they'll give you.'

'And where'll I go while they're regenerating?'

'They help you find somewhere. We're moving next month.'

'Where to?'

'Over the river, to Billingham.'

'That's fair distance.' Vincent looks at Scott. 'I'll bet you're over the moon about that, aren't you, sunshine?'

'No,' Scott says.

'I'll bet you're proper fucking made up with your dad here, for uprooting you?'

Scott says nothing.

'So you'll have to change schools?'

Scott nods.

'Will your mates be going?'

Scott shakes his head.

'You got a lass?'

Scott nods.

'And is she going with you?'

Scott says nothing.

Vincent whistles. 'Fuck me. Sorry, son.'

'Anyway,' Frank says, 'this side of the estate's the last phase, so you've got a while yet.'

Vincent's eyes narrow. 'And then what? You think I'll be selling up and moving out? These slick cunts with their clipboards reckon they can swoop in and take what's mine? I *bought* this place off the council, fair and fucking square…' He stares at his boots. When he speaks again his voice is softer. 'It's all going away, isn't it?'

Frank answers as blandly as possible. 'I don't know.'

A switch flicks and suddenly Vincent's animation and brightness once more. 'Well, enough morbid shite! Where were we?'

There are two possible exits from the room. The back door and the door they came through. That one at least, Frank knows, isn't locked.

Vincent says, 'We'll get to your boy in a second, but first I need one final favour.'

'It's getting late,' Frank says.

'It's not that late, Frank. Look, we do this, Scott says his piece, then we shake hands and off we all fuck. Deal?'

'We really need to be off.'

'Ah, Frank. Five minutes.'

'What is it?'

Vincent smiles. 'Good man. This is a quickie, no heavy lifting, scouts honour. It's to do with the coming of Amadeus, Ludwig's replacement. I like giving them names like that. It lends an air of sophistication.'

Frank thinks of Ludwig chewing on a human testicle, and nods.

'I can't be without a dog,' Vincent says. 'Never have, never will. It'd be like being without my cock. I mean, what would I play with?' He laughs at the joke. 'My mate Beech is sorting me out with an Irish wolfhound, a big bastard.'

Something is coming, Frank thinks. Something is coming, but what?

Vincent says, 'I've always kept dogs outdoors. That's where beasts belong, but as I was just saying, I'm going a bit soft. I'm finding myself craving company at nights, so I've decided Amadeus is going to be able to come and go as he pleases.' Vincent produces a stub of pencil from his waistcoat. 'Which is why I'm putting in a dog door.'

Frank scrambles to find Vincent's angle.

'Thing is, though,' Vincent says, 'I can't get hold of Beech to ask him exactly how big Amadeus is. Sackless of me, really. I don't want to put all the graft in then realise the hole's too small, or worse, that I've sawed a massive fucking hole in my door.'

'So what do you need?' Frank asks.

Vincent licks the tip of the pencil. 'So what I need you to do, Frank, is be a dog.'

Frank is back at the bottom of the well, in a universe of mildewed darkness, watching himself move in slow motion.

'I reckon a grown man on all fours is about the same size as a wolfhound. Get down on your hands and knees and I'll mark you off.' He nods at Scott. 'Your lad here can be the judge.'

Frank's mouth is dry. He knew this was coming, knew as soon as Vincent rang this afternoon, yet he *still* came. Through all the fights and stress these past few months, his argument for moving had been that he was doing it for the good of the family, that he was doing what any decent, responsible father would do. But dragging his son here, into this kitchen…that wasn't responsibility. That was something else entirely.

'Maybe I'll take you on a quick lap of the kitchen too,' Vincent says.

'Vincent, this isn't happening.'

Vincent stands straight. His head almost touches the ceiling. He picks up Ludwig's collar and leash.

'But Frank,' he says, 'I'm not asking.'

—

Rob cracked first. Frank's mam was friends with his mam, and he'd only been in the house half an hour before the phone rang and, a few minutes later, his name was being shouted up the stairs. Bernie, his dad, was at the kitchen table, his hands spread wide either side of the empty fruit bowl, and his mam – who had supposedly packed them in for New Year – was stubbing a cigarette out in the sink.

He was in for it.

As he spilled his guts, his parents' eyes formed a protective glaze against the calamity their only son had brought to bear. When Frank started in with the excuses – *I had nowt to do with it, I'm just a hanger on, I don't even like Tommy Greener* – his dad put his hands over his face. His mam reached for her cigarettes.

'Why him?' Bernie groaned. 'Why *his* boy?'

A decent question, asked at the wrong time.

Frank shrugged.

The next day, his father rang Vincent. Vincent didn't want to talk over the phone, so Bernie said he and Frank would go over. When Frank refused, Bernie literally dragged him there. It was the first and only time his dad had ever laid hands on him, a fact which exponentially deepened Frank's trepidation as he was marched across the estate.

'Don't bullshit him,' Bernie said. 'He'll know if you bullshit him. Just put your side across – things got out of hand, *you* were the one what saved him, right?'

In the Barr front yard, cement mixers showed the knock-through was underway, but no renovation was being done that day. The house was shut up, dead.

His dad banged on Vincent's red door and while they waited, Frank recalled some of the juicier Vincent rumours he'd heard down the years: that the man slept with a machete under his pillow, that he'd broken a card cheat's spine in a poker game. That he had two hearts. Insane stories, but at that moment Frank believed them all.

They heard footsteps and locks turn and then Vincent was standing before them.

His dad started talking – *Hello, I'm Bernie Hulme and this is my son Frank. We spoke on the phone earlier and…* – but Vincent kept schtum. Despite himself, Frank felt a frisson of excitement. He'd never been this close to Vincent before; his long black hair was etched here and there with comet-tails of white, and his teeth, flashing occasionally from within the thicket of his bushy black beard, were those of a conger eel. But more than anything, it was the eyes. Twin blue Calor-gas flames flickering all over him.

Vincent retreated into the house and left his dad hanging mid-sentence, so they followed. Inside was gutted: bare boards, stripped plaster, loose wiring snarling from the walls. The dividing wall had been brutally sledgehammered and the ceiling propped up on telescopic jacks. The place reminded Frank of the waterworks the rare times he and his friends had dared creep inside. Vincent's footsteps receded towards the back of the house, and every few seconds his dad glanced over his shoulder to ensure Frank was still behind him.

The back room, like the rest of the house, was a husk. Lengths of timber stacked alongside tubs of plaster and primer and white spirit. A power drill cord snaked between a few scattered Guinness crates being used as furniture. Godbeams of sunlight flooded through bare windows and engulfed the room, engulfed Vincent, who was waiting for them along with a woman. Vincent's wife, Alan's mother. So small was she next to Vincent that she appeared almost as an optical illusion, a trick of perspective. She was rolling her shoulders as if about to step into the ring.

'This him?' she said.

'Jean,' said Vincent. 'Calm.'

She stalked right up to Frank and locked her furious eyes on his. '*What kind of human being does what you did?*' she hissed. Frank had never had so much rage directed towards him, and he was suddenly acutely aware of his own heartbeat, his breathing, all his internal rhythms clattering against each other.

'Hey,' she said. 'I asked you a question.'

His dad put a hand on his shoulder. 'Jean, I–'

'Don't Jean me, Bernie,' she said. Fat tears trembled on her eyelashes. 'He crawled home. Literally *crawled*. They say he might not walk right ever again.'

'He's alright?' Frank said. Only then did it dawn on him he had been entertaining ideas otherwise.

'*ALRIGHT?*' Jean screamed, 'Oh you rotten shite! You awful, cowardly rotten *shite*!' Her spit landed on his cheek. Vincent guided her out of the room. Frank heard them talking quietly in the hallway.

'Five minutes, son,' his dad said as Frank wiped his cheek.

Vincent came back alone, pointed at Frank. 'Right, talk. Now.'

So he talked, just as his dad had told him to: about Tommy's game and the football, and how he didn't know what they were planning. How he – Frank – had been the one who'd pulled Alan – *saved* Alan – from the well. He explained that all the other boys had ran and then how he, too, had finally ran, abandoning Alan to darkness and fate, bleeding and alone. Frank knew he had to meet Vincent's gelid eye while he said these things, but it was orders of magnitude harder that it had been with Jean.

Vincent listened pensively. When Frank finished, he sighed. 'I know what you see when you see Alan,' he said. 'You see weakness. Softness. You laugh, don't you, when he minces by?'

182

'No, sir,' Frank said.

'You think he's ripe for humiliating. Don't think I don't fucking know.'

Out of the corner of his eye, Frank saw his father. He looked nervous.

'And you know what?' Vincent went on. 'You're right. Sometimes I look at him and I'm like, who the fuck *are* you?' He loomed over Frank. 'But the thing is, he's got my name and that means something. That means when you humiliate him, you humiliate *me*.' He bent down, those magnetic eyes of his filling the world, and Frank began to shake. 'So remember this – when you see my boy, you see me. *You. See. Me*. And next time you think about pushing him, know it'll be me pushing back, and I'll fucking *murder* you.'

'You can't say that,' his dad said.

The black beam of Vincent's rage swung onto Bernie. 'You're telling me what I can and can't say in my own house?'

His dad held his hands up. 'All I meant was, that was a little strong. He's just a boy.'

'So he's not accountable for what he's done?' Vincent took a long step towards him.

'No, yes, of course he should be…It's just, like I said he—'

'You're a bit on the small side, aren't you Bern?'

'What?'

'Small. You. See, them trousers Alan had on were brand new. Jean just got them last week, and C&As aren't cheap. They were ripped all up the leg and the blood, well, I know from experience that doesn't come out in the wash.'

Vincent's boots on the floorboards sounded like boots in old Westerns: the haunted outlander from the Wastes who pushed through the batwings and hushed the saloon. His father backed away.

'Now,' Vincent said, 'I don't see why I should have to fork out for another pair just because your spotty, cunt kid reckons he's going to humiliate me, do you?'

His dad pressed up against the wall. 'I'd be happy to pay for some new trousers.'

Vincent shook his head. 'I've got money, Bern. It's your trousers I want.'

In a watery voice, his father said, 'I'm not doing that, Vincent.'

Vincent nodded like this was all part of a reasonable interaction, as if the world wasn't capsizing. 'Well, *someone's* getting their kit off…' He looked over his shoulder and winked at Frank.

'You don't,' – his father swallowed – 'you don't touch him.'

Vincent picked up the power drill and revved it. There was a plank between two beer crates which formed a makeshift bench. Frank thought about using it, but what if it wasn't like in the films? What if instead of knocking Vincent out cold, the board broke harmlessly across the compact muscle of the man's back? What then?

Bernie fumbled at his belt buckle, kicked off his shoes. '*Fine*,' he said, 'you want them? Have them, you sick bastard.' He was wearing saggy, once-white Y-fronts with loose elastic dangling from the waistband. His fine blonde leg hairs were filaments in the bright sun. His foot caught in his trouser cuff and when he tore it free, the change fell from his pockets. Frank watched a 10p coin vanish between the floorboards.

His dad threw his trousers at Vincent.

'His shirt was fucked, too,' Vincent said.

Bernie, stricken, looked at Frank. 'Get out of here.'

'Don't you fucking move,' Vincent said. With his non-drill hand, he grabbed a fist of Bernie's shirt and literally ripped it from him.

'Stop it!' Frank screamed.

Vincent laughed and pulled down Bernie's Y-fronts, grabbing him by his testicles. 'I don't reckon you should be having no more bairns, Bern.' He revved the drill as Frank's father beat wildly against Vincent's head. Frank ran to the plank, but when he tried to pick it up its unexpected weight sent him tumbling.

'Bernie!' Vincent roared. 'You dirty fucker!'

The urine splattering on the floorboards sounded like staccato bursts of distant gunfire. Bernie crumpled slowly, eyes open but abandoned. Vincent stepped back to shake off his hand – topaz droplets in shafts of dust-dense light.

'I wasn't going to fucking *do it*,' Vincent said. 'Who'd you think I am?'

His father cupped himself and turned to the wall. Frank, too, made to turn away.

'No, lad,' Vincent said. 'See this well. From now on, when you think of your dad, think of this.'

Frank had splinters in his hands. He picked up his dad's trousers.

'Leave them,' Vincent said. 'Leave it all.'

His dad stood up. Frank did and did not want to look at his father's nakedness. Nothing felt real as he led the way through the house. Outside, they scuttled along the back of the shops, through the late-summer stench of the bins. When they reached the alley unseen, Frank took his

T-shirt off so that his dad could attempt to fashion some kind of garment. Bernie gave up after several tries.

At the far end of the alley, on the Green, came light and voices: laughter, footballs, radios. People settling in for the day.

'Stay here,' Frank said, 'I'll find a washing line.'

His father muttered something.

'I said stay and–'

Bernie Hulme walked into the light. The first jeers rang out seconds later.

Frank stayed in the alley for a very long time.

—

Ludwig's leash and collar hang from Vincent's tattooed fist.

Scott is frantic. 'Mr Barr, I'm sorry I was on your allotment and trampled your roses. I'm sorry for drinking. I didn't know it was yours and I shouldn't have been up there and I'll work for free or do anything you want. I'm really, really sorry, please.'

'Shut your kid up Frank, before I do it for you.'

'Scott, go. I'll catch up.'

'Stay where you are Scott,' Vincent says. 'You'll want to see this.'

Frank and Scott circle Vincent around the table. Despite everything, Frank feels vaguely ridiculous.

'You remember how this works, don't you?' Vincent says.

'You sad, sick old fuck. This whole estate can't wait 'til you're dead.'

'What estate?' Vincent says. 'Didn't you vote to flatten it?'

Frank rotates past the kitchen counter and snatches Vincent's empty bottle.

Vincent chuckles. 'What you going to do with that?'

'Don't tempt me.'

'You're a fanny, Frank. Your da was a fanny.'

Beside his father, Scott looks as if he's about to puke.

'*Go*,' Frank whispers.

'Don't, son,' Vincent says and, with a strength Frank cannot even begin to comprehend, he heaves the heavy oak table into the wall. Nothing now separates the three of them. Frank brandishes the bottle and steps in front of his son.

A man enters the kitchen.

He looks older than Frank. Jowls and chins and grey-speckled stubble, a belly peeking from beneath a stained T-shirt. Frank is momentarily confused, but then he sees the man's leg. He's wearing cut-off sweat pants and there, above his right knee, disappearing up towards his groin: smooth, thick welds of scar tissue.

Alan is wearing headphones and hasn't heard a thing.

His surprise, when he becomes aware of the melodrama unfolding in his kitchen, reminds Frank of the TV soaps he pretends to his wife he doesn't also enjoy. Behind his thick glasses, Alan's eyes dart between the three of them. When he grins that bloodless grin of his, all the years between then and now concertina into dust. The cassette Walkman he is listening to is a museum piece snapped to the elasticated waist of his cut-offs; bright orange foam headphones attached to a thin metal headband. Frank catches a snippet of Kate Bush's 'Running up that Hill' when Alan tugs them off.

Alan holds up an empty glass. 'I...wanted milk.'

Frank hasn't seen him in decades. He had always just assumed Alan had got the hell out as soon as he was legally able. Who wouldn't have? Had he – Alan – been living in this house all this time? With *Vincent*? Dear God…

'Alan,' he says. 'It's Frank.'

'I remember,' replies Alan.

'And this is my son, Scott.' He exerts a small amount of pressure on his boy's back. Scott and Alan shake hands briefly.

Printed on Alan's shirt is a large, hirsute man in an unsettling leather mask. The man's demented grin is missing teeth and there's a filthy sock puppet on his hand. Scott's eyes flash recognition. 'I watch Mankind's matches on YouTube,' he says.

'You do?' Alan says. He puts equal emphasis on both words, as if he hasn't spoken aloud for some time.

'Yeah, his 1998 Hell in the Cell with The Undertaker is mint.'

Like his father's, Alan's grin has started to rot. 'Well, I'd agree that, ah, what he did that night wasn't quite human, but as far as a display of *wrestling* goes, it, ah, it wasn't his best. If you want to see what the man was truly capable of, I suggest you view his bouts with Terry Funk. Now those are, ah, *real* artistry.'

'Aye?' Scott says.

Vincent speaks to Alan. 'Didn't I tell you about coming down when I've got people?'

'I just wanted milk. I, ah, I didn't know.'

'That's 'cause you're always listening to them fucking tapes. What've I told you about them tapes? They're not yours, they're your mother's.' He stomps over to the fridge and removes the milk. 'Here, give me your glass.' Gripping Alan's hand, which is itself still gripping the glass, he slops in the liquid. It splashes over both their clasped hands and onto the floor. 'Milk, milk, milk!' Vincent chimes, 'For healthy teeth and fucking bones!'

When the glass overflows he puts the milk on the side with a trembling hand. For the first time, he sounds like a man his age. 'You can go back upstairs now.'

Alan watches milk droplets tremor on his hairy wrist. Then he looks at his father and, though it lasts less than a second, Frank and Scott both see it: Alan's eyes narrow and Vincent *blinks*.

Then it's over. 'Bye,' Alan says, and limps heavily from the room.

Vincent leans against the counter with his hands across his chest. He stares blankly at the ceiling. Frank realises he's still holding the ale bottle.

'Just go,' Vincent says. 'Both of you. Before I change my mind.'

Neither of them need to be asked twice.

—

From Vivienne Avenue there were several ways his father could have got back to their home on the other side of the estate, so Frank picked the longest one and walked it slow. He let himself in through the back door. Only the kitchen and living room were on the ground floor, and only his mother was upstairs, getting ready for work. Frank told her everything at Vincent's had gone fine – Alan was OK, no hard feelings. She seemed to buy it, just as she swallowed the line when, asking after her husband's current whereabouts, Frank said he'd gone to Fat Gary's to pay the papers.

He went downstairs again. Their house had a cellar that you entered from the kitchen. It was where his dad kept his fishing gear. In those days, Bernard Hulme was a keen fisherman who tinkered at his workbench most days after work, recalibrating reels and making bright, feathery fly lures. Fish liked those lures because they thought they were insects. They didn't realise the cold steel hook until it was too late.

Frank opened the cellar door and gagged on the moist, graveyard funk wafting up from the below. A faint light emanated from down there and, for some reason, there was a great deal of shredded tinfoil on the steps. He found his father at his workbench, his back turned to him. Bernie was wearing the decorating overalls he kept on a nail down there. More tinfoil by his stocking feet – big scrunched balls of it – and to this day, Frank does not know where it came from. Sometimes, late at night when he can't sleep, he still finds his thoughts turning to that foil.

'Dad,' Frank said. 'Dad.' He felt moronic repeating the word, but it was the only neutral thing he could think to say; anything else would have fallen on an incline and sent them rolling towards God knew what.

His dad turned, and maybe it was the greasy light coming off the old bulb, but he looked ghastly. His face was all creases and channels, his scalp pallid beneath thinning hair. Shadows had amassed under his eyes and in the hollow of his throat. Bernie Hulme was a lurching corpse, a Hammer Horror.

'I'm busy, son. What do you want?'

Only Frank could now no longer think of a way to say what he wanted to say, so he left his dad to his fishhooks and made for the surface.

—

Hood up again, Scott walks ahead. After what's just happened in Vincent's hot, bright house, the night seems huge and cool. Frank looks up at the sky, but the streetlights have sunk the stars. When was the last time he'd seen stars? The spotlights of the greyhound track continue their slow scissoring over the dual carriageway. In the blocks, there are still some lights on, still some signs of life, but not many and not for much longer. Soon, like the rest of this place, the high rises will be nothing but a rubble.

'Scott,' Frank says.

Scott stops, turns around.

'Take that hood off, man. You look like a thug.'

He tugs it down.

'Are you alright?'

He shrugs.

'Because I'm not alright.'

He's going to front it out, Frank thinks – part of him *wants* Scott to front it out – but then his son buries his face in the crook of an arm and cries. Frank hesitates, but when he finally does hold him, Scott doesn't pull away. His hands, Frank realises, fit perfectly between the blades of his son's shoulders.

Scott rubs his eyes with his sleeves, embarrassed.

'You were right,' Frank says. 'I should never have taken you there.'

'Guy's a dick.'

'A massive dick.'

'I feel bad for Alan. What's the point of having a kid if you're going to be a dick?'

Frank says nothing.

Scott says, 'Did you see how his leg was all messed up, Alan's? Did Vincent do that?'

191

'No, but if you want, I can tell you how it did happen. I owe you that.'

He nods. 'Were you friends or something?'

'Me and Alan? No.'

They head towards the alley on Tan Row.

'Are you going to tell Mam about this?' Scott says.

Frank laughs. 'Are you?'

Then Scott laughs. It is a good sound. One Frank has not heard in a while.

—

Frank's wife Pamela – Scott's mother – had been a secretary at the paint factory where Frank used to be employed, until it was sold to a Norwegian company that laid off half the workforce a fortnight before Christmas one year. Frank, a Clearasil-soaked virgin of nineteen, finally gathered the guts to ask her to the cinema. Pam was out by the fire doors, smoking with the rest of the girls. They all watched him approach, and their giggling was almost enough to send him veering through an open loading bay. In fact, the only thing that stopped him from doing so was imaging himself through Pam's eyes. He projected a strong, capable man; a man who didn't know what it was to lose. A man who bent the wills of other men to his own. Through her eyes it was Vincent she saw coming her way, Vincent asking her to the pictures that Saturday, and Vincent playing it cool when she said yes.

The night of the date, Frank bought a new shirt, polished his brogues, and styled his hair in a way that covered as much of his forehead acne as possible. His mam wouldn't stop fussing. Such a handsome boy, she kept saying, seemingly blind to his carbuncles. So handsome. You remind me of Bernie when he was your age.

At the mention of his name, Frank's father did not turn from the television, though Frank saw his hand flex tighter around his can of Stones.

Frank never did figure out how to tell his dad what he had wanted to tell him that day in the cellar. Perhaps, he thought, when he got a little older, it would come to him, and so he had waited. He waited twenty-two years until a series of crippling strokes took his father's life.

But Bernie's question: Why *his* boy? Why Alan? Sometimes Frank almost believes what he had told Vincent, that they had just been stupid kids, that things had got out of hand...but it doesn't quite sit right. There's always that memory of Alan, unconscious and falling into the well, and he knows that for an instant he'd wanted it to happen. Had wanted it more than anything.

—

The streetlights don't penetrate the alley and their footfalls ricochet against the tall brick walls. They pass Lily Butler's *Missing* poster. Vincent had said she wasn't coming back, but Frank hopes otherwise. He can't imagine what it must be like to lose a child.

Scott leads them across the Green. Every third or fourth step Frank must jog to make up the difference in their strides. Soon, he thinks, they'll move away from here, and when – *when*. Not *if* but *when* – they come back, the house Scott grew up in will be gone, along with the boy himself. Pam says this is just how it is – that Scott will one day worry about his own children in the same way – and he tries taking comfort in that, but he's afraid. What if the distance he's felt opening up between them soon gapes like the void separating Vincent from Alan? From his own father and himself? A void so deep you can't hear the rock land?

There's still traffic on Hollis Road. Thankfully, Scott's too focused on finding an opening in it to see how his dad is looking at him. The miracle of him.

It won't happen, Frank thinks. Not to them. No matter where Scott goes, he won't let that gap widen. Even if he ends up on the other side of the world.

Like Manchester, say.

HEART
OF
CHROME

Corina Clarke of Peelaw Bank

Mould is an affliction around here. Only so much deluge can council brick take before waterlogging ensues, before the Judith Krantzes bloat on the shelves, before colonies of green fuzz take up residence in the grooves of your Kate Bush LPs, and your alveoli choke with spores. In this respect, Corina's house is worse than most: Petri-dish blooms of the stuff have crept across her bathroom walls to the extent that she now loathes turning her back while showering, unable to fully discount sentience.

She squeaks a swathe through the bathroom mirror fog and applies a layer of foundation, two ticks of eyeliner. Her tongue, when she pokes it out, is wine-black and sour. Work clothes consist of bobbled black leggings and a black top, an aliceband to secure her shower-damp hair (the blonde now the drab fawn of old chamois leather with two inches of grey root showing). Finally, she pinches the back of her hand. In some magazine or other she once read that if the skin there snapped back instantly, you were still young. There was still time.

The kitchen table is how she must have left it the night before. A sozzled Olympic parody of interlocking wineglass rings, two empty merlots sharing the podium with an overflowing ashtray. Her phone lies face down in the mess. She flips it over and sees the waiting text message:

HEART OF CHROME
DONT SAy I never giveyou nowt. Beech x

Beech. She lights a cigarette and re-reads the message while the kettle boils. What did Beech want? She's no closer to an answer by the time she sits down with her instant Gold Blend.

The kitchen doesn't get sun until teatime, yet the air is already coagulating. Another scorcher on the cards: an Easter heatwave, so the radio had said the night before, that was due to last at least until the schools went back, not that you'd know they were even out. The streets were silent. Any other year – even at this hour and with the windows shut – she'd be hearing the shrieks and yells of school-free children, but two recent events had changed things. Firstly, phase one of Rowan-Tree's 'regeneration' had already moved many families away, and, secondly, Lily Butler's disappearance had spooked everyone. It seemed parents in homes which had not yet been bulldozed were keeping a close eye on their offspring.

She drops her cigarette hissing into a wine bottle, splashes lukewarm coffee into the sink, and puts the milk back in the fridge (glimpses her barren shelves: those few mushy inches of cucumber, that bit of gnarled ham). The painting on the fridge door belongs to her granddaughter Una-Lee, named after an artist who had apparently come from this very estate. Corina had stolen it from her parents' flat last week; the work freakishly good for a five-year-old: the red-eyed, green-skinned witch reaching up out of the toilet is capable of raising hackles. The witch's emaciated fingers end in long, yellow claws and her teeth are black jags. The poor girl being grabbed has her knickers round her ankles, utterly doomed, her mouth an aghast 'O' of horror. Somehow, Corina thinks, her mother – Una-Lee's great-grandmother – must still be at it with the Peg Powler stories. The willies she'd put up she and Jim when they'd been Una-Lee's age; the two of them clinging to each other under the duvet as Mam stage-whispered: *Peg's in the pipes…she's in the pipes and her arms are LONG.* Of all the things for her mother to have forgotten – the names and faces of loved ones, what year it was – so strange that Peg remained.

The fridge door creaks shut. Her head pounds.

Still, time to get on.

Corina lives at the top of Peelaw Bank, and each descending step replaces the warm dome of sky with a stagnant palette of greys and browns. Abandoned houses with steel sheets bolted over windows and doors; whale ribs of exposed roof joists where the tiles have been stripped. An easy £500, Max had once told her. The lead, too. At the bottom of the bank, all the streets to her left – Charnwood Street, Feltnam Street, Durham Close – streets on which she'd had friends and clients – have been replaced by a vast building site. A builder, naked from the waist up, exits a portakabin and, tilting his face to the sun, slaps his sizable gut as if it were a ceremonial drum.

Hollis Road is quiet as she lights her second cigarette of the day. She crosses onto Stanhope Street, then walks the long bow of The Crescent until it gives out onto the precinct of shops on Tan Row. The glass frontage of *Yvette's* is the first of eight units and, as usual, Yvette is at the hotplate frying rashers and pucks of black pudding. She doesn't look up. Gary's newsagent is three units along from *Yvette's*. The narrow door is open, but the window shutters are down – have been for years – and it's too dingy inside to spot Gary himself. Save for hers, the rest of the units are empty. Behind each door a yellowing pile of unopened circulars and final demands, the husks of flies, bellies up. In the unit neighbouring her salon, someone has attempted to reverse-write **SHAZ IS A**

199

SLAG in the window suds, but got the *S*'s and *Z* backwards.

Hair by Corina is the final unit. She rummages in her bag for her keys and clatters up the shutters.

Inside, the place smells of scalp, shampoo, and mildew. Three chrome cutting chairs glint in the morning light, matched by an equal number of hooded dryers against the back wall – brainsuckers, Jim used to call them – their Perspex domes the colour of burnt sugar. A desk with moneybox, phone, and appointment book. Framed, hand-drawn hair model sketches on every wall. By all appearances just another humdrum Friday, but not for Corina. Today these objects are charged with significance.

She boils the kettle in the backroom. Along the far wall runs a strip of reinforced glass letting in subaquatic daylight from the alley beyond. Below this is a slapdash stack of cardboard boxes, some stencilled with logos and brands: **DRAX DOMESTIC BLEACH, MEGA SAVE WIRE SCOURERS, McADAM'S MEATBALLS IN RICH GRAVY.** There's no paracetamol in the drawers so she takes her coffee onto the salon floor.

Did she do something last night? Deep into her second bottle, she'd done something. A phone call? To who? To Beech? Is that why he'd texted? She goes to check her call log, but her phone isn't there. Must have left it on the kitchen table. Bravo, Cor.

Her coffee is cold by the time the old woman enters. Despite the heat, she's wearing a heavy beige mac and fixes Corina with eyes, or eye – one is a scuffed prosthetic – sunk deep into her rumpled head. She doesn't cover her mouth when she coughs.

'My tubes,' the old woman finally says, 'are murder.'

'Good morning Mrs Terry. How are you?'

Mrs Terry doesn't respond. Her stiff fingers work her coat buckle. Corina hangs the mac on the stand next to the dying yucca while Mrs Terry lowers herself into the reclining sink chair. It's always strange to see the elderly like this, looking up at you with their heads resting in the salmon-pink basin; the position does something to them, makes them younger, their skulls re-materialising from beneath sloughed flesh. The pipes vibrate violently when Corina turns on the water. An agonised groan – iron twisting, whales dying – rumbles up from deep below their feet.

'You need to get them pipes seen too,' Mrs Terry says.

'They've been getting worse.'

'Mine are going the same way.'

'Just old, I suppose.'

Water quivers mercurially in the creases of Mrs Terry's forehead. The remains of her grown-out perm darkens, sags. 'Not that they'll be your problem after today though, will they? I seen Pam Hulme on the 551. She says you're shutting.'

'That I am,' Corina says. 'After today.'

'Gillian?'

'I let her go last month.'

'So it's just been you?'

'Just been me.'

Clients often nod off under the warm water, but not Mrs Terry. The old woman's good eye remains trained on her throughout and her hand is lumpen, crustacean, when Corina helps her out of the sink. She shoots Corina a crepuscular look in the mirror as she settles into the cutting chair. 'You're better off alone,' she says. 'Folk aren't worth it.'

Corina snaps on the radio.

It's always tuned to a local station, *Shine FM* 107.3. They're half way through a news bulletin: *…sentenced to eighteen months in prison for the destruction and illegal disposal of greyhounds estimated to be several thousand in number. The remains – discovered in a field north of Nunethorpe during housing construction – are believed to be connected to the racing industry. The court heard how the animals had been bludgeoned and mutilated to avoid identification, before being buried in large pits. Vincent Barr, 74, was found guilty of multiple counts of animal cruelty and conspiracy to –*

'He's wrong 'un,' Mrs Terry says. 'That whole family's nowt but scunners.'

Vincent.

She'd once asked Beech what happened to the dogs when they could no longer race; what befell the rest of the litter that never even made it to the track. Beech had smiled. Don't worry, he'd said. People took care of them.

The bulletin ends and the DJs attempt some awful banter. Corina wraps Mrs Terry's hair in endpapers, winds rods tight against the roots, slathers the hairline in barrier cream. The stink of the perm lotion no longer even registers. Mrs Terry has been having the same perm since Corina opened for business back in the late 1990s. In fact, most of her remaining clients are perms. Over the past twenty years, how many perms is that? Too many, and that's one problem with the job – as with life in general, people tend to stick with what they know. The Blank Slate, that person with the thick tresses who says, 'it's up to you' – that person is rarer than condors.

Corina stretches an elasticated plastic cap over Mrs Terry's head so that the chemicals can do their work.

'Fetch me my bag over,' Mrs Terry says.

Corina fetches.

Mrs Terry takes out a Mills & Boon paperback. The hunk on the cover sports *Wham!*-era George Michael hair and a five o'clock shadow. A ghostly slip clings like the thinnest of atmospheres to the full chest and hips of the blonde swooning in his arms. The book is titled *Behind Drawn Shades*.

'I prefer the doctors and nurses ones,' Mrs Terry says.

Sat in her elevated chrome chair, her head bulging under rods and plastic, the old woman looks like a high-priestess of some ancient, extra-terrestrial race. She licks her thumb, opens the book at page one, and begins to read.

———

Speaking of the cosmos…

In New Jersey, 1964, physicists Arno Penzias and Robert Wilson pointed their Matterhorn-shaped radio antenna at the universe and accidentally discovered what scientists had hypothesised since the end of the WWII: Cosmic Microwave Background Radiation – CMBR for short – the 13.8 billion-year-old thermal radiation left cooling in the wake of the Big Bang. The implications were startling. CMBR, they realised, was everywhere, evident in all directions at once, lacking any central point of origin, and thus utterly inescapable. It was a phenomenon which resisted relegation to the twin, frosty realms of interstellar space and academia because it penetrated to the very marrow of our collective existence. CMBR was – *is* – all around us: turn on the radio or television, and it's the snow between channels. Reach out to touch someone, it's the air between your fingers. It's in our lungs. Our hearts.

This somewhat oblique aside is pertinent because, out of all the stories before you here, Corina's is perhaps hardest to tell. A life lived in the afterglow of its own past is extremely difficult to unpick, to sequence in a way that will make sense to anyone, including that person themselves, simply because everyone they've ever been is everywhere, always. *N* states superpositioned and entangled to the detriment of linear narrative; Time's Arrow supplanted by every boomerang ever thrown since the Dawn of Man, all hurled skyward at once. This has consequences. Yes, in one way, when Corina sees Mrs Terry's copy of *Behind Drawn Shades*, she is slung back in time to the early 1990s, to memories of her apprenticeship at *In-Val-Uable*; but in another, more accurate, sense she doesn't go anywhere at all. Her distinctions between *past*, *present*, and *future* have long since begun to collapse, meaning that the young woman Corina was at twenty-two is right there beside the Corina of the present, and co-mingling with all the other Corinas she has been or will become. And there are others with her too: Annabelle and Max and Una-Lee – figures who may, to the untrained eye, appear to be gone, but who are in fact as omnipresent to Corina as CMBR. They fall like snow through the events you're about to witness, dusting what passes for Corina's present with the half-life of their absence.

One such person is Val, proprietor of *In-Val-Uable*, who kept a stack of Mills & Boons for customers to muck-mine while they waited for their appointments. On slow days, Corina leafed through them herself, and one in particular stood out: *Black Forest Lust*. The plot, she recalls, concerned a wager made by two jaded Bavarian princes who lived together in an isolated castle: who would be first to defile

Ophelia, the raven-haired climber their flunkies had yanked half-dead from a remote ravine after a rockslide? The princely creeps employed all manner of subterfuge. They cut the phone lines to stop her calling her diplomat daddy, they slipped knock-out drops into her Chablis (which, thanks to her third kidney's superior toxin-metabolising abilities, failed) and once, while she was bathing, resorted to actual *Scooby-Doo* eyeholes cut into an ancestral portrait. Things looked bleak for Ophelia until, that was, she encountered the shirtless underling Klaus, the princes' stable hand, who rescued her honour, stole her heart, and popped her cherry (because Ophelia was a three-kidneyed, international mountaineering virgin). Ridiculous? Perhaps, but there was a scene in chapter three which crackled with enough premonition to give Corina pause. The moment Klaus and Ophelia met for the first time: *Shadows swung wildly in the stable of spooked, bucking colts. A bolt of lightning split the sky just as Ophelia's cerulean eyes met his russet ones, and at that moment their two worlds exploded...*

Val leered in the staffroom doorway. Wouldn't mind riding bareback on that Klaus, she said.

Corina threw the book onto the pile, embarrassed. It's all bollocks, she said. That's not how people are. They don't *explode* when they meet.

Fuschia pink lipstick smudged Val's fag-stained teeth. You sound so sure, she said.

And Corina was. Back then at least. Before Max.

Because who can predict when their life will go kablooey?

—

Enter Gary. Newspapers tucked under one arm, sweating buckets.

'Thought I'd just pop these round,' he says. Then, registering the old lady in the chair, 'Good morning, Mrs Terry.'

In the mirror, Mrs Terry's good eye crests the edge of her book.

Corina motions to the papers under his arm. 'You needn't have.'

'Oh, it's no bother. Really, I just wanted to stop round to say you'll be missed.' His green sweater is speckled dark with perspiration and stretches nigh to transparency when he bends to put the papers on the waiting table.

'Are you feeling any better today?' Corina asks.

'Oh, never better, never better. Though I had to get rid of Danny, so I'm on the hunt for a new paperboy. He's been pilfering the *Sunday Sport*, grubby little sod.'

'Fourteen-year-olds and boobs, Gary. It's a dangerous mix. How much do I owe you?'

Gary waves a stubby hand. 'No, hinny, please…'

She brandishes a fiver from her purse, but almost recoils at how hot and clammy his hand is when she forces it on him. The man is burning.

'But we're friends,' he says.

'You're running a business, same as me…same as I was.'

Wispy tufts of hair dust the sides of Gary's pear-shaped head. Small, twinkly eyes; child's eyes in a flushed face. 'Promise you'll pop in from time to time.'

'Scout's honour.'

'Because me and Suzy will – wuh – *gakh*…'

'Gary? *Gary*?'

His face is a boiling red lozenge.

'Gary, I'm calling an ambulance.'

He pincers his chest with one hand, wagging a finger violently with the other. White stuff flecks his puckering mouth. Corina runs to the phone on the desk but before she can lift it, Gary unleashes a series of coughs – hard and wet and absolute, like bones breaking deep in their meat – that bend him double. Saliva dangles from his chins. Gradually, it passes. The blocked blood drains from his face and he starts breathing again. Just.

The pipes shudder and clank when Corina fills a mug with water from the backroom. A few years ago, the council had finally got around to filling in the worst of the potholes on Peelaw Bank. There'd been a cement mixer outside her house for several days, and the rough grozzle of spades in gravel sounded a lot like Gary's chest.

Gary takes the cup with both hands. 'I'm fine,' he says. 'Fine. Just a nasty cough I can't shake,' he says. The mug trembles. 'Something going around.'

'Come and sit down a sec.'

He sips the water, hands it back. 'Pet, I've got to get on. The place'll be ransacked by now. Do you need any more boxes?'

'I'm fine, Gary, thanks.'

Once the door closes behind him, Mrs Terry speaks. 'That man is not long for this world.'

'Would you like a cup of tea?' Corina says quietly.

'My Colin went the same way. Dropped dead.'

'Or coffee, maybe?'

Mrs Terry licks a thumb, turns a page. 'Two lumps.'

In the back, Corina reads the boxes while the kettle boils: **CLINK FARMS BACON GRILL, ECONOMIX NON-BIO DETERGENT, BLASZCZYK HERBATNIKI WAFEL WANILIA**. Gary did fourteen-hour-days in that sarcophagus of a paper shop, with no help. She'd once picked up a tin of garden peas in there and it had been two years out of date. Nevertheless, he did better business that either her or Yvette for the simple reason that he was the only off licence on the estate. Over the years she'd seen every type of drinker imaginable cross his threshold, from the functioning citizen in for a few tins after work, to the sweat-soaked shambles counting out a can of special brew in coppers.

The kettle rumbles to climax. Corina spoons granules and wonders where on that scale she fell.

Where did Jim?

—

Twenty-four-year-old Corina on the settee in her new house on Peelaw Bank. She had one bloodshot eye on the TV, massaging from her temples ten hours of *In-Val-Uable* where, after the completion of her apprenticeship, she now worked full time.

The soap was just going to the adverts when Jim clattered home.

He said, Who the fuck do you think you are?

What?

You know what. Fat Gary.

Jim I –

You've been on at him, haven't you?

I'm worried about you. I asked him because I'm worried.

The wheezing in his chest sparked a coughing fit. He wiped his pulverised mouth with his pulverised hand. It's like being back home, he said. Like I'm a fucking child – worse – a *thing* what's got to be kept locked up.

208

You think I don't know about the bottles under your bed? Jim, you *clink*.

So? What else is there, eh?

On TV, a young couple ran through a meadow in a washing powder advert.

There's me, she said.

Jim's scars were still pink then. They flexed as he laughed a laugh that sounded like vomiting. He said, But for how long?

What do you mean *but for how long*?

Pretty soon Max'll be moving in, then it's curtains for me.

Max has nothing to do with this. This is your home.

He thinks that too, does he?

He's not family.

Jim teetered on his crutch. Not yet he's not, but one day…or if not him, someone. Then what about me? Am I going to be Jolly Uncle Jim? For fucks sake, can you imagine your kids wanting to sit on my knee?

He staggered back when she stood up.

They should've left me down that well, he said.

Don't say that.

They should've left me with *her*.

With who?

His gaze drifted to the television. A radiant teenager was applying spot cream to a face that would never require it. He Parka-sleeved tears. Nowt, he said.

Jim…

Promise, he said. Promise me.

She ignored the roiling in her stomach, that hallmark of lousy gamblers everywhere. I promise, Jim. Of course I promise.

He lurched to the stairs and said, Tell Gary next time he doesn't serve me, I'm putting his windows through.

—

'*Ta.*'

Mrs Terry takes her drink without looking up from *Behind Drawn Shades*. Corina goes to the window. Across the green, people are moving furniture out of a house on Alexandria Terrace and into a dirty white van.

'Godspeed,' Corina whispers.

And then, just like that – it comes to her.

She spreads Gary's newspapers on the waiting table like a croupier would cards. The back pages, the day's race information; her fingers brush the columns of names and times, odds and form, and there it is: the 8:39pm at Stockton, 515m flat. Heart of Chrome – an A4 bitch at 30/1. Her heart thumps at the thought of the wall-safe in the back, embedded in the cupboard under the sink. The month's takings inside, just shy a grand.

Think of what you could do with that kind of money.

Cor, no.

No more dealing with housing association and council bastards. You could get Mam in somewhere nice, somewhere private.

Listen to yourself.

You could –

A woman in a floral-print sundress steps into the salon, fanning herself with a polaroid. Her hair is mousy, streaked white and pineappled atop her head with the kind of thick elastic band postmen drop everywhere.

'Can you fit me in?' she asks. She's a big woman, husky,

smelling of Nivea and sweat when she hands Corina the photograph.

Corina wrinkles her nose. 'Are you sure? Christ, I haven't done one of these since my apprenticeship.'

'I'm sure, pet.' The woman shakes her hair loose. 'Sorry it's a bit greasy.'

The polaroid is of the woman decades younger, at a barbeque by the looks of it. She's wearing a lurid knitted jumper and the sun lights up her Whitesnake hair-metal hairdo from behind, making it holy. Corina shows the woman to the sink chair. Unlike Mrs Terry, she closes her eyes as soon as she's reclined. The floor judders when Corina turns on the showerhead.

The woman chuckles. 'You should get that seen to.'

Her hair *is* greasy. Corina lathers it up and, for a while, the silence holds, but she can tell the woman's a talker...

'It's for a play, the hair,' the woman says.

'Come again?'

She cracks an eye. 'We're putting a play on at the Civic Hall. It's set in 1992, hence the hair. Mickey said I could wear a wig, but I want immersion. Like whatjimicallim? That actor. The squinty one.'

Corina shakes her head.

'It's called *Right to Live*. It's about the first time the council tried palming the blocks off onto that housing association.'

'Did you live there?' Corina asks.

'Still do. I've been in Palmerston thirty year now. We were actually going to perform it there, but the Rec. centre's been condemned.'

'My parents are in Asquith.'

'I know, pet. You're Nora's lass.'

211

'You know my Mam?'

'I wouldn't say that. She was still part of the group when I was just getting involved, which is going back ten, fifteen year now. I was only there a few months before she stopped coming. Everyone loved her though. How's she keeping?'

The Terrible Thing spilling from the soft click-click of her mother's knitting needles had spread across most of the living room carpet, almost to the bar fire.

'She's fine.'

'Tell her I'm asking after her.'

Hair washed and towelled, Corina sits the actress in the cutting chair next to Mrs Terry. The necessary hairdryer-break in conversation will, she hopes, carry over into the rest of the appointment, but as soon as Corina turns off the machine the actress says, 'I'm the lead you know. Well, co-lead. It's me and a man a called Peter, who's from the housing association. His character I mean, not him.'

'Are you nervous?'

'Pet,' she said, 'I'm a natural show off. But seriously, confidence comes from believing in the material. We didn't want to tell other people's stories anymore, especially as this year's going to be our last. We wanted to tell *our* story, so we did, we wrote it. Well, Mickey – that's Mickey who ran it with your Nora – he did most of it, but we all chipped in. It's an important play. People need to know what that government did to the working class.'

Corina makes one of the listening noises she's perfected over the years and curls random sections of hair with hot irons. Controlled chaos, that's what this style is all about.

'The eight months we've spent putting this together have been wonderful,' says the actress. 'It really brought back how folks used to look out for the community.'

Beside them, Mrs Terry spits something nasty into a tissue.

'Do you want to know what it's about?' The actress asks.

Corina reasons saying yes will at least keep the conversation mostly one-way.

'Well,' the actress says, 'it's not going to sound as good when I tell it, but I play Maureen Taylor, the heroine. Picture the scene: its 1992, and she's been made redundant from the steelworks where she's been a secretary for umpteen years. Her husband, done in by the dole, has drunk himself into an early grave, and a Fiesta's just gone over her cat. All she's got left is her little flat in Lloyd George, but it's dropping to bits. Windows loose, boiler knackered. Damp across the walls.'

Corina thinks of spores watching her as she strips naked in her own bathroom.

The actress goes on. 'Plus, there's all these' – she makes air quotes under her nylon shawl – '*students* and *squatters* and *druggies* moving in. Maureen complains to the council, but they say they've got no money to do owt, and that's when Mr Blenkinsop – that's Peter – comes along. He's from the new housing association. *They* can fix everything, he says, but on one condition – everyone's got to transfer tenancy over to them.'

'Rowan-Tree,' Corina says.

'In the play they're called Sandhurst, but aye.'

'Mam was part of the Tenants' Association what fought them.'

'I know she was,' the actress says. 'And good on her. You can't have something as important as housing in private hands. Transfer, or forget about getting your hot water fixed? Tell me that's not blackmail.'

Mrs Terry turns the page, pretending to read.

'Well,' the actress continues, 'that's it for Maureen. First, they took her marriage, then they took her job, and now they're trying to take her *home*. Enough is enough. Something snaps in her, and she decides to take on Blenkinsop – and Sandhurst – head on…'

Despite herself, Corina is intrigued. 'How?'

The actress winks in the mirror. 'Come and find out. It's at the Civic Hall next Tuesday, 7pm. Tickets are £3.'

'I'll see,' Corina says.

They listen to the radio and, little by little, Corina's hands take over. They hairspray scrunched layers of hair, set them with blasts of the dryer.

'I think we're done,' she says.

The actress inspects herself in the mirror, grinning. 'Oh God, this is a *scream*.'

'Is it OK? It's been a while.'

'OK? Pet, it's hideous!' She bounces the spray-tacky curls. 'You're a genius. I tried doing my own fringe once and nearly ended up in A&E.'

'It's not hard,' Corina says, slightly embarrassed. 'You just find the shape and bring it out.'

The actress plucks a folded twenty from the coin purse hanging between her substantial breasts. 'You know, I've walked past here a million times, but once the play's over you can bring me back into the twenty-first century.'

'I'm afraid today's my last day.'

'I thought this side of the estate wasn't being knocked down until next year?'

'It's not that,' Corina says. 'There's just not enough business.'

The actress shakes her head. 'And why's that, eh? We

214

might've beaten them in '92, but we always knew they'd try again. All they had to do was wait until things got bad enough again. It took twenty year, but things did.' She drops her purse back into her cleavage. 'Me and my husband will be gone by end of summer. Your folks are the same?'

'Aye.'

'Once the estate's pulled down, it'll be three and four bed family homes. Most folk left in the blocks are older or live alone. How many of us do you think will get to come back?' She looks out over the green to Alexander Terrace. The removal van is now being loaded with the final few possessions. 'What'll you do next?'

Heart of Chrome. Open a Post Office account in Una-Lee's name, for when she's eighteen. Annabelle won't have a say once Una-Lee's eighteen.

Corina says, 'I'll be alright. Anyway, break a leg.'

When the actress is gone, Mrs Terry lowers her book. '*Save the blocks?* She's not right in the head. They should've been pulled down yonks ago. They're not fit for human beings, never were.'

Corina begins cleaning her scissors.

'But then,' Mrs Terrys says, 'I don't have to tell you.'

—

Whenever Corina thinks of the blocks – as she often does, as she does then – it's invariably 1992, the year she finally cracked. Crude protest banners hanging a hundred feet up between windows. Spray painted bedsheets limp with rain:

215

**SAVE OUR FLATS! SAY NO TO TRANSFER!
THATCHERISM = RACHMANISM!
TRANSFER IS PRIVATISATION!
FUCK OFF H.A. SCUM!**

She thinks of Mam at the kitchen table, chopping flyers into Seabrook Crisp boxes, ready for meetings and demos. Dad seething in the other room, eyeballing *Bullseye*, sucking on the last of his teeth. His ash-filled orange peels, the tabloid crosswords he can't finish. She thinks of poor Jim, how for three years after the accident he barely left his room. How when she tried talking to him, his eyes were clouded, distant. How he didn't watch his horror films anymore and how she'd scour the *Radio Times* for late-night Frankensteins and Wolfmen – films she herself found ridiculous, but which she'd sit up late watching in the hope he might decide to join her. He never did. How one night he hurled all his tapes from his fourteenth-floor bedroom window while Dad hammered on his bedroom door. She thinks about how she never saw Alive anymore. About being twenty-one with no clue as to what she was doing with her life. How the sinking feeling was on her even before she'd opened her eyes in the mornings. She thinks about the lunacy that was four fully grown human beings living in a handful of concrete boxes in the sky. How the flat became a psychic tension map burning red in her mind: the muffled crump of her brother's crutch in the hall after everyone had gone to bed, the squeaking hinge on the cupboard next to the fridge, the spectral clonk in the pipes whenever someone turned on the hot tap – how it all betrayed her whereabouts and left no place to *be alone*. About how that wasn't even the worst of it, how there was some ambience the walls took and amplified – the default sound of life itself that went deeper than mere sound, an inescapable clamour that never, ever *stopped*. How it scraped against her sanity like frayed violin strings. She thinks about how she would lie on her bed with a pillow wrapped round her head in a vain attempt to block it all out, fantasising wrecking balls and caved ceilings and thousand-volt cables whipping death. About Asquith House toppling in a God-fist of dust.

About the futility of such reveries.

—

The actress has forgotten her polaroid. Corina picks it up. That jumper she's wearing in it… when they were young, back when she was still capable of coherent garments, their mother had knitted such attire for herself and Jim. Jumpers that, in her burgeoning pubescence, she had gone to extreme lengths to avoid wearing.

She puts the picture by the money box. If the woman wanted it, she'd be back.

The Rowan-Tree letter she'd received yesterday is in her cluttered handbag. She ignores it, rummages for cigarettes. Mrs Terry doesn't acknowledge her as she steps outside.

The precinct is hot and her head thumps in protest as she lights up, inhales. The distant sound of pneumatic drills on the breeze. Getting closer each day.

Exhale.

Across the green, the figures emptying the house on Alexander Terrace close the van and lock the house. Corina squints through smoke as they pull away

No, she won't be going to the actress' play. No point. She already knows how it ends.

—

Due to its relative position across the green, *Hair by Corina* offered front row seats to Alexander Terrace's demise. Harbinger: the house centre-left, the one with the green door. Vans came and went, and come nightfall the dark windows made the house a punched-out tooth in a grimace of light. Emptiness rippled out from the abandoned geometry of its rooms, disseminating foreboding, drip-feeding Omen. First to fall to the hoodoo was Mrs Hill, who lived at the top of the Terrace and came in for a shampoo and set every two months with the reliability of an atomic clock: 'We've got no choice but to move,' she said, three months before actually doing so, 'negative equity, pet.' Her departure was followed by Mrs O'Shaughnessy (Helen Mirren bob) at Number 19 for the same reason. A month after the O'Shaughnessy's left, someone – kids probably – set fire to the house. Soot raked up and out of the shattered, blackened windows, as if someone had attempted to mascara a giant skull. Mrs Veitch (amber tints) lived next door to the O'Shaughnessy's, and her house was so badly damaged that she and her family had to stay in a B&B while the insurance came through. When it did, the Veitchs moved too. The council began shipping new people into the vacated houses – younger people mostly, on (if gossips was to be believed) housing benefit. Which was fine, Corina had no prejudices; she just wished they'd come in for haircuts.

Then came Rowan-Tree with their majority vote for transfer and 'Regeneration'. Langland Way and The Avenues were first to be put to the wrecking ball, her regulars on those streets rehoused miles away, their homes and histories smashed; that sound bricks make when they break rolling thousand-fold across the rooftops became the first thing she heard in the mornings. The air took on mass, sat on her chest. Popperwell Avenue went next. Hayrick Walk. South Ponds Rise. Windhorst Avenue. Mrs Laville (Anjelica Houston's do circa *The Postman Always Rings Twice*) lived on Windhorst: 'I don't open the curtains anymore because the living room looks onto the site. Those men don't wear tops, and the *language*…They start banging at the crack of dawn. I rang the council, said my husband's got epilepsy. They said it's nowt to do with them, said to ring Rowan-Tree. So I did. It was like talking to the speaking clock.'

That was the last time Corina cut Mrs Laville's hair.

Mrs Vose (cut and blow dry) lived sandwiched between two vacated houses over on Somers Street, until the council bused in new neighbours. She was in tears as she told Corina about the syringe her daughter found in their yard. The Voses left two months later.

Watch them fall: Halfrey Road, Roman Way, Loom Street. Fences went up around the building site to stop the pinching of bricks and timber, to keep teenagers from heavy petting in the clawed buckets of diggers. The hoardings and billboards: Daddy with one arm round Mummy's pregnant waist, the other hand paternally resting on his son's shoulder, the three of them watch the youngest daughter gambol with a chocolate lab on the front lawn of their immaculate new-build:

ROWAN-TREE HOMES:
IT'S WHERE YOUR HEART IS.

Rowan-Tree sent her a leaflet explaining their plans for the bulldozing of her home, for the easiest methods of selling it to them so that they may do so. Included was a map of the prospective new estate: houses and streets so *other* to those she knew that they simply failed to compute. The blocks, her home, her salon – all erased, replaced by a Rowan-Tree utopia dovetailing with the detached houses of Moorside, where her daughter Annabelle, her boyfriend Kyle, and five-year-old granddaughter Una-Lee now lived.

Meanwhile, Alexander Terrace continued to empty. Goodbye Mrs Barker (perm), au revoir Mrs Lobe (perm), auf wiedersehen Ms Killkerry (shingle bob). Soon, her one remaining Alexander client was Mrs Enright (perm) at Number 30. Mrs Enright who grew Red Hot Pokers in her front garden and glued hand-painted seashells along her wall. Mrs Enright who burned with defiance, her voice powdery from laryngeal cancer. 'I've lived here forty year and I'll be damned if they're turfing me out now.' But the cardboard signs in her windows reminded Corina of the same clapped-out sloganeering on the Tenants' Association flyers her mother used to distribute: **UNITED WE STAND, DIVIDED WE FALL** and **UNITE AND FIGHT AGAINST ROWAN-TREE SOCIAL CLEANSING!** And ultimately, even Mrs Enright caved. Around the time Corina lost a week's takings on a reverse-forecast at Monmore that should have been *nailed on*, Mrs Enright took the home-loss cheque. The knotweed rose up to murder her Red Hot Pokers and, one-by-one, kids prised the seashells from her wall, to skim through her windows or carry off to destinations unknown.

—

Corina ponders the whitewashed window next door as she crushes her cigarette. Who *was* Shaz? Why was she a slag? Further questions without answers. The place had been a laundrette up until a few years ago.

She should go back in, sweep up the actress' hair, rinse the chemicals from Mrs Terry's head, but she lingers. The sun works on her hangover. It must be horrible for the kids off school, cooped up inside by abduction-fearing parents on a day like this. What would Una-Lee be up to right now? Drawing, probably. According to Dad, that was all her granddaughter did when Annabelle took her to Asquith for visits timed meticulously to never coincide with her own. Una-Lee is the only thing capable of cracking her father's carapace these days.

Smashing little drawer, he said, last time Corina was round. A right little Mona Lisa (Corina didn't correct this). She must get it from Annabelle.

Uh-huh, Corina said.

Don't know where Anabelle got it, he said. Not you.

Uh-huh.

———

A month or two after the cataclysmic New Year's Eve 1993 explosion, she woke on Max's settee to find him sketching her on the back of an envelope. They'd been making love. She must have dozed off.

What are you doing? she said. Let me see.

So he did, and she was astounded. It looked just like her.

Only prettier, she said.

He rolled his eyes. Then: you do me.

I can't draw.

221

Everyone can draw. It's a skill, same as hairdressing. It's about shapes.

The post must have come while she slept. He picked up a fresh letter, one with a plastic-window, the kind nobody enjoyed opening.

Right, he said, here's how you do a face. It's like an oval, then you do a cross like *this*. This is your guide. Now do another horizontal two thirds down the vertical – here – and that's the mouth, get it?

I get it. But can you do animals?

The graphite tip of his pencil whipped out a circle, a rhombus tapering.

She said, Your tongue pokes out when you concentrate. It's cute.

He slashed out more lines and something began to take shape – a deep chest, a tucked waist, powerful haunches.

A dog, she said. A greyhound.

Yep. And this?

More assured lines, the way a pencil had never been in her own hand.

A bird. A hawk. How come you're a steelworker and not some artist type?

There's an art to steel, too. Now what's this?

A rabbit!

Aye. Now, once you've got the shape you need to fill it in.

His pencil looped and lutzed inside the rabbit, forming eyes and nose, mouth and teeth. Flattening the tip against the envelope, he rubbed to create light and depth; the tail a delicately shit-stained pompom so real-looking she could've sunk fingers into it.

We never had pets growing up, she said. There was nowhere to put them.

He passed her a fresh envelope. OK, now you.

I can't. What can I draw?

I told you, me. He offered her his chewed HB and splayed out amongst the settee cushions, one languid arm unfurling fern-like above his head. *So…how do you* want *me?*

Stop messing about.

Something in her voice halted his clowning.

Aye, just sit like that and be still.

The oval and cross were fine, but when it came to filling them in…The left eye, that delicate fold under the ridge of eyelash – how to capture that? She sketched it as best she could before moving onto his right eye, but soon realised because she'd spaced them too far apart, his nose appeared wonky. The pencil had no eraser. Failure was permanent, and with each new line the mess compounded. Sweat broke out on her lip. She flattened the pencil as Max had done. Sunlight brushed the left side of his face and he was beautiful, more beautiful than she'd thought possible. But on her envelope, he was dead. Mouth dead. Eyes dead. Hair an assemblage of Death. By the time she got around to shading his cheeks, her armpits were damp. Why did it matter so much that she got this right?

Let me see, he said.

She pressed the envelope to her chest.

Come on, let me. Peeling it from her like a bandage from a wound.

She couldn't look when he looked. She knew why it mattered.

He studied it for what seemed like a long time. You forgot my neck bolts, he said.

Fuck you.

He flopped on top of her, laughing. I love it.

I couldn't do the insides.

You'll get better, he said, slipping her top off over her head and kissing the hollow of her throat…

—

'Time for stage two, Mrs Terry,' Corina says.

'I'm just finishing this page,' she says, turning a fresh page.

'Take your time, Mrs Terry.'

Corina helps the old woman back into the sink, peels away the plastic cap, and starts rinsing off the perm lotion. As ever, Mrs Terry's good eye remains flinty and alert.

Corina says, 'So what's the book about, anyway?'

'Why?'

'Just asking.'

'Well,' Mrs Terry says, 'I supposed I don't mind. There's this sculptor, see, what's in love with the statue of a girl what his enemy's done. Only this sculptor's blind, and he's fallen in love by feeling it, and his enemy won't tell him who she is, the lass he carved.'

'That's not on.'

'Oh, he's a proper scunner. So now the blind sculptor's going round touching everyone up. You wait, though, he'll end up with his assistant. It's not my usual, as I say. I prefer the doctors and nurses ones because whatever else they get up to, at least they're still putting a shift in. But the van didn't have none. They never have what I want nowadays.'

'That library van's still going? How come I never see it?'

'It's down to once a month now, and only parks outside the Civic Hall. It's all computer games and them *DDV* things.'

'Me and my brother used to wait for it outside the blocks when we were little.'

'That would've been Henry. He drove it for nigh on forty year.'

'I think I remember. Elvis hair, yeah?'

'Lovely man.'

Corina pats dry Mrs Terry's head before adding the neutraliser. Mrs Terry asks for her book again.

'You must be a romantic,' Corina ventures.

Mrs Terry chews on the word like chop fat. '*Romantic*? I read 'em because I get through 'em quick, that's all.' And with that, she returns to her story.

—

She and Max sketching and making love is, to Corina, intrinsically entangled with the night they first met: Krissy Mackenzie's New Year's Eve party, 1993 – the night of the bomb. Corina was in a corner with a rum and coke, brooding on the bust-up she'd had earlier with Jim. Their fighting was becoming habitual since he'd moved in with her. Even though she doubted it herself, she'd said to him, Why don't you come tonight? It'll be fun. But Jim was already wasted and refused to budge from the confines of his room. Blaring that same acid tape for the millionth time.

The music stopped at Krissy's party. The room took up a slipshod countdown.

Ten! (he'll be passed out by the time I get back) – *Nine!* – (OK, like I get what happened to you was awful) – *Eight!* – *Seven!* (but you need to stop pointing the finger) – *Six!* –

225

Five! (take control of your life) – *Four!* – *Three!* (enough of this martyr shite) – *Two!* – *One!* ('cause you're starting to remind me of Dad) – *HAPPY NEW Y* – and it was then, on the literal final syllable separating present from past, then from now, that she glanced across the room and into his eyes and the world exploded: a concussive THUD! knocked the room off its feet, and an earth-smashing BOOM! rolled over the houses, shattering windows and shuddering bone. Party goers screamed and clawed at each other as heavy things thumped against the roof. Lights flickered. Outside, a cacophony of car alarms and howling dogs.

He made his way across the room and knelt beside her. Are you OK?

I'm OK, she said. She felt OK, anyway.

I'm Max, he said. I make memorable first impressions.

Somehow, she was under a chair. Get me out of here.

The front door was drunk on its hinges, and out in the street it was snowing. Fine debris winnowed down amongst the flakes. By the looks of it, every window in every house on the street was blasted out. Across the road, the front of a Nissan Sunny lay flattened beneath a large, smoking boulder.

She gripped his arm. Is that…is that an *asteroid*?

He picked something off the ground and whistled through his teeth.

In his palm was a blood-flecked wisdom tooth.

She heard herself say, I had mine out a couple of year ago. The gas made me funny. I told them I wasn't getting out the chair until I got a sticker.

I had mine out during my GCEs and missed my German oral.

226

Couldn't you retake?

Oh, ja.

He looked older than her by maybe a decade, and his eyes were brown and soft. Such a queer sensation, this; already she knew where they were headed. She said, I'm Corina by the way. Happy New Year.

Max dropped the tooth into the settling snow and smiled. Happy New Year, Corina.

Sirens rose in the distance. She noticed something attached to the doorframe directly above their heads. Mistletoe.

Look up, she said.

—

Neutraliser rinsed, Corina removes the rods from Mrs Terry's hair and replaces them with bright pink rollers. As usual, Mrs Terry sits under the far right brainsucker, which rattles when Corina turns it on.

The clock on the salon wall is a cat with oscillating eyes, a murderous grin, and a swinging pendulum tail. It's almost noon. Meredith isn't due for an hour.

She takes the backroom phone into the toilet, closing the door on the cord as best she can. She wriggles her leggings and underwear down and rests her forehead in her left palm. It occurs to her that this could be the last time she ever uses this toilet, a thought as vertigo-inducing as it is prosaic.

Calling Bev would stop this going any further. Bev was the first person she'd met when she walked through the doors of Gamblers Anonymous five years ago, the woman who had helped her through the first jagged weeks and months. Recently, Bev had even put Corina's name forward to chair a new chapter over in Yarm, but that was before Corina started drifting away from meetings.

She tinkles into the bowl, dials with her eyes closed.

Years ago, Max had made her delete all her gambling contacts. You can't keep doing what you're doing, he said. It's tearing us apart – look, *look* at your daughter (ten-year old Annabelle at the kitchen table, head bowed, rubbing her eyes under a fringe as dark and impenetrable as a motorcycle helmet visor). Max slid her phone through the crumbs on the tablecloth. This is symbolic, he said. A first step. So she deleted everything right there, in front of both of them, safe in the knowledge that every number she'd ever need was already seared onto her secret heart.

The phone rings and a woman answers.

'I'd like the odds for Heart of Chrome tonight in the 8:39 at Stockton.'

A keyboard clacks. '30/1,' the woman says.

Corina hangs up. No betting surges mean either the dog's as dud, or it's been made to look like a dud. Beech told her how it worked. Stop a fast dog with drugs to lengthen its odds. Then, at the right time, in the right race, run it straight and clean up.

But if that's this, why is Beech telling her now?

She flushes the toilet. A mildew vortex – wet and rotten – swirls up out of the U-bend.

Beech, what are you after?

—

Max had managed to get the Saturday night off and it was all planned: an Indian in town, maybe a drink somewhere, then back for an early night. Annabelle – five now – was staying at Asquith with Corina's folks, so they had the place to themselves. As soon as they got back, Corina slid a hand round Max's neck and put her January-bleak lips to his. He responded sluggishly. She pressed his palm and led him upstairs.

He flopped backwards on the bed. Grey skinned, his eyes slits in periwinkle pouches of flesh. She got to her knees. Like her lips, his thigh was wintery to the touch.

Her hand moved in languid, crotch-bound circles. I had a nice time tonight, she said.

He didn't respond. She undid his fly.

Nff...s'tired...

She stopped. He propped himself up on his elbows.

What?

Now you show signs of life.

Eh?

I didn't marry an idiot, Max.

You just said you were having a nice time.

You barely said anything to me the entire meal, and you drank like four pints.

And? I've been at work since 2am. It was the only way I could get tonight off in the first place, so I felt like a drink, right? Doesn't mean I don't enjoy being with you still.

Still?

What?

Being with you *still*. Like I've got a sell-by-date.

He collapsed back. Jesus, Cor.

On high heels, she wobbled to her feet. You can't just enjoy *still* being with me.

He made a mask of his hands.

She said, You know, I've started second guessing myself. Thinking, well, this's what's supposed to happen after you've been married a few years, isn't it? You drift off into your own bitter little world, while I get old and ugly.

Cor, what the fuck are you on about?

I'm *on about* you not being interested in me. In *us*. Your head's somewhere else.

He rolled off the far side of the bed. His chin was on the edge of the sea-green duvet in such a way it was as if she were arguing with his freshly guillotined head. He said, You want to know where my head's at? It's at that fucking factory. It's on the double-shifts and the people getting the chop *every single week*. And how I'm too shit-scared to say owt in case I'm next. Does that not show you I care? – she heard him zip his fly – Or do I still have to get my cock out?

You think it's easy for me either? What? What's that?

What's what?

That smirk.

Nowt.

No, haway, Max.

Fine. It's that place.

The salon, yeah? And?

Well it's hardly been the empire-starter you planned, has it?

Building a reputation takes time.

I told you opening on the estate was a bad idea.

What are you trying to say?

I'm not *trying* to say anything. We barely see each other, that's a fact. And Annabelle spends more time round your parents than she does here.

So you want me to, what? Stay home? Get a nice little pinny and make pies? This isn't the nineteen-fucking-fifties.

You're doing it again! Can't we have a rational

conversation about this? I just think it's time you thought about cutting your losses.

You just can't take the fact I've done something for myself, can you? That it's my name above that door? What's your name on, eh?

His head dropped out of sight. Our marriage certificate, he said.

Next thing he was on the landing, calling her back – *Cor, come on, Cor* – but she was already halfway down Peelaw Bank, already relinquishing control to the streets that tacitly led her to the bus idling at the stop on Stanhope, as if waiting for her alone. Their fight multiplied within her like mirror reflecting mirror as she was carried through the estate and onto the dual carriageway, towards the spotlights of Stockton Dogs, where, without quite knowing why – not then at least – she pressed the bell.

—

Hungover or not, she's *ravenous*. All the instant coffee, the cigs – her stomach is sheep-shanked.

'Mrs Terry?'

Under her brainsucker, the old woman's good eye swivels in her direction.

'I'm just popping to Yvette's. Do you think you'll be alright?'

'Not like I'm going anywhere, is it?'

'If anyone comes in, tell them I'll be back in half an hour.'

But Mrs Terry's already gone back to her book.

The midday news bulletin comes on. Corina clears out before they reach the part about the greyhounds.

—

His first words to her: *Penny for them?*

She was staring at the race, the dogs on the track like clockwork things wound to breaking.

Huh?

He leaned against the railing, an oddly school-boyish gesture. I said penny for them.

Sorry, I was just watching the race.

So I see. Owt juicy you're willing to let me in on?

The black dog in the blue jacket took the tape, the rest finishing a split second behind.

Never seen you here before, he said.

I've only been once, with my husband.

Is he here tonight, your husband?

On the track, the last races' dogs were bundled off at one end while the upcoming animals were walked on at the other. A tractor pulled the traps to the starting line.

Not tonight, no.

They both watched the tractor for a moment, then he turned to face her. Despite the cold, he was sweating profusely. My name's Derek Beecham, he said, but my mates call me Beech.

Dog number 6 was a speckled grey. It dug its haunches so deep into the sandy track that the handler was forced to wrap the leash double around his fist and yank the animal clean off the ground.

And you are? he said.

Corina looked at him askance and told him.

That's a pretty name. Scottish, isn't it?

I don't know what it is.

The handler moved behind 6, side-footing it towards the

traps, which, to Corina, resembled car-crushers in miniature. Beech abandoned the rail and stood full height. Even in her high heels, she was at least a foot shorter than him. She shivered in her thin dress.

So, Corina, are you having a punt?

A what? No, I'm just watching.

You said you'd been here before. You bet that time, aye?

Once, yes.

How did you get on?

I won, Corina said. At 50/1.

Nice, he whistled. Very nice. Maybe you could bring that insight to this next one?

That was just luck.

Beech lit a thin cigar. Still, who do you fancy?

I don't know, she said, turning back to the track. Number 6.

Out of the corner of her eye, she registered Beech scribbling something. He folded the scrap of paper and held it out to her with the tips of his nicotine-yellow fingers. Corina took it warily.

As he walked away he said, No peeking 'til the fat lady's sung.

Number 6 was last into the trap. Silence fell. A feeling like fingertips on skin, then the rabbit shot past and six muscular dogs sprang loose. People all around yelling; an old man in a fishing hat screaming: *YES YOU GO YES YOU GO YES YOU GO YES YOU GO* with the last shreds of his voice as – *cut my losses?* – wind-flared muzzles, black gums, white ribbons of foam, the dogs hit the first bend at impossible speeds – *he exaggerates that fucking job, I KNOW he does* – opening up on the straight, thinning out, number 6 somewhere in the middle but –

so he can justify staying away – losing ground – *GO YES YOU* – coming up to the final bend, bug-eyed and grinning with exhaustion – *is it another woman?* – not even dogs anymore, really – *YOU GO YES* – but things flayed from the belly of the world, things – *younger?* – from nightmare – *no kids?* – and then it was – *GOOOOOOO* – all over. The dogs streaked across the line and pounced on the rabbit, tails whipping.

The boards announced the race. From first to last: 2, 5, 1, 3, 4, and, finally, 6.

She unfolded Beech's paper:

Any order:

1 , 2 , 5

there is no LUCK
(I'm in the bar)

She said aloud, He must think I'm stupid. Then she went looking for the bar.

Down on the track, number 6 was being dragged from the spotlights and into the dark.

—

Outside on the precinct, the heat is a clenched fist. Tendrils of BBQ smoke stitch the air, along with, fainter, the frigid brine of the North Sea itself. Seagulls pinwheel high above, their calls far off, dream drugged. She's tempted to look in on Gary for paracetamol, but the idea of swapping the warmth and light for his sepulchral newsagent carries her past his door and on to *Yvette's*.

Yvette's was the first business to open on the Burn Estate, and its founder, Yvette's father, celebrated the occasion by painting his new-born daughter's name across the front window in cardinal red and gold. The window itself is a marvel; miraculous in that it has never been smashed in over 60 years (Corina's has been done twice, Gary's so many times that he stopped pulling up his shutters altogether). Inside, too, things have barely changed since Corina was yea-high: the faded Formica tables and chairs bolted to the floor, the fruit machine flashing in the corner, the wheezing sauce bottles – the sauce itself off-brand, too red and vinegary – the fruit machine flashing in the corner, the chrome tray-rail running the length of the counter past cottage pies and casseroles in glass hotboxes, the fruit machine flashing in the corner. The only real difference came with the cigarette ban; now only grease hangs in the air.

The fruit machine flashing in the corner.

Yvette, putting a sausage butty in front of a Hi-Vised builder, looks up when the door jingles. 'I was hoping you'd stop in today, pet.' Her face is marshmallow pink; her hair beneath the net scraped into the severest of buns. Apron clean, but threadbare. She goes behind the counter and picks up a Styrofoam cup.

Corina raises a hand. 'I'm going to sit in today.'

'And why not?' Yvette says. Then, 'How are you holding up?'

'Ah, you know.'

'And then there were two, eh?'

'Maybe another unit will come along?'

Yvette's scans her clientele, the handful of equidistantly-spaced OAPs sitting silently save for the low chink-and-scrape of cutlery. 'Who'd set up shop in a place due to be knocked down?' She nods over to the Hi-Vis cramming sausages into his mouth. 'He'll be swinging the hammer.'

'You don't know that. Nobody's said anything to me about the salon yet.'

'They will,' Yvette says. 'It's a shame you couldn't hang on 'til they bought you out.'

'Aye,' Corina says.

Yvette lowers her voice. 'Have they made an offer on your house yet? I don't mean to pry, it's just I've been hearing things.'

'What things?'

There's a melodramatic tinge to Yvette's voice. 'Well, that they'll try to shaft you. It happened to someone the other day, Tracey Dyer. She lives round your way. Do you know her? She's a bit bottom heavy?'

'Sorry.'

'Well, she got her house independently valued, and when she told Rowan-Tree, they sent their own people in for a second appraisal. She got the letter last week. Fifteen thousand *less* they're offering, and she's got to accept – apparently it's against the law to sell to anybody but them once transfer's been agreed.'

Corina thinks of the letter in her bag.

'I don't know how these housing whatsits live with themselves,' Yvette says. 'Don't take this the wrong way, but I'm glad I moved to Hemlington when I did. What are you going to do?'

There's a place she's found on the internet, somewhere in Queensland, Australia, that is doing *ground-breaking Alzheimer's research* – their words – with a protein called TDP…PTD? She doesn't claim to understand, but what

236

she does know is that Heart of Chrome would let her fly Mam out there.

'I'll figure it out.'

'If they think they're short-changing me on this place when the time comes, they've got another thing coming...'

'Gary dropped the papers round this morning and he didn't look well.'

Yvette repositions her apron straps over her breasts. 'Well, he's been in for tests.'

'What? When?'

'Last month. He wasn't due his results for three weeks, but they rang him straight back wanting to arrange a consultation *immediately*.'

'Christ. What's wrong with him?'

Yvette glances around conspiratorially. 'Well that's just it – he won't go, will he? I says you're being daft, Gary, I says you need to go in, but he says, they know nowt, doctors, and I says, *Gary, you need to go in*. You're grafting dawn till dusk, man. You're no spring chicken. You need to go in, see what they say.'

'What did he say?'

'What did he say? He says, I'm scared. I says, of what? Of being told it's the end, he says.' Yvette presses her thumb onto a stray crumb on the counter. When she moves her thumb, the crumb is gone. 'I says, we're all scared of that.'

'Maybe I can have a word?'

Yvette shakes her head. 'He doesn't want people knowing. Anyway, what'll it be?'

'A BLT with mayo...no, no mayo. And coke. Diet coke.'

'Pop's in the fridge, I'll bring the rest over.'

Corina takes a can from the chiller and sits at a back table. The sun streaming through the front window spangles her hungover eyes, suffusing everything with a honey-gold light; *Yvette's* projected backwards across the empty table tops. As a bairn, Mam used to bring them here for breakfast on Saturday mornings before food shopping in town. Corina always had the same thing: a raspberry Crusha milkshake and toasted teacake burned brittle at the edges. Jim copied, but picked the currants out of his. They discovered a strange thing about their mother on those Saturday mornings. She wouldn't sit anywhere else but along the back wall; would march them straight out again if those tables were occupied. An obstinate streak in an otherwise pliant soul, they had ripped her for it when they got older. For example, she and Jim had watched an old gangster flick on TV late one night – some paranoid mobster who always sat at the back table at restaurants, and the one time he didn't a rival hood snuck up and blew his brains out. Mam was heavily involved with the Tenants' Association by this point, and went to meetings at Yvette's every Friday afternoon. As she headed out the door with folders and notebooks under her arms, the two of them would glower from beneath the tilted brims of imaginary fedoras.

Jim: Don't be no rat, Ma.

Corina: Yeah, you disrespect the Gambinis, you better sleep with *both* eyes open.

Their mother's face crumpling in confusion, Why do you keep *saying* that?

But they'd be too busy cracking up to explain.

There's some spilled sugar on her table. Corina begins shaping it into a spiral with the tip of her finger. The Hi-Vised builder burps loudly.

The Tenants' Association. It was the climbing frame

238

which first got Mam involved with it. That climbing frame, what did people call it again?

—

The Thunderdome. A rung-rotten scaffold in the centre of the communal green, a rusting gallows that had taken its pound of flesh from generation after generation of block kid. Its most recent victim was Irene Donaldson's boy Ricky, who had earned a trip to A&E, sixteen stitches, and a tetanus needle in his arse. Irene had been demanding the council get rid of the edifice ever since.

They don't give a shite, she said. Might as well be speaking Swahili.

Irene was their left-hand neighbour in Asquith and often popped round for a cuppa with Corina's mam (sometimes Corina joined them, most times she didn't. Not that that mattered – from her room she heard every word). Irene wore sovereigns on each finger and nibbled the corners of her shortbread like a rat.

And do you know *why* the council doesn't listen, Nora?

Why's that? Corina's mam said.

Because Westminster's told them not too. If they start making places like this habitable again, folk will want to stay, and that's the last thing they want. Same with the steelworks. They could've put money into it, could've stopped your Morris losing his job, but they want everyone off their books. Someone else's problem. It's a conspiracy against the working class.

Mam slurped tea. Yes, I see.

But then men did come for the Thunderdome, felled it in sheeting sparks. Irene was giddy. It's that new Tenants'

Association, she said. Them Peel House people. They've sent the invoice to the council with a list of signatures, in case the buggers try for criminal damage.

Peel House? Mam said. Aren't they the graffitiers?

Murals had been appearing in the stairwells of Peel House. Murals that flowed together like half-sunk dreams. Murals that were, in Corina's opinion, gorgeous.

They're good people, Irene said. Don't listen to the gossips. They give a monkey's, and that's more than most. They want to see this place back to how it was. Remember that? Remember when we had *clout*, Nora?

I remember, Corina's mother said.

Well, Irene said, there's a meeting tonight…

Which is how Mam got involved, and soon she was staggering in with two thousand leaflets to cut and fold for a demonstration, her thick glasses fogged up, long after tea time had come and gone. She spent nights sorting tinned pineapple from tinned butterbeans for Christmas food donations. She arm-twisted local journalists into covering community clean-ups on the slope behind Attlee House, where knackered settees were set to burn black oblongs into the grass. Indefatigability personified – and all while clocking forty hours at her cash-office job down at the industrial estate.

After Jim had his accident, she added carer to her list of duties. Constantly fussing around him, making sure he ate and did his exercises, standing outside the toilet while he was in there. One night he swung his crutch at the tray of chucky eggs she carried into his room, and it was Corina who'd held her mother's yolk-tacky cheek to her chest.

I don't know what more I can do, she wept.

Corina, speeding towards crackup herself, said, There isn't anything. You have to start doing things for yourself.

Which was how the acting started.

Some people in Peel House had set up a theatre group and applied for funds to the Tenants' Association, who rejected the idea. The grapevine was ashiver with rumours the council were planning tenancy transfer to a housing association, and they would need every penny to fight it. It was Mam who finally convinced them to sign off the funds, and to say thank you she was offered a part.

This was Final Straw for Corina's dad.

Nora, you've lost the fucking plot! First they were just taking advantage of your soft nature, but now they've got you making a tit of yourself.

They were in the kitchen, Corina her bedroom, but the walls carried their argument – mixed it with TVs and toilets and wailing children – and piped it directly into her ears with stereo Walkman fidelity.

I like being part of the community, Mam said.

You're part of this family, Nora, first and foremost.

So I don't get to do something for myself, ever?

And that's what you want to do, is it? Prance about?

I've always enjoyed acting.

Since when?

Since school. I was in lots of plays at school. You never forget, Mickey says.

A pause. Corina braced herself.

I've heard about this Mickey, Dad said. He's one of them druggies what's took over Peel House. That place used to be for normal people.

They just want a roof over their heads, Morris, same as everyone. They'll be good for this community. You'd see that if you got involved.

Corina can picture the sneer on her dad's face when he

said, Let me tell you about *community*. Community is fucked. There was one, years ago, but freaks like them wrecked it. Now everything's out of control.

Through the wall she shared with Jim, Corina could hear the relentless beat of acid music.

You're a hateful man, Mam said. When did you become such a hateful man?

What? You're talking like them! Nora, *they are the ones what ruined our son!*

Her mother made a high, wounded sound. Corina rolled off her bed, left her –

('*You.*')

room and exited the flat, heading for –

—

'You.'

(*for* –)

'Hey, you. I know you're listening.'

An old woman a few tables over glares at Corina through bi-focals.

'Yes?' Corina says.

'I know you.'

'I don't know you, sorry.'

'You're that pervert's sister.'

Others are eavesdropping. The builder looks furtively up from his butty. Only Yvette is still oblivious; lost to steam and sizzle behind the counter.

'I don't know what you're talking about,' Corina says.

'He snatched that poor bairn and now he's God knows where with her, doing God knows what. How can you show your face?'

'Shut up,' Corina says flatly.

The old woman flashes pomegranate gums. 'Or what?'

'I'm just trying to have lunch.'

'I will *not* shut up, not when me and mine have to rub shoulders with *kiddie fiddlers*.' The woman's magnified eyeballs are pink-yellow ruptures.

'My brother had nothing to do with that girl.'

'Is that right? Then where is he? Why'd he scarper?'

A memory of Jim in his kitchen the last time they had spoken. He was so thin and bent in all the wrong places, making black tea with his dead hand. And then another, later, after he had vanished, of walking into the disturbing contents of his living room. All those strange pictures on the walls.

Corina says, 'Maybe he bolted because of old cunts like you who've got nowt better to do than spread nasty rumours.'

The old woman rears up from her table. 'You see? You see what she says? Threatening me because I dare say what we're all thinking?'

Corina starts to shake. 'It was people like you who ruined him.'

'Leave her be,' the builder says, though who he's addressing, Corina can't say.

A chapped hand on her collarbone.

'Everybody relax,' Yvette says.

The old woman crows, 'When they catch him, I'll be there to watch him swing.'

'Phyllis, I think you better leave,' says Yvette.

'*Me*? It was her what said that awful word. Everyone heard!' Phyllis casts around for allies, but all eyes are on mug and spoon, yolk and crust.

'It's for the best, love. Just for today.'

The look in Phyllis' eyes is cauterising. She trembles with indignity as she gathers her things. 'I've been coming here since your dad's day, and this is how I get treated? Well, I won't be back.'

'Don't be like that Phyllis. You're welcome here any time.'

But Phyllis is gone.

Corina says, 'You can't afford to be losing customers on my account.'

'Pet, all she ever has is a cream slice. She's got no teeth.' She slides the BLT under Corina's face. 'Eat up.'

The sandwich is typical *Yvette's* fare: the bacon fatty, the L and T limp. But Corina, doesn't notice this because she's got her eye on something else.

The fruit machine in the corner.

—

Corina escaped the flat and was now battling the headwind on the sixth-floor walkway of Palmerston House. She buzzed for more than a minute before his muffled voice came from the other side of the door.

Yeah?

It's me.

Who?

Corina. Open up.

A series of clicks and clacks, and then the door opened just enough for Alive to peer around. Cor, what are you doing here?

Jacketless, her teeth clattered. She said, I was just thinking it's been a while since we hung out. I don't know, I thought I'd surprise you.

Alive glanced down the walkway in both directions before opening the door a little wider. Yeah, well, he said, I appreciate it, but I'm a bit busy.

Only then did she register he was dressed in vest and boxers, and that the boxers were on backwards. His dilated pupils were polished volcanic glass. Ambient techno drifted from his bedroom, a room she'd never seen. There was a high-heeled shoe in the hallway behind him.

Hey, he said, maybe give me a ring after the weekend, aye?

Her smile felt carved into her face. Aye, no worries.

He shut the door without saying goodbye.

She took the cold, echoing stairwell down and stalked across the central green. All around her, encircling, enveloping, towered the blocks – a million windows blazing. Up in Peel House, a party was getting underway; an electronic beat pinged and ricocheted around the horseshoe. Her dad was right. This place *was* out of control.

She stood in the centre of the green, in the circle of bald earth where the Thunderdome had once spilled blood, and thought about what Irene Donaldson had said. How it was time to get their clout back.

—

She steps out of *Yvette's* and hears the click of a crutch behind her. For an instant she thinks it's –

'Meredith! What happened to you?'

Meredith's right foot is bandaged twice its normal size, a tartan slipper shod over the bulk. 'I did it getting out of the bath.'

'My God, are you alright?'

She shifts her weight and winces. 'So they tell me.'

245

In the salon, Mrs Terry, her head still densely packed with rollers, has moved to the cutting chair. 'Money's in the box,' she says without looking up from her book.

'Thanks.'

Meredith sits awkwardly in the waiting area.

'A man rang,' Mrs Terry says.

Corina begins removing rollers. 'Did he leave a name?'

'He wouldn't give me one, but he had a mouth on him.' She looks at Corina, searching. 'He said he was a friend of yours. Then a young lass come in. I told her what you told me, but she took off.'

'Is she coming back?'

'How am I supposed to know?'

'Thanks Mrs Terry. You're all done.' She removes the final roller. The old woman's hair now resembles curls of sheered steel. Mrs Terry scrutinises herself in the mirror and nods. Then, instead of leaving, she settles in the waiting area with her book. Corina turns to Meredith. 'So, shampoo and set?'

Her foot makes it tricky to get Meredith comfortable in the sink. Her skull thin like a blown-egg. The pipes scream when Corina turns on the water.

'Goodness,' Meredith says, 'you should get that seen to.'

'When did you hurt your ankle?'

'Last Wednesday. I had to crawl to the phone.'

Meredith's hair is long and white, and brittle like loft insulation when Corina starts shampooing it. 'That's awful. Have you signed up with the property pool yet?'

'I'm on the phone every day, and every day they tell me the same – not successful, better luck next time. It's horrible. I don't like competitions. I don't even play bingo.'

Corina knew. She was trying to organise her parents'

move ahead of demolition, but her mother needed specialist sheltered housing, which meant Dad had to be found a one-bed somewhere nearby. The process was nightmarish; an endless cycle of buck-passing between Rowan-Tree, the council, and the hospital. She needed to be assessed, they said. You need this form, that department. Last week she'd raged at a housing officer for not turning up to an appointment, only to learn Dad had cancelled it. When confronted, he'd said, She doesn't need people looking after her! Nobody knows her like I do, isn't that right Nora? But all Mam could manage in reply, as she sat knitting her shapeless monstrosity on the settee, was something about how Jim had been *very rude today*, how she'd *banged on his flat for half an hour*, and he hadn't answered. Talking about it like it was yesterday, not a decade ago.

Meredith says, 'All I want is somewhere dry. I've got mould everywhere.'

'You should see my bathroom,' Corina says.

Meredith closes her eyes. 'I looked into getting one of those dehumidifiers, but they're so dear.'

'I had one once. You wouldn't believe how much moisture was in the air.'

'I'll bet, hinny. I'll…bet.'

'Meredith?'

But Meredith is asleep. Her nose whistles delicately.

'The damp,' Mrs Terry says from the waiting area, 'plays havoc with my tubes.'

—

The dehumidifier was a story she used to tell back when she still went to meetings:

My daughter Annabelle had bad asthma growing up, and our house was – is – really damp, especially in winter. And I mean *really* damp. Like trickling-down-the-walls damp, which obviously did her chest no favours, so we got a dehumidifier for the upstairs landing. The amount of water it sucked out of the air…like, it would beep when it was full, and there'd be six litres in the tank. Six litres every couple of days. It's a wonder we weren't wearing snorkels.

If any attendees of the Gamblers Anonymous meeting ever found this funny, they never laughed.

Annabelle was always so keen on emptying the tank, but six litres is a lot for a twelve-year-old. She'd slosh half on the floor before she got to the bathroom, but that was Annabelle all over, always wanting to help. Me and Max – my husband – we worked different hours. He'd been a steelworker, but was laid off and the only work he could get was in a frozen food factory. He hated it because they had him doing splits, nights. And my business wasn't doing so well either. I had to take work where I could get it, which meant staying open later. But when I got back, Annabelle would've done the hoovering, or tried cooking tea, no matter how many times we told her not to touch the oven. She just took it upon herself. How many kids do that?

So one day I open the paper to check the races, like I did every day, and two dogs jump out at me. I still remember their names: Mr Wu and Phantom Limb, and as soon as I see them, I know they're the ones. I'd been losing all that winter, totally lost the touch. You know the touch, aye? When you look at a race and you just *know*…

it's weird…it's less like predicting the future than it is controlling the present. So when I see these dogs, I feel, like, *finally*, someone – *something* – is acknowledging my shitty run. I owed money to people – well, one person – a man – let's call him B – who I'd met literally only the second time I ever went to the track. At first, he was nice, he showed me the ropes, and when I hit rough spots he'd lend me money. I know, daft, but he was so nice about it in the beginning. It wasn't until my losing streak went on that I started getting the feeling he wouldn't be so nice forever. All I needed was one win, to get it off my back. And that's when I saw those two dogs…

Sometimes, to win big you need to bet big. My employee's wages are in the safe and I try to resist, you know, I try keeping my head down, but some days there's literally no customers and I spend hours mooning out the window. And that's the dangerous bit, that's when your worldview gets bent. Gambling becomes part of something more elaborate, doesn't it? You *had* to have lost all those times, to pay your dues. It was vital you gambled the mortgage repayment and covered it with that secret credit card, otherwise you weren't worthy of The Big Win. Even with what B'd told me about how common race fixing was, this was how I was still able to give myself the edge in my head. *There is no luck*, that's what B liked to say. And maybe he meant it one way, but I took it another because to me, all that shady stuff was the insignificant work of mere humans, while my wins and losses were something more… I can't think of the right word…

In the dusty church hall, nobody offered pertinent vocabulary.

I'm sure you can guess what I did next. It's weird, isn't

it? It's like you're watching yourself going into the bookies and filling out the slip. You're totally invested yet totally detached at the same time. Two yous – and in the space between, that's where the bet gets made. It's only after you hand the money over that they smash back together and the doubts flood in – What'll I tell my employee? What'll I tell B? What if this is the fuck up that lets Max find out?

So I go home. Max is due back from his shift, but Annabelle's still home alone. I run a bath. I just need time to get myself together. I find that the hardest part of addiction isn't dealing with the fallout of your actions, it's maintaining a semblance of normalcy the rest of the time. Just, like, eating a meal with your family, or having a conversation with your partner, or helping your daughter with her times-tables. Being *present*, you know? The constant stress of bring present.

I have a soak, and when I come out there's a wet patch at the bottom of the stairs and my bag is turned inside out on the hall radiator, and it's *empty*.

I'm like, Annabelle, what's happened?

Christ, she looks panicked. She says the dehumidifier beeped, so she'd tried emptying it herself – one less job for me, like – only as she was carrying it down, she stumbled on the last step and spilled the whole thing into my bag. She took everything out and put it on the radiators to dry. Naturally, I freak out. Has she seen the betting slip? Does she even understand what it is?

Then Max comes home. I'm like, *Where is it?*

And she's like, Where's what?

A little square of paper with writing on it. Which radiator?

She's like, Mammy, I don't know. And why would she? There's so much crap in my bag – business letters, all kinds

250

of crap. I grab Annabelle…I grab her wrists and she…she yelps…then I go into the living room just as Max's coming through the other door. I can see the slip on the radiator, a foot away from him. The pen's run but it's still readable. My secret self, there in the open. All he has to do is look down, and if he had, maybe things would've gone different. But he's knackered, as usual. He goes upstairs and I stuff the slip in my dressing gown.

Annabelle was so sorry, she was only trying to help. But I'm livid, and not because the slip's ruined – bookies have a policy for that – but because if I'm exposed, gambling would've got a lot harder.

Anyway, long story short, the dogs came in and my employee got paid, and B eased off a bit. Annabelle had trouble holding her pen at school the next day because she'd sprained her wrist – *I'd* sprained her wrist – and when Max asked her about it, she was like, I think I did it playing hockey…So maybe you're wondering how I can live with the guilt? It's…I'm sorry…

Take your time, said Bev. Take your time.

…Thanks. I'm OK…But here's the thing about guilt. When you're gambling, guilt doesn't factor. The streak is all that matters – either breaking a losing one, or keeping a winning one going. Winning becomes this eighteen-wheeler with fucked breaks going down a hill, gathering speed, and you'll jeopardise everything before you jeopardise that. So yeah, maybe what you've done is bad enough for you to knock it on the head for a bit – like I did – but it never truly goes away. It always comes back worse. Which it did. Much worse.

Bev put her hand on Corina's knee.

Annabelle's grown up now and we haven't spoken for a

long time. She has a daughter of her own who I've never met. My husband left, too…he wants a divorce and is trying to get me to sell the house, but I'm dragging my feet because I don't want it all to be over. This is why I'm here today, for them. If I can admit I have a problem maybe I can win them back… (but she doesn't mention how, of late, the old feeling had returned. Like being chained to a cement block dumped into a canal, the sinking sensation was on her before she even opened her eyes in the mornings).

Maybe, for the first time, I can win without leaving it to chance.

—

'I've got things in my walls,' Meredith says, eyes closed.

'Things?' Corina says.

'Mice. Rats. They scrabble around at night.'

'Have you set traps?'

'Oh, I don't want to hurt them, it's not their fault. The empty houses attract them.'

From *Behind Drawn Shades*, Mrs Terry says, 'Vermin is vermin. You can't be soft. They got into my brother's wife's kitchen once and carried off her gammon.'

Meredith opens one eye. 'Her gammon?'

'Her gammon,' Mrs Terry replies, ominously.

Meredith looks up at Corina. 'I saw Gail Barnett last week. She's been offered some lovely sheltered accommodation in Thornaby.'

'Lucky her,' Corina says, handing Meredith a towel.

'So I asked them why *I* couldn't be in Thornaby. I said, I'm sure I've been on the list longer than Gail Barnett, but they said they couldn't discuss individual cases. I said, but I'm seventy-three and I've got *things* in my walls. One of these days they'll find me dead in my chair.'

'Meredith,' Corina says.

'I always thought I'd end my days here,' Meredith says. 'I remember even after David and I were married, we still couldn't get on the list because we didn't have children. That was the rule. We had to live with his mother, and I can say this now because they've both passed, but she was a bitter, bitter woman. I think I prefer living with mice than I did her.'

Hair damp against her head, Meredith looks even tinier. A preserved peat-bog woman. Corina helps her into the chair.

Meredith says, 'But even once I was in the family way, Rosanna was almost born before they gave us a house. That's how prestigious they were.'

'I got my two-bedroom place no questions asked,' Corina says.

'Oh, but they were *lovely* when they were first built. All round here, you wouldn't believe me if I told you. The council even had leaflets on how to cut your grass and scrub your doorstep. You needed written permission to put up a picture hook! It was a month before David could hang his auntie Florence over the wireless…'

As Corina rolls and pins Meredith's long hair, she tries to imagine the estate like this – rows of brand new houses gleaming beneath a Cold War sun, the gardens shimmering with Cabbage Whites and Red Admirals. But she can't. It feels flimsy, two-dimensional, like the family on the Rowan-Tree billboards. Her own house is draughty and damp, the brickwork seamed with mother-of-pearl slug trails and a raw-boned cold pulsing off the solid cement floors. Yet when she'd first moved in – her own home! – such things had seemed inconsequential in the face of the sheer silence greeting her each time she turned the key in the lock. It was a silence she thought would also do Jim some good, though Mam protested at first. Corina argued that a new environment – even if it was just the estate – might help him out of himself. But Jim kept sinking. She would come home slack-jawed from college, or *In-Val-Uable*, or her weekend checkout job, and put her head round his door to see him passed out with an empty bottle, twitching in dreams. Lips moving. Shattered hand caressing something she herself could not see.

Meredith is still talking. 'People were *respectable*. You left your door open and folk'd pop their heads in. Everyone knew everyone, not like now. Now new folk move in and six months later they're gone.' Meredith looks at herself in the mirror. 'How things change.' She turns to Mrs Terry. 'Folk were nicer back then, don't you think?'

Mrs Terry makes a show of finishing her sentence before studying Meredith thoughtfully. 'How's your memory?'

'A few holes,' Meredith says, 'but sound enough. Why?'

'So I take it you'll recall the events of the second of July, 1968? Around midday?'

Meredith looks troubled. 'Should I?'

'Aye, you should. Second of July, 1968 – the Day of the Dark.' She looks at Corina. 'You mightn't have been born.'

'I've never even heard of it.'

'No, I remember now,' Meredith says. 'I was visiting my auntie in Cromer that week, but my mam kept the Gazette for me.'

'It was in the paper?' Corina says.

'Have you ever woken up in the middle of the night and can't move?' Mrs Terry says. 'You're paralysed, and you *know* something's coming up the stairs, getting closer? Well it was like that, this feeling creeping over the estate. It started mid-morning. First the sky went green, then black. Dogs howling, all the birds taking off at once – huge, black balls of birds. Colin was on shift, so I was in on my own. I told myself, don't be daft, lass, don't be daft. It's just some bad weather, just a thunderstorm, only it kept getting darker and darker. I felt like I was being buried alive.' Mrs Terry massages her tortured hands and neither Meredith nor Corina speak. 'But then the rain started and the lightning blew the lights, and I knew it wasn't no ordinary storm.'

'What did you do?' Meredith whispers.

'I went to the upstairs window and it was like midnight outside. Darker even, because there were no streetlights. I looked up the street and in the lightning flashes I saw a river rushing. Bikes, sheds, bins, all sorts being swept away. The hailstones were big enough to crack the roof slate.'

'Why the hell have I never heard about this?' Corina says.

Mrs Terry plucks at the hairs on her chin. 'Folk don't like to remember what they don't like to remember.' She coughs into a hanky and continues. 'Nathan Deacon was our next-door neighbour. He was a quiet lad, with a young wife and bairn – a boy, I forget his name – no more than four or five at the time. Nathan was out in the storm, on his knees, in his front garden. I banged on the window but the wind was too loud, so I pulled the bedding over me and went out. I was young then, light on my feet, but the hail still nearly flattened me. Nathan was in some kind of trance and when I slung a blanket over him, I realised he was praying. *The sixth seal's broken*, that's what he was saying. *The sixth seal's broken* – something, something, *blood*. Oh, and I should mention he was only wearing his briefs.'

'Goodness,' Meredith says.

'I got him into his house and lit a candle – folk still had candles in them days – and he looked like he'd gone ten rounds with Jack Bodell. Welts all over him, his eyes closing up, gore all down his face. I'm not sure he knew where he was.'

Corina thinks of Max, what those men did to him; his blood, his eyelids fluttering. The rose petal stuck to his cheek.

Mrs Terry says, 'He thought it was the apocalypse, and he wanted to get square before it was too late. That's when he told me how, when he was a lad, he used to take his little brother down to the coal shed and rape him.'

Corina gasps.

'And how, when the bairn got TB and died, he'd been relieved.' Mrs Terry reclines in her chair. 'So I left him there, in the dark. I went home and locked the door and waited for whatever was next. I'm not religious, but I'll admit I said a prayer.' She shakes her head at herself. 'Then the storm let up, the hail stopped, and the clouds went away. Half an hour later it was like nowt had happened.'

'What caused it?'

'The storm? I'm not going to sit here and say it was owt but bad weather, but I'd be lying if Nathan's Biblical business hadn't crossed my mind.'

'And Nathan? What did you do about him?'

'Took him off the Christmas card list for starters. Aside from that…I'd seen what the dark had done to him. That was enough. Besides, they moved away not long after.' Mrs Terry looks at Meredith. 'So in answer to your question as to whether folk were nicer back then, I learned it takes the end of the world to see inside another.'

The radio plays a jingle for pet insurance. Mrs Terry picks up her book.

'Cromer was lovely,' Meredith says. 'The crabs were delicious.'

Hair rolled, pinned, and netted, Corina puts Meredith under a brainsucker before slipping into the back to ring the bookies. Heart of Chrome's odds haven't changed, but all it takes is a handful of inordinate bets for the system to flag a dog, slash odds. How long can she hedge this?

The phone rings as soon as she hangs up. The line is awful. 'Hi? Hello? Hello? Are you there?'

'I'm here!' Corina shouts.

'Oh, good. Can you fit me in today?'

'Yes, yes.'

'Hello?'

'Hello, yes. Yes I can. When are you coming in?'

'In about fift–.'

'Fifteen minutes? That's fine. What's your nam–'

'Yes.'

'Yes. What's your name?'

'That's won–' the line goes dead.

In the salon, Mrs Terry is almost half way through *Behind Drawn Shades*. Meredith sits serenely under her brainsucker, hands folded in her lap, bandaged foot jutting like some monstrous cartoon golf club. The sun begins its slow slide. Corina wanders over to the desk and turns the pages of her appointment book. Her first client of the year, she reads, had been Mrs Minto, another former regular.

Between Mrs Minto's name and Meredith's, the pages are mostly blank.

The phone rings.

'Busy today,' Meredith says.

'It's probably that woman again. Good afternoon. Hair by Corina, Corina sp-'

It isn't the woman. 'Not answering your phone these days?'

A feeling like falling.

'I said you're not answering –'

'It's in the house.'

He eats as he talks. 'Some bitch picked up before. Haway, ask me how I've been.'

'How've you been, Beech?'

He chuckles. 'Keeping my pecker up.'

'Did I ring you last night?'

'I can't remember the last time you rung me, and it cuts me up. Did you get my message?'

'...Aye.'

'And?'

'And what?'

'Don't fuck around. You know *and what?*'

'OK, then. No.'

A pause on his end. Noises, voices in the background – a pub probably. 'You do understand what this is? This is gilded. This is from Martha, to me, to you. No bollocks.'

She looks up. Mrs Terry is a split-second too slow in going back to her book. Corina goes into the back and takes Beech on the phone there. 'You think you can ring me up after what those men did to Max?'

Beech swallows whatever he's chewing. 'Listen, they worked for Martha, not me. Selling on debts is pretty standard practice, it's how you stay liquid. You–'

'But I—'

'You owed me money – quite *a lot* of money – and I could've been a cunt about it, could've got nasty, but did I? I gave you all the time in the world, but I've got my own shite on the go n'all.' His voice so close in her ear she can almost smell him. The thin cigars, the empty junk food wrappers in the footwell of his Vauxhall.

'So why now? Why Heart of Chrome?' she said.

'Because we're mates.'

'We were never mates.'

'Haway, this is my way of saying sorry. This is a whatsit? An olive branch.'

'I've got to go.'

'I know you haven't forgotten what it's like,' he says. 'Waiting for them traps to open. The rush of it.'

She cups the receiver so hopefully neither Meredith nor Mrs Terry can earwig. 'That's why you did it, isn't it? Because I wouldn't sleep with you? You tried it on, I shot you down, so you let me get as deep as I did. I lost everything because of you.'

'Pet, you did that all by yourself. Think about tonight, eh? This dog's a real rocket.'

'I'm with a customer.'

'I'll ring again in a bit,' he says and hangs up.

In the salon, Meredith and Mrs Terry are watching her.

'Hold the fort,' she says weakly, and leaves before either woman can respond.

The newsagent is deserted.

'Gary?'

No answer.

'Are you in the back?'

259

He's probably nipped upstairs to check on Suzy. He does that. She works her way between the shelves to where the paracetamol ought to be, but there isn't any. In fact, looking around, there isn't much of anything. Behind the counter, a beaded curtain separates the shop from the storeroom and the steep flight of stairs leading up to Gary's flat. Is that a radio coming from up there? According to Gary, Suzy prefers Radio 4 in the daytime and Smooth FM at nights.

'Gary? It's Corina...'

Should she pop up? Or nip into the back for the tablets and leave the money in the till? She considers both options, but the catacomb gloom in the newsagents is fast draining what little life force she has left.

The *rush* of it. Of course she hadn't forgotten.

She calls Gary's name, counts to six, and leaves.

The bulletin is on again: ...*conspiracy to pervert the course of justice. Alice Powel, from the organisation Track Watch, who attended the sentencing today, said that it was the most appalling case of animal cruelty she'd ever encountered: 'Once again, these graceful, loving animals have been sacrificed to man's greed, discarded once their purpose had been served. So yes, with today's imprisonment of Vincent Barr, we may have won a small victory, but violence towards animals is systemic in our society, and until that changes, we, as a society, do not deserve to call ourselves civil.'*

That's all for the hour, we'll be back at three with another bulletin...

Corina lifts the brainsucker off Meredith and helps her back into the cutting chair. A wave of satisfaction washes over her when unwinding the curls. It's come out good, even if she does say so herself.

A woman with dark, shoulder-length red hair enters. Late twenties, maybe a few years older than Annabelle. In her corner, Mrs Terry gives her the once over.

'I'll be with you in a minute,' Corina says.

The woman looks up and smiles.

Meredith pays and limps to the door, which Corina holds open. She should say something; Meredith's been a regular since the start and, in many ways, a friend. But she can't think of a thing to say. Meredith lingers on the precinct, perhaps engaged with similar thoughts, but in the end neither women says anything as the door closes slowly between them.

The young woman already has a picture of herself ready on her phone. In it, she has the wavy, short-medium style popular nowadays. 'That's from two Christmases ago,' she says as she reclines in the sink, 'I was chubbier in the face then. I'm a mince pie fiend.' Her accent is southern. 'I'm Rachel.'

'Corina.' She lifts the showerhead. 'Brace yourself.' This time the entire salon floor buckles in corrosive misery.

'Turn that thing off!' Mrs Terry yells.

As soon as Corina touches the tap, the shrieking stops.

'Yowzers,' Rachel says.

The tiles around the sink are sunken and cracked.

'I had an appointment at my usual place in town,' Rachel says, as Corina starts washing her hair, 'but then the husband called to say his meeting was overrunning because the satellite link to America was down and blah blah blah – I tune out when he's in suit-mode – so I had to stay with our daughter all afternoon, meaning I wouldn't be able to get into town, get back, *and* get ready in time.'

For the final ever time, Corina deploys her profession's most profound question: 'Going anywhere nice?'

261

'The husband's taking me out for dinner and dancing. Got to keep the romance alive somehow, don't we?'

'I suppose,' Corina says.

'I searched for salons closer to home, but they were all booked solid. This was the nearest place with a slot, so I decided to risk it…' Her words hang in the air. Corina glances over at Mrs Terry, who, for all the world, appears to be reading.

'That came out wrong,' Rachel says. 'What I meant is you build a relationship with your hairdresser, don't you? They know what you like and it takes the anxiety out of things. You understand, don't you?'

'It's fine,' Corina says. 'So where're you coming from?'

'Not far, really. The other side of Moorside, just past Seamer.'

'Nice area,' Corina says tonelessly.

'We can't complain. We're relatively new, we were in Peterborough before, but my husband was asked to run the northern office.' Corina asks no further questions, but Rachel carries on talking. 'Moving's a wrench. There'll always be people you're sad to say goodbye to, but all-in-all it wasn't too bad. I'm freelance graphic design, so I can work anywhere, plus our daughter Nina hadn't started school at the time. This is her first year, actually. She's in Riverside Primary.'

'In Thornaby?'

'Do you know it?'

'My granddaughter just started there. Maybe you know her? Una-Lee?'

Rachel's grin is worthy of a toothpaste ad. 'She and Nina are as thick as thieves! The last day before Easter, they came barrelling out the gates with their coats over their heads yelling, *We're Lyre birds! We're Lyre birds!* And Una-Lee nearly took someone's wing mirror off! I don't know what they're teaching them in that place!'

The pipes continue to sigh even after Corina turns off the water. 'How's Una-Lee getting on in your opinion?'

'She's like Nina, really into art. Take it from a professional, your granddaughter's a wonderful artist.'

'She gets it from her mother.' Corina points to the framed sketches around the room. 'She did these.'

Towel dried, Rachel's hair sticks out at all angles. 'You must be very proud.'

Corina picks up her scissors. 'Keep your head straight, please.'

—

We were worried sick.

Four words passed down the generations like Crohn's disease and hammer toes. Four words now uttered by Max.

Annabelle hadn't said a word since calling from the train, a silence that stretched from the station, through the ride home, and was now unspooling in the living room. She perched on the chair with the bad angle to the TV. Corina stood in the doorway, uneasy. Max paced the rug.

Another chestnut: *What were you thinking?*

Annabelle, from beneath her thick, dark fringe, said, It was the last weekend of the Una Cruickshank exhibition.

It's *London*, love, Max said. You're fifteen. The look he gave Corina said, *Why aren't you saying anything?*

Because this was her mess. Knowing Max was on double shift, she'd rung Annabelle from the salon to say she'd just booked a late appointment and wouldn't be home until after ten, that there was a pizza in the freezer. Fine, Annabelle said, take your time. I'm just going to work on some charcoals. Her unconcerned tone encouraged Corina, smoothed the jagged edges of her lie. It made slinking off to Stockton Dogs that much easier, as if mother and daughter were complicit in the deception. This would, in fact, turn out to be perversely accurate: upon returning home some £200 down just before 11pm, she found Max in the kitchen. The fume extractors at work had packed up and everyone had been sent home. He'd just got back. Where was Annabelle? Where were *you*? But before Corina could commence lying, she was saved, in the finest hackneyed tradition, by the bell – Annabelle calling from the train.

Corina came fully into the room. You've been completely irresponsible, Annabelle.

But it was important! Neither of you would've taken me. I thought I'd be back before you got home. I didn't know the train would break down where there was no signal.

The point is you took advantage, Corina said. And where did you get the money?

I saved up. I wanted to get back bef–

We must be giving you too much! Well, from now on, you get nothing. And you're grounded too, until you–

Cor, Max said.

can be *trusted!*

Cor!

Max was looking at her strangely. Annabelle tugged at a thread on her sleeve, a black tear spilling down her cheek. When had she started wearing mascara?

Love, Max said, why didn't you just ask?

I did, she said. Remember?

Corina couldn't, and by the looks of him, neither could Max.

This isn't like you, he said.

The bag of rolled prints from the gallery was between her feet. So what *is* like me?

I'm sorry about not taking you, Max said. But we're both working. He glanced at Corina.

You both like it like that, Annabelle said.

What do you mean? Max said.

Dark bags under Annabelle's eyes. It means you don't have to see each other, or me.

They let her go upstairs. Corina didn't have enough fingernails left for them to dig into her palms.

Hopefully she won't do that again, she said.

I rang your phone, Max said quietly. Then I rang the salon. You weren't there.

Corina didn't reply for a second. Then: I was. I just had perm lotion on my hands.

—

'That reminds me,' Rachel says, 'congratulations on Annabelle getting into uni.'

'Huh?'

'She told me at the gates. It'll be a good way for her to meet people once they move down and, really, she's barely even a mature student. I'm originally from Hove myself. It's a lovely place.'

What sounds like TV static – the beginning of the universe – squalls in Corina's head and heart.

'Kyle's doing well, isn't he?' Rachel says.

'What?'

'I said Kyle's doing really well. Annabelle said he's been fixing a bridge? Or extending a bridge? Something to do with bridges, anyway. It all sounded very technical.'

'He's an engineer,' Corina hears herself say.

'So when's the big move?'

The back of Rachel's head blurs. Why is this woman here? This can't be a coincidence. No, this is…this is….

Rachel sees Corina in the mirror. 'Oh my, are you alright?'

'Aye…hay fever or something.'

'My husband's the same. I have antihistamines?'

She wants this woman gone. 'No, I'm fine.'

When she resumes work, Rachel says, 'I'm so jealous they're off to Barbados next month. We haven't been anywhere since Bali. Bali's gorgeous. The people are so warm and friendly, and the *food*. Have you ever been?'

'No.'

'Oh, promise me you will.'

Mrs Terry leans forward in her chair. 'Rachel, shall I tell you about my last holiday?'

Rachel has evidently forgotten all about the old woman in the corner. 'Err…of course. Where did you…?'

The mocha iris of Mrs Terry's good eye is flecked with saffron and gleams under the salon lights. 'Blackpool. Have you ever journeyed?'

'I can't say I have. Is it nice?'

'Back in the 70s, the sea was like unsieved gravy. I went with Colin.'

'Colin's your husband?'

'Was. He's dead now. Heart attack.'

'I'm sorry.'

Mrs Terry shrugs. 'He used to be on the forklifts – well, until he went in blotto and crashed one – and he only got a fortnight off a year, which he'd spend down the pub or on fishing trips with his mates. Only he never came back

266

with any fish. For years I was on at him to come away. Nowt flash, mind, I've never fancied going abroad. Just somewhere nice, but he never got round to booking. So one year I booked us up for Blackpool. Our hotel was called the Sea View, but all you could see out our window was the bins.'

Rachel's smile is strained. 'Still, you never spend much time in the room, do you?'

'True,' Mrs Terry says. 'In his case, he was mostly in the bar.'

'Well that can…be fun too,' Rachel replies.

Mrs Terry coughs into her hanky. 'What's your husband's name?'

'Eric.'

'Say that after you wake up to Eric relieving himself in the bedside drawer.'

Corina's head pounds worse than it has all day.

'Robert Goulet was singing at the Pavilion,' Mrs Terry says, 'but Colin wouldn't come. He didn't like music, so I went on my own. A beautiful man, Robert, with a beautiful voice. You won't hear his like again.' Something has softened in Mrs Terry's voice. Corina tries to imagine her as a younger woman.

'Only,' the old woman continues, 'I couldn't enjoy him. Something was *gnawing* me. So after the show, I took a turn along the pier, and that's when I saw him. Colin. He was on the tin-ducks with the barmaid from the Sea View.'

Rachel can't keep it up any longer; her smile collapses as Mrs Terry goes on. 'He was trying to win her a teddy, but the sackless drunk missed every single duck, and I was *furious*…but not at him or her. I was furious at myself. Furious I'd ever wanted to come away. Furious I'd thought things could be different, even for a few days.' She pauses, her remaining eye as dry as its glass counterpart. 'Then he put his hand on that tart's arse. Now, I meant to walk away, go back to the hotel and pack my bags, but I heard myself saying his full name: *Colin Lewis Maurice Terry*, the way he'd told me his dad used to do before he took the belt to him. His dad did that most days, and Colin still whimpered in his sleep. Nightmares and whatnot. He was aiming the rifle at the ducks when I said it, and he span round and the next thing I knew I was on my back and folk were screaming.'

Rachel is grey. 'What…happened?'

'What *happened*? Jesus, woman!' She pulls her eyeball out of her head and thrusts it towards Rachel. The eye is alive, somehow; the darkness inside Mrs Terry's vacant socket perfect. Corina burps BLT.

'*This is what happened!*'

Rachel mumbles into her own lap. 'I don't know what to say.'

'Then say nowt.' Mrs Terry works the eye back into her head. 'Just do us all a favour and say absolutely *nowt*.'

The rest of the cut passes in silence. When she's finished, Corina holds up the mirror.

'Its fine,' Rachel says weakly. 'Thank you.' She pays quickly and leaves.

'Awful woman,' Mrs Terrys says. 'People like her don't know what this world is.'

'Was that story true?'

Mrs Terry runs her tongue along her dentures. 'The man couldn't hit a single duck for that tart, but one shot at me…'

'I'm not sure I'd be able to forgive someone if they did that to me.'

'Oh, pet, it was easy enough. I even started making him his favourite dinners to show there were no hard feelings. He liked his fry-ups, lots of black pudding, corn beef hash, parmos with extra cheese and chips. I got him his favourite stout, too, as much as he wanted. I'd never let him before, on account of his angina. He actually died at the dinner table, face down in a tray of chow mein…' she touches her new perm. 'Poor sod.'

'I'd better sweep this hair,' Corina says.

'Lass, I know all about it.'

'About what?'

'When you're asking strangers about your own granddaughter, something's not right.'

Corina grips the counter. 'Haway then, what's the word? That I drove my family away? That I'm some compulsive gambler? Things got out of hand, that's all. I just want everything back how it was.'

Mrs Terry frowns. 'Come September, it'll be eighteen years since Colin died, and I still catch myself missing him. It galls me, that. I think, you dozy old mare, you should never have married him in the first place. But then I think it wasn't a mistake, it was a choice.' She taps her false eye gently. 'It weren't no accident, weren't no bad luck. A choice.' Then she picks up her book.

Shadows creep towards the brainsuckers. The TV aerials of Alexander Terrace are alien characters stencilled against the sunset. Annabelle's framed heads glimmer in their frames.

Corina gets the broom.

—

Two conversations with Annabelle.

Her first: the three of them at Redcar beach, channelling grey curds of seawater to sandcastle moats. Eighteen-month-old Anabelle squealing as the castles tumbled. Supertankers squat against the horizon. Gulls riding the convergence zone, dive-bombing their chip cones. Still twenty-some years from closure, the steelworks towards South Gare were shrouded in serpentine billows of smoke and steam. Corina curled into Max on the blanket, his sandy hand stoking her spine, watching as Annabelle collected shells into her plastic bucket. One moment of perfect, absolute peace which was over the instant Annabelle threatened to pick up a rusty beer can. But it was enough.

On the train home, Max slept with his temple against the glass. The sun was setting and Corina had Annabelle on her lap, the treasures found by her daughter that day laid out on the table before them. Annabelle picked up a small, fragile thing and said clearly: *S'ell.*

Corina's heart accelerated beyond the dusk train. That's right! It's a shell! And what colour is the shell?

Annabelle's eyes were bright.

'*Ink!*

Their last conversation, seventeen years later: Annabelle wracking through hangers in her wardrobe, tossing jumpers and skirts into a suitcase on the bed while Corina stood in the doorway.

Can't we talk about this? she said.

Annabelle took out a burgundy cardigan, held up a sleeve, put it back.

Belle, please talk to me. I didn't mean for any of this.

Then: Just say something.

Then: Love, please.

The prints from her trip to the Una Cruickshank exhibition years before still covered her walls: large blue-grey regions that seemed, on closer inspection, to be foggy riverbanks; the occasional figure glimpsed – or maybe not? – distantly in the mist. They unsettled her, but they were nothing compared to the poster of the witch-thing above the radiator. The awful way it held its hand over its face, leering from between skeletal fingers.

Corina said, I've tried talking to your dad, but he won't listen.

Annabelle laughed. I wouldn't either, if I was him.

It wasn't all me, we had our problems before this.

She threw a skirt venomously into the case. Those scumbags nearly kill him, and then he pays them off with his life savings. Don't put any of this on him.

OK, I'm sorry. I need help, I admit it.

Annabelle wheezed as she pressed the case down. How... *brave* of you. You...got caught, that's all. I'm fed up of... hearing it.

But it's the truth! I swear, I'm done with all that. I'll never gamble again. I'm – what's wrong?

Her daughter's eyes bulged. She rifled through her bedside table for an inhaler, from which she took several whistling drags. When she could speak again, Anabelle said, In...in the three months since I've been...at Kyle's. I haven't had a...single attack. But ten minutes back...here, and...

It's the damp, Corina said.

No, Anabelle said, shakily zipping the suitcase shut, it's not.

Love, try to understand.

But that's just it, Mam. I do. Understanding makes no difference.

You're angry.

Annabelle was taller than she was, and her brown eyes were Max's. Maybe when I was younger, she said, but not anymore. Look, I just came to get the last of my stuff – I didn't think you'd be here – but seeing as you are, I'll tell you this. My whole life I thought my existence took something away from yours, that I was just some unasked-for complication. So I tried to fight it, I tried to be the best daughter I could be…but no matter what I did, no matter how good I was, you wouldn't see it.

She held her right wrist in her left hand and said, Even when you were there, you weren't there.

I promise I'm here now. I love you.

Annabelle pushed past her and made her way downstairs.

There had to be something Corina could say to make her stay, some lie or half-truth or distortion to employ. For years, had she not been master of that? The abstract future sacrificed to the tangible present? Perhaps, but that had been before she was caught, before she faced the one consequence all addicts dread: the complete discreditation of their words right when they needed them most.

I'm starting meetings, she said.

In the hall, Annabelle paused. So?

So? So I'm going to meetings and going to get better.

Don't do this for me, she said.

It was raining out. Despite the dehumidifier, the damp was profound.

When can I see you? Corina said.

You can't.

Belle, you don't mean that.

Annabelle wrenched the swollen front door open with both hands. Outside, the estate was saturated in grey, vinyl-crackle drizzle.

Do you want to bet? Annabelle said.

Corina watched her daughter leave. The hand not holding the suitcase was pressed to her still-flat stomach. Una-Lee would be a month away from entering the world before Corina even learned her daughter was with child.

—

The rest of the afternoon passes quietly. As she approaches the book's final pages, Mrs Terry slows her pace, however, like all stories, The End eventually arrives. When it does, she closes the book and drops it into her bag without fanfare.

The phone rings again but Corina doesn't answer. When it rings off, she asks, 'So did the blind sculptor find the statue-woman?'

'Aye, but she was a wrong 'un. He got with the assistant, like I said.'

'Good for them.'

Mrs Terry looks out at the precinct. Petrol-blue night descending, a faint persimmon lustre across the rooftops. 'I'd better get on.'

Corina helps her into her mac. 'What are your plans for tonight?'

'Dinner and dancing,' Mrs Terry says. 'Got to keep the romance alive somehow. Take care then, lass. I've liked it in here all these times, and I appreciate you letting me sit. You know what I mean.'

'I've liked it too.'

'I don't know where this Rowan-Tree is shifting me. Like that mouthy cow said this morning, there's not going to be much scope for little old ladies on housing benefit, so I don't know if I'll see you again.'

'I'm sure you will,' Corina says, though she's far from sure.

Mrs Terry shuffles to the door. 'And whoever's on that phone, remember what I said. You've got a choice.' With that, the old woman steps outside and melts into the night.

Corina locks the door and breathes. Time to get to work.

She takes down the top row from the cardboard box wall in the back room (**OAKFIELD TINNED CARROTS, NON-TOXIC FIRELIGHTERS, McADAM'S CHICKEN IN WHITE SAUCE**) and starts packing any stock that can be sold back to the wholesaler. The phone rings but she ignores it.

Box by box, the back wall reveals itself.

The final box (**McADAM'S HEARTY IRISH-STYLE STEW**) hides the dent. It's barely there, really, the dent – just a little hole in the plaster, easily attributable, say, to a careless boot or hastily moved chair. The ghostly brown stains around it the result of mud or bike-oil.

—

She never told Gambler's Anonymous this.

Two men muscled the door at closing time, just as she was turning the lock, one wearing a baggy grey suit and eyebrows like two fat strikes of permanent marker, the other in cuffed denim, a long porpoise face grinning in anticipation, his right-front tooth blue-green and dead.

You know what this is, Suit said.

As Corina backed towards the brainsuckers, a bewildering peace washed over her. That it was all finally coming to a head was almost a relief.

My husband will be here any minute, she said.

Deadtooth spat on the floor. Good one.

You owe Martha, Suit said.

I don't know any Martha. What is this?

Suit spoke as if she were a slow child. You owed Derek Beecham. Derek owed Martha. He sold you. Now you owe Martha.

I've got some things lined up, she said. I'll have what you need then.

He got closer and Corina realised Suit's eyebrows were actually an inexpertly plucked monobrow.

Nah, man, he said. That's not how this works.

The back of her head touched a brainsucker. Over the approaching men's shoulders, across the dark green, the intermittent lights of Alexander Terrace twinkled. She saw herself reflected, cornered. No, this wasn't a relief at all. Now everyone was going to know. She ran into the backroom, but the door's latch was no match for Deadtooth's brawn.

Don't play silly buggers, Suit said.

Corina grabbed the phone and Deadtooth twisted her arm flush against her spine.

This lad gets a bit carried away sometimes, Suit said.

Air rushed into the salon. They hadn't locked the door behind them.

Cor?

Max. Why was he here? She'd lied before – Max wasn't coming. They hadn't spoken since their last fight a few days ago. It had been years since he'd stepped foot in the salon.

Deadtooth's hand reeked of kebab meat when he clamped it over her mouth. Suit went out to meet Max.

Corina only heard the next part: Max saying *and you are?* followed by a series of grunts and slaps. Deadtooth threw Corina into the table and went to help. They dragged in Max by his armpits, his chin pitter-pattering blood. Inexplicably, there was a rose petal stuck to his cheek. They hurled him at the wall head first. Deadtooth went back into the Salon. There were voices. He returned.

Bill, there's a fat cunt out there says he's called the police.

Bill turned the jet discs of his eyes onto Corina. Consider this your only warning, he said. Then they left.

The dent in the wall above Max's head ran with blood. He lay unconscious and contorted, made cubist like a figure in Annabelle's art books. She touched his cheek and flipped through a mental Rolodex of denials and half-truths, running damage-limitation scenarios, postulating blame.

Gary huffed into the doorway.

I saw them, he said. I saw. The police are on the way.

The whole scene felt unreal, had a sea-shell echo. Gary helped her to the sink where, catching a whiff of the mildew rising from the plughole, she vomited.

Stem roses lay trampled on the salon floor, along with a card written in his dainty hand: *I'm sorry. I love you. Max.* The petals were the same colour as his blood and made it difficult to separate the two…

…and as she looked at the crushed roses, she remembered this:

Max sniffed the rose on the table their first night at Stockton Dogs.

Sorry, Cor. I think it's plastic.

I prefer that. I feel bad watching them die.

They were celebrating the grand opening of *Hair by Corina*. Max's treat: a two-course meal (Corina had lamb, Max half a roast chicken and chips) with a complimentary bottle of Asti Spumante. But why the dogs? Plain curiosity, really. Those spotlights had been carving the night her entire life, and yet she'd never once been.

A bookie came to take their bets.

Go on, Max said. Who do you fancy?

She opened her programme to the next race. It was baffling, but a name leapt out.

That one, she said. Klaus.

Max frowned at his own programme. Cor, it's 50/1.

She gave the bookie a pound. Klaus to win, please.

Max bet on the second favourite and the bookie went away.

Why Klaus? he asked.

She sipped her wine. Something told her that whatever was at work would unravel the moment she tried putting the significance of the dog's name into words.

Max ate some chicken skin. Why are you smiling?

—

Product sorted and boxed, Corina fills a bucket with warm soapy water (pipes rattling) and goes to work on the brainsuckers and chrome chairs. When they're clean, she starts on the counters.

The actress' polaroid is still by the phone. The woman is singing into a beer bottle as if it's a microphone, the loose sleeves of her jumper rolled to the elbows. The jumper is test-card pattern awful. She looks at it a moment longer before dropping it into the bin bag.

—

Like most single-digit children, Corina was largely indifferent to how she was dressed. At that unselfconscious age, the concept of fashion simply didn't register except as an external evil to be endured. What child has not been lectured against grass-staining their 'good' trousers? Not felt the crushing disappointment of realising that there, under the tree, Santa's left a *cardigan*? However, all that changed for Corina come comprehensive school; come crops tops and lipstick and pierced ears and boys. Boys who only liked mature girls, not ones in jumpers knitted by their *mams*. Imagine a boy she liked *seeing her in one*? She'd, like, literally *die*.

At first, she simply stopped wearing them. Pushed them to the back of the wardrobe, and was vague when her mother asked why she no longer wore them. But her mam wouldn't take the hint, and soon Corina would walk into her room to find the pullovers laid out on her bed, arms thrown wide as if expecting a deep embrace. It was too much.

They had to go, but how?

Plan A was brutal. She stuffed the pink zig-zag number – knitted for her last Christmas – into a bin in town and, when Mam enquired as to its whereabouts, she told her she'd left it on the bus. Her mother was disappointed, but beyond a brief chastisement, nothing further was said. There was now one less horror in the wardrobe. Success! But while the tactic was effective, the guilt she felt over the callous disposal of the sweater eclipsed her joy at being rid of it. She took the next one to a charity shop in the city centre, thinking at least that way someone might get some further wear out of it. She told Mam someone had stolen it from the swimming baths; the one after that from the back of her seat at the Ritzy. Her mother rang these places – *Hello? Yes, has anyone handed in a puce sweater with lime green triangles down the arms?* – but while Corina's guilt remained palpable, it was at least now at manageable levels. Until a new problem occurred. Several jumpers were now in circulation around the city. What if, say on one of her Saturday shopping trips, Mam came across one? Draped over a Salvation Army mannequin, even?

It consumed her. She existed crouched in a state of readiness, prepared at a moment's notice to reel off excuses from that mental Rolodex of denials and half-truths she would one day put to a very different use.

But then she opened her wardrobe and the jumpers were gone.

I've taken them down the rec. centre, Mam said. You're too old for them. I didn't think you'd mind.

A strange feeling dwelling in the Venn intersection of Regret and Shame crept over Corina. For the first time, the true effort her mother had put into those jumpers hit home; all those knitted hours, all that purled love, thinking – *hoping* – that her only daughter might love them too. It was almost enough for her to ask her mother to knit her another, but to have done so would have been to crack the seal on a swell of emotion she wasn't sure she could even articulate.

Not that her mother put her needles down. Far from it. If anything, her output increased. There was always Irene's boy Ricky who could do with some new mitts, or an Aran cardigan for Old Tommy down the Labour Club, who lived in a one-bed and couldn't afford to run his heating in winter. Then there were the never-ending rounds of

Tenants' Association fundraisers requiring a steady stream of scarves and booties and hats and jumpers and knitted animals for prizes. Not to mention Jim's new-found appreciation. Once acid music sunk its fangs into him, the only clothes he'd be caught dead in were luridly baggy.

But something was wrong. Gradually, Corina noticed what was issuing from the ends of her mother's needles wasn't quite right. One arm of a jumper a little too long. Slightly fin-shaped mittens. In the tried and true tradition of one not wishing to engage with the awfulness festering beneath the surface of things, Corina put this down to her mother's prolific output. She was cutting corners, winging it, dropping stitches – that was a knitting thing, right? – because she feared letting down the community she was now so deeply involved in.

Mam, she said, they're taking advantage of you. Dad's words coming out of her mouth.

So she continued turning a blind eye to the scarves ballooning like impacted intestines, the drooping, eight-fingered bogeyman gloves, the Cyclops balaclavas. Baby booties which sagged with woollen tumours. The socks fit only for a creature from one of Jim's monster films, something of cloven hoof.

It's these bloody patterns, her mam said. The people at *Knitting World* need shooting.

Thus began The Era of the Terrible Thing: the amorphous waves of shapeless wool spilling across the carpet, until Corina, able to kid herself no longer, finally picked up the phone and called a doctor…

—

Sirens interrupt her thoughts. Corina goes to the window just as the ambulance passes. The police officer standing beside Gary's newsagent waves the vehicle in, its lights now flashing silently.

Two medics unload a stretcher and guide it swiftly through the narrow doorway, past the officer who steps aside. The officer is a young woman with a brunette chop under her cap. A community support officer, actually, not police proper. Corina's seen her around. Beside her, Yvette stands stunned.

'What's this?' Corina asks.

'I just went in for some beans,' Yvette said, 'but the shop was empty. I got one of my feelings, so I went round the counter and he was lying there, on the floor.'

'On the floor?'

The support officer looks Corina up and down. 'A man's been found collapsed on the premises.'

'What do you mean *collapsed*?'

'That's all we know for now. Please move back.'

'But I know him.'

There's sympathy in her voice. 'I understand, but you have to move back.'

'I just went in for some beans,' Yvette says.

A police car pulls up and two regular PCs get out. The driver is a tall woman with a simple, mousy ponytail. The other is a young man who looks barely out of his teens.

'He's in there,' the support officer says, letting them inside.

Yvette moans.

Corina cranes her head round the door. The stretcher is wedged between the depleted shelves, below the blank gazes of the women on the covers of the pornographic magazines. The medic's heads bob up and down behind the counter as the older PC prompts the younger to ask if there are abrasions, contusions, or suspicious marks of any kind on the body.

The body.

The support officer gently but expertly pulls Corina away.

'I knew it,' Yvette cries, 'I *told* him! And for what, eh? For what?'

Moths flit in the ambulance's headlights. Corina lights a cigarette. 'I nearly went behind myself today for paracetamols…what if he was already there? What if I could've helped?'

A few minutes later Gary is rolled out under a sheet. They put him in the ambulance and drive away, sirens dead, lights dead.

The older PC has faint acne scarring at her temples. Her radio hisses with words Corina identifies as English, yet are still somehow incomprehensible. 'Did you know the owner?' the PC says.

'He's dead?' Yvette asks.

'I'm afraid so. It was most likely a heart attack.'

Yvette turns away. The PC ignores her. 'Our system tells us Mr Kinnear lived in the flat above, is that right?'

'Aye,' says Corina.

'Does he have any next of kin? Nothing's coming up.'

'He never said. It was just him and his wife, but she died years ago.'

'What about the keys?'

'On a hook behind the beaded curtain. Should be, anyway.'

The PC thanks her and turns back to the shop.

'Wait,' Corina says. 'Suzy. He's got a budgie.'

The PC hooks a finger.

Inside, the rookie is bagging up the till. Corina follows the older PC behind the counter (not looking at the floor there), through the beaded curtain and up to the flat. Suzy isn't hard to find – they just follow the radio. The powder-blue puff ball cocks her tiny head as they approach her cage. Corina signs a chit to say she's taken the bird and then they leave, but not before Corina sees how Gary lived: the stacked cases of Irish-Style Stew in every corner, the water stains on the ceiling reminiscent of MRI-scanned brains. On one wall there is a framed picture of a young woman holding aloft a giant marrow. It, like everything else, is veiled in dust.

But more than anything, it's the smell.

Mildew.

—

She didn't need to find the divorce petition on the kitchen table to know Max was gone – the stench of mildew in the hall told her everything she needed. Nevertheless, she went from room to room saying his name, testing the tensile strength of her new reality.

That first night she lay awake in Annabelle's bed. An orange bar of streetlight from the imperfectly drawn curtains cut across the poster of the witch-thing above the radiator. Staring down at her through its fingers. Corina stared back.

You win, bitch, she said.

—

Corina puts Suzy on the salon floor, below the clock-cat's psychotic eyes. The bird peeps mindlessly and hops from perch to perch. The long nights the two of them must have spent together: Smooth FM on in the background while Gary ate tinned food and Suzy pecked her seed. Yvette had offered to take the bird, but half-heartedly. It had been difficult to extricate herself from Yvette's company after the PCs locked up Gary's shop and left. She was obviously distressed, but Corina had plans for the rest of the evening which were, frankly, more pressing.

Nearly 7:30pm – still more than an hour to go. She dumps her handbag out onto the backroom table, ignoring the Rowan-Tree letter as if falls to the floor. The month's takings are in the safe, plastic-wrapped hundred stacks which she counts into the bottom of her handbag. The odds are the same when she calls the bookies. If she catches the 551 from Stanhope Street, she can be there in twenty minutes.

The salon door opens. She has forgotten to lock it.

Thick, snotty breathing. She picks up the broom, peers round the door…

But it's only Alan. He hasn't seen her yet. Sitting awkwardly in the waiting area in a blue cagoule, the right arm of which hangs loosely by his side. He seems to be reciting something quietly under his breath, and for some reason Corina is reminded of the prayers said by Mrs Terry's neighbour Nathan, during the Day of the Dark. Silently, she retreats into the backroom and flushes the toilet. Then she counts to ten, musters what she hopes is a friendly smile, and walks briskly into the salon.

'Alan! I didn't hear you come in! I'm sorry hinny, but I'm closing up now.'

Despite her generous heads-up, Alan is apparently

bewildered by her appearance. 'Oh, right. That's, ah, fine.' His right arm bulges at the elbow when he stands. Something reasonably large has been shoved down the arm of his coat. 'I heard it was your last day?'

'Yep,' Corina says.

His grey jowls sag. 'In that case, I'd like to thank you for your, ah, stellar, ah, follicle management. Ha ha. Joke. But really, I've always enjoyed, ah, talking to you. Good luck in the…' then, touching his protruding joint: '…I was. Hmm, no. I was recently, ah…*puddings*…' a pained expression ripples across his face. 'It doesn't matter. Well, goodbye.'

She watches him gingerly take the six or seven paces to the door, noting how he avoids stepping on the tile-joins. Glancing at the cat-clock, she says, 'Alan, come back.'

'I don't want to put you out.'

'Don't be daft. Come on, sit down. I'll get my things.'

By the time Corina's located her scissors and shears in a box that once contained **HERE BOY! CHICKEN 'N' LIVER DOG FOOD**, Alan has hung up his coat. Whatever is in the arm stays wedged in the sleeve. Something is different about him. For starters, he's wearing a collared shirt, though it's creased and some of the buttons are in the wrong holes. She's afforded a peek of his swarthy belly and catches a whiff of the smell enveloping him. Like spoiled milk, she thinks.

'You're a bit early, aren't you?' she says, fastening the nylon cape around his neck. 'You were only in last month.'

He fumbles the picture out of his pocket. 'Yes, ah, but I thought I'd try something new.' It's been cut from a glossy magazine, some blandly-handsome actor or other.

Alan is watching her surreptitiously in the mirror. 'This is do-able,' she says.

His eyes are tiny new-born panda eyes when he removes his glasses. Corina places a number-one guard on the shears, pushes away her misgivings, and begins shaving. He flinches when the blades touch him.

'What made you decide on the change?' she asks.

'I've never had a trendy, ah, hairstyle before.'

'Hot date?'

He shifts uneasily in his chair.

'Anyway, so how have you been keeping?' she says.

'Busy, ah.'

'Yeah, me too. Busy busy.' Fine hair and flakes collect on the backs of her hands.

Alan says, 'May I ask why you've decided to close?'

'It's pretty simple. I'm not making any money.'

'So what'll you do?'

She moves the shears in fluid strokes up his head. 'Take some time out…you know, think about my next step. All that stuff.'

'You live on the estate, don't you?'

'Yep.'

'Do you think you'll come back after it's rebuilt?'

Heart of Chrome would let her pay Max what she owed him, both for the gambling debts, and for his half of the house she had been putting off selling back to Rowan-Tree. The letter they had sent her said the bastards wouldn't give her what it was worth, but the extra money from the race might be enough to make up for it.

'I fucking hope not,' she said.

Alan starts at that.

'Excuse my French,' Corina says. 'It's been a long day… Gary's dead.' Alan's face becomes grave as she recounts the day's events.

'I just saw him today,' he says.

For a while the only sounds are the razor and the radio.

'I'd leave if I were you,' he says, and does Corina detect a trace of self-pity in his voice? 'Really, what's there to stay around for?'

'Well, if we're being serious now, there's my daughter and granddaughter.'

'And your brother,' Alan says. 'I haven't seen him around for a while.'

She snaps off the razor. 'Are you seriously telling me that you haven't heard the rumours?'

His shoulders tense. 'That's not what I meant.'

'So you *have* heard?'

He manages a brittle second of eye contact in the mirror. 'But I don't believe them.'

'Why not?'

'Because I know what people can be like. I'm sorry, we don't have to talk anymore.'

But after today, who will she have to talk to? 'He's been missing three months now.'

'Do you have any idea where…?'

She shakes her head.

'Sorry,' he says.

'That's what really gets me, actually. Like, we'd been so *close*. Growing up, we always had each other's back. But then we fell out.'

'How?'

'I made some promises, but then I had a family and things changed. He didn't forgive me, but I was stubborn too. I let it fester. We never really got right after that…I stopped knowing what was going on in his head.'

She puts down the razor, picks up the comb.

287

'Like, I had to clear out his flat before they knocked it down. I found all this weird stuff, all these maps and sewer plans and a picture on the wall of this awful witch-thing. This monster. I'd seen it before, the picture. It was by Una Cruickshank, my daughter's favourite artist.'

Alan looks troubled. 'I…read about her once, Una.'

'She was supposed to have lived round here. My granddaughter is named after her. Anyway, I stood in Jim's living room and there was all this *stuff*, and I felt sick. I knew something awful had happened.'

'You don't know that.'

'No, listen. After he vanished, I got desperate. I went round an old friend's to see if he knew how to get hold of these two people, Adam and JJ. Jim'd been friends with them – more than friends – but my friend he –'

'Who's your friend?'

'Everyone calls him Alive, but his real name's Clive.'

'Clive Alive?'

She smiles. 'He's still on the blocks. Well, he's not my friend anymore. Or he was. I don't know. We haven't seen each other in a long time…' Alan is looking at her strangely in the mirror. 'But Alive didn't have a number for either of them, and he was like, oh, your mate Dave was round not long ago. I was like, Dave who? I don't know any Daves. He was like, you know, *Dave*? Your mate who had the car accident? Apparently, I'd given Dave Alive's number so he could buy some drugs…'

'And that was Jim?'

'Who else? It's all connected – those maps and posters, this "Dave" business – something awful's gone on, I know it, but I'm never going to know what.' She shakes off her comb. 'I'm sorry, Alan. I don't mean to vent.'

'You can always vent at me,' he says.

Suzy cheeps and flutters in the cage.

She says, 'He used to have this tape.'

'A VHS?'

'He had loads of them, horror films and that. But no, this was a cassette. Acid music, you know? *Doosh doosh doosh.*'

'I know. I believe, ah, it originated in Chicago in the mid-1980s, gradually mutating on its way over here.'

'You're into it?'

'Oh, no. I read about it. I'm a reader.'

They usually are, she thinks.

'I was into hip hop,' she says. 'Old school stuff. Not anymore, though. I always hated acid, but I'd recognise that tape anywhere – he listened to it over and over. So when I saw it in his house, I packed it up with everything else and took it home, but for weeks I couldn't face it. Do you understand?'

'I think so,' he said.

'What finally gave me the guts was that Jim had had this belief in the music, how it connected people. So I thought – ah, it's daft – but I thought maybe if I really listened, maybe I could connect with him. Wherever he was.'

'That's not daft,' he says. 'I do the same. My mam loved Kate Bush.'

'So anyway, I put it on.'

'And?'

'And,' she sighs, 'it was still just noise.'

The news bulletin comes on, but Corina's thoughts are elsewhere. They hear Vincent's name before she thinks to turn it off.

'Sorry,' she says.

'It's OK. I heard it this morning.'

'How are you holding up?'

Alan speaks slowly, feeling his way through his response. 'The police thought I was in on it too, because I wasn't shocked when they told me. But then shock, surely, comes from believing you know something to be true, only to have that reality whipped out from under you. My reality is that I've never known him. I couldn't answer a single *effing* one of their questions. About anything, then or now.'

Several strands of Alan's hair come out by the root with every stroke of the comb. He has to be around her own age, Corina guesses, but looks older.

The cat says 7:50pm.

'What do you mean *then or now*?' she asks.

He shifts in the seat. 'Well, like Jim for instance. What people say Dad did to him.'

'That was an accident. Jim was on drugs.'

'Maybe,' Alan says, 'but you didn't think that at the time, did you? You came round the house, remember? I was in the kitchen, but I heard you arguing. What did he say?'

She shaves the hair growing out of his neck. 'He wanted me to keep my voice down in case I woke your mam up, but I was ready to kill him. I tried to hit him with an ashtray. He pinned my arms and I thought he's going to crush me, but he just held me there. He said he knew what it was like to have something awful happen and the world keep turning. He'd felt the same when his dad died.'

'In the blast furnace.'

'Aye. He said he remembered seeing him go off to work, like he'd done a million times, and then he was dead and there was nowt left of him to even bury. He was like, It just

290

doesn't make sense. Same as when his brother got in a plane and was never seen again. He said he kept thinking about it, your dad, thinking how it couldn't be that simple. Like there *had* to be more to it. Only, even after all those years, he was still none the wiser. So he said to me, you've got two choices – you either let the loose ends drive you mad, or you tie them together in whatever way lets you keep going.'

'I didn't know that,' Alan said.

Fine, translucent hairs drift to the floor around her feet. 'Then he was like, So if blaming me lets you do that, then blame me. Only after that, I couldn't.'

'But what was he doing at a rave in the first place?'

'You've never asked him?'

Alan says nothing.

'Why not take your own advice?' she says. 'Get away from here?'

'Dad says I've got to protect the house from Rowan-Tree while he's away. Whatever they offer, I'm to say no.'

She doesn't mention the letter she has received. The poor soul has enough problems. Instead, she says, 'You know, I had dreams for this place. It was going to be the first of a chain across the whole country. And not on poxy estates, neither. I'm talking city centres. Main drags.'

'I'd never be able to do that,' he says. 'I don't have a business brain.'

'It's a skill,' she says, 'like any other. You work at it. But anyway, it never happened…Then, when me and Jim fell out, I said some things I shouldn't have. I said the only reason I'd ever stayed around here was because he needed looking after. It was a shitty thing to say and it wasn't even true. Really, I was just afraid. I was young and this was the only place I knew.'

With tiny clippers, she defines the hairline around his large ears.

'Truth was, I envied him,' she says. 'I envied how he disappeared for days on end to London or God knows where, going to parties, meeting different people.'

Finally, she holds up the mirror and reveals to Alan the back of his own head. His hair is too thin and his face shape is all wrong. The style heaps another five years on him.

'I love it,' Alan says.

It's just gone eight. She'll need a taxi if she's going to make the bookies now. She nips into the back to grab her bag and wash her hands, yelling, 'Thanks for listening to me prattle on.' Alan makes no response, either because he hasn't heard her over the deafening plumbing, or because when she comes back she finds him occupied by the coat stand, tugging furiously at the blockage inside the arm of his cagoule.

'What are you doing Alan?'

The coat rips, and a thick white goo splatters onto the floor. Even from across the room, the smell is abominable. Suzy throws herself against the bars of her cage.

Corina thinks, You hear about this kind of thing, don't you? The quiet soul who kept himself to himself. That's what the neighbours always say on the news, once the sex-dungeon has been discovered. The bone-jumbles under the floorboards. The skin-suits.

She says, 'Alan, you're giving me the willies.'

He looks mortified as he yanks the cagoule off the hook. His hands are covered in a cottage cheese-like substance. He freezes, as if under arrest, and then flees the salon with the coat bundled into his chest, leaving a trail of the stuff behind him. There is some kind of kerfuffle on the precinct and, a moment later, a young woman enters. Corina's heart stops.

'That nutcase nearly went straight into me,' Annabelle says, inspecting her clothes for splatter. 'Who *was* that?'

Has there been a day these past five years when Corina hasn't imagined this moment? Any possible permutation of word or deed as yet undreamt? Then why can she think of nothing to say? Why is she frozen to the spot, her heart about to detonate?

'Mam, are you alright?' Annabelle asks.

Her daughter. Her daughter *here*, standing in front of her. She's less gangly than she used to be, and her hips have filled out. Eyes luminous like the spots on the wings of the rarest butterflies. Corina pinches the skin on the back of her hand.

'You pierced your lip,' is all she can think to say.

Annabelle's leather jacket creaks when she brushes her fringe from her eyes. 'A few years ago, yeah. What's the bird called?'

'Suzy.'

Her daughter watches the bird hop around the cage. 'I came in before but this one-eyed woman bit my head off.'

'Mrs Terry,' Corina says. 'She does that.'

They both fall silent for a while. Annabelle crosses her arms. 'So what is it then?'

'What's what?'

'The voicemail you left me. The thing you said you had to tell me in person. I figured it had to be important, considering you haven't rang me in five years.'

Then Corina knew who she had called last night. Not Beech, but Annabelle. Everything falls into place a second before it does for her daughter.

Annabelle shakes her head. 'I knew it. I *knew* you sounded drunk.'

'But I do want to talk,' Corina says. 'All this time, that's all I've wanted. I'm just stubborn and stupid. I swear I've tried.'

Silence again. Corina thinks of the eraser-less pencil Max once held out to her. Failure was permanent. 'How's Una-Lee?'

'She's good. She's started school now. Look, what do you want?'

'To say sorry. I want things to go back to how they were.'

'How they were was horrible, Mam.'

'Which is all my fault. I just…I don't want us to still be like this when you move.'

Annabelle blinks slowly. 'How do you know about that? Actually, never mind. Nothing stays quiet round here, does it?'

'When were you going to tell me? *Were* you going to tell me?'

Annabelle shrugs.

'When are you going?'

'June, probably. His job starts in August. He's basically in charge of all the projects on the South Coast. Like, he's only thirty-one. People fifteen years older than him struggle to get to that level.' Corina can hear the pride in Anabelle's voice. 'And I've got a place at Brighton Uni to do fine art, part time.'

'You were always a wonderful artist.' Beside her, on the wall, is one of the framed heads. 'Do you remember these?'

'I can't believe you still have them up.'

'Of course I do. So your dad knows, does he?'

'He's happy for us.'

'How is he?'

'Mam, things are good for me. I'm looking forward to the future. This is the opposite of that. Are you still going to meetings?'

'I am, yes.'

'You're lying. Fuck this, I'm leaving.'

'Annabelle, please.'

'Just tell me one thing.'

'Anything, love. Anything.'

'When's the race?'

'What?'

'You've been sneaking looks at the clock since I came in. You did it all the time when I was growing up, only then I didn't know why.'

The eyes of the heads drawn by her daughter are all on her. She takes a breath.

'It's in twenty minutes,' Corina says. 'If I ring a taxi I can just make it. I'm betting the takings. Usually, I bank them every few days, but this last month I kept putting it off.'

'Why?'

'I don't want your sympathy, but recently I haven't been doing well. I got a letter from the housing association saying – never mind. The point is, all this stuff – all these memories – have been going round and round in my head, and I can't stop them. I don't know if I *want* to stop them. Then this morning there's this dog, out of the blue, and I think, *coincidence*, really?'

'You're still the same, aren't you?' Annabelle says.

Silence again. Even Suzy keeps quiet.

'I'd better get off,' Annabelle says.

'When was the last time you had your hair done?'

She glances at herself in the mirror, 'I don't know. A while.'

'Come on, I'll do it.'

'Mam, I have to get back.'

'Please.'

Her daughter doesn't move. Corina feels the familiar constriction in her chest, just as she used to in those terminal seconds before a race, straddling two competing futures.

Annabelle frowns. 'But what about your dog?'

'I want you to be my last customer.'

Still Annabelle doesn't move. For a moment which stretches to the horizon, Corina thinks her daughter is going to leave, but then Annabelle takes off her jacket and sits at the sink. She looks up at Corina warily, as if expecting to be the butt of a prank. 'This will be the first time I've actually had my hair cut in here. You always did me at home.'

Corina rummages in a box for shampoo and conditioner. 'And afterwards you'd jump on your dad and there'd be hair everywhere.'

Annabelle closes her eyes. 'I don't remember that.'

'I do. So what'll it be?'

'Whatever you think.'

It's almost twenty to nine. At that very moment, Heart of Chrome is tensed in her trap, ready to be shot into the universe.

Corina picks up the showerhead. 'The pipes are going mental today.'

Dreamily, Annabelle nods.

But when she turns on the tap, nothing happens. Nothing but clean, warm water. So she washes her daughter's hair.

UXO

Douglas Ward of Campbell Road

N.B. – The following is comprised of transcribed conversations conducted with several residents – or former residents – of the Burn Estate, in connection with the infamous 1993 New Year's Eve explosion. Interspersing these testimonies are the journals of one Douglas Ward, the man who, on that very same night, came into my home armed with a kitchen knife, and spilled my mother's ashes all over the rug.

This document exists because I believed Douglas to be the thread which would guide me not out of, but *into* the labyrinth of my family's history, a history superimposed like acetate over the world I see each day outside my window. I have sensed this labyrinth my whole life, but have always lacked the ~~opportunity~~ courage to enter, because I know that deep in the dark of it, someone – *something* – awaits me.

I should acknowledge that the following does not encompass the entirety of my investigations. Rather, I have selected and arranged portions in order to attempt a narrative. My reasons for this, I hope, will become self-evident; yet this is not to say that I have in any way manipulated or supressed anything within the portions themselves. In my chest does not beat the grey heart of the censor. On the contrary, I have remained verbatim throughout, even when it has hurt to do so.

Alan Barr

Conversation with Ian Pavel. Billingham
Social Club. 17th April 2016 [1]

---

[1] At a loss as to where to begin this document, I forced myself down to the Labour Club to ask the older patrons whether they remembered a Doug or Douglas – I didn't know his surname at this point – a gangling, stooped young man with dirty-blonde hair who would have last been seen in these environs in the early 1990s. Unsurprisingly, my enquiries were mostly unsuccessful, although I did drink two blackcurrant and sodas – a cardinal error for someone with a bladder the size of mine.

I visited the urinal and positioned myself an acceptable distance from the only other user, an elderly gent relieving himself in erratic spatters. During a lull in micturition, he turned to me and growled (paraphrasing): "I know who that Doug knocked about with. Little fat fella. Ian summat. Last I heard he was in Billingham. I've been wanting to get my hands on that cunt for twenty-five year."

So I decided to try and find this Ian, but how? In the American procedural shows I watch, supermodel-attractive detectives momentarily click-clack computers to bring up detailed files, addresses, mugshots etc., so as to speed the story onto the next exciting scene. In reality, however, the process was exceedingly protracted as I had little more to go on than the mumbled hearsay of a man betraying symptoms of Parkinson's, sprinkling the toes of his slip-ons with his own greenish urine.

To find Ian, then, I decided to bend the truth. I made up some notices which read:

Local Historian wishes to speak to former residents
of the Burn Estate, near High Leven.
Especially interested in anything pertaining to the
1993 New Year's Eve Explosion.
Remuneration for genuine information.

followed by my phone number and email. I put them up in Billingham library, the local pubs and W.M.C.s, and waited, all the while chastising myself for using the words 'pertaining' and 'remuneration'.

I began receiving a dribble of calls (no emails). I introduced

Is it on? It's like being down the cop shop, with the tape recorder and that.

It's, ah, it's an mp3, Ian. There's no actual tape in it.

Call me Pav. Everyone does.

OK…Pav. Well, as I said on the phone, I'd like to talk about the New Year's Eve explosion of 1993. You said you knew him, the man who was killed?

Doug, aye.

Doug, yes. You were friends?

----

myself as Alan Healy – not my real name, of course – and asked the caller who was speaking. If it wasn't an Ian, I'd thank them for their interest and regretfully inform them that my project was now complete. If I'm honest, I knew the chances of such a plan working were astronomically slim, but I sleep easier with at least the illusion of proactivity between myself and the knowledge that I am orchestrator of my own inertia. So you can imagine my surprise when, after more than three months, he called. His surname was Pavel. He sounded cagey.

Ian: 'What kind of remuneration are we talking?'

Me: 'Well, Ian, that depends on what you know. After checking the archives, it seems that someone died when the bomb went off. Is that correct?'

'Aye. Doug. I knew him.'

'Would you be willing to tell me about him?'

Pause. 'Depends. I'm a busy man. I'd like to sort payment first…'

He point-blank refused to return to the estate, so we agreed to meet in the Billingham Social a week later; another bus ride 10 miles up the dual carriageway, across the strip of scuffed pewter that is the River Tees.

Nah. I used to do a bit of driving for Tubby down the scrap yard, and he'd be lurking about, hawking bits and bobs for drink. I felt bad for the lad, so I looked out for him. What are you going to do with this tape?

Nothing. It's just for me, so I don't forget. Sometimes I'm forgetful.

You're getting old. We all are. Are you writing a book or something?

I have an interest in local history. You may be aware that the estate's being knocked down as we speak.

I'd heard something. You live there, like?

No. As I said, I'm just a local history buff. Social housing history, to be precise. But I'll be sad to see the estate go. Once a community is broken up, the culture and stories – the oral histories – it's all lost. I'm just doing my bit to preserve it.

Nobody in their right mind would want to read a book about that shite.

Well, like I said, it's just for me.

I could do with another pint of bitter.

[Pause while it dawns on me] *Oh, right. Of course.*

[Inaudible. Time passes. Background pub chatter. I return].

You're on the lemonade?

I don't drink, I've never, ah, liked the taste. So, Ian, what can you tell me about Doug?

Well, he did. Drink, I mean. He was what you'd call a *wreckhead*. The kind of bloke you forget exists 'til you see the fucker picking up ciggie-ends outside the shop. He drank, and when he wasn't drinking, he was getting money for drink. He did this through not entirely legal means. That's how he got into trouble. I mean, if you think about it, that's how it all kicked off.

How all what kicked off?

The bomb. Bear with me. There was this jumper, right? This awful brown and yellow stripy jumper. I can see it now. Christ.

Sorry Ian, I think you've lost me.

Robbing from a proper shop's always going to be a gamble, only people from round the estate were too sackless to realise. Like, they'd go into Levis or John Lewis and start shoving stuff up their coats, in full view of everyone. That's how they got done. That's how Doug used to get done.

We're talking about, what? Stealing? Shoplifting?

Aye. So I was like, to Doug, if you *are* going to keep robbing, why don't you do it the other way round? Nick the cardboard tag, yeah? You know, the little cardboard tag-thing on the string? You could steal as many of those as you wanted because they're small, they don't have the beepy thing.

So the tags were stolen from the shops, but the clothes...?

Charity shops. You'd be surprised what labels turned up. And the best bit was them places didn't have CCTV, or security neither. Half the time there's only an old biddy behind the till. Easy to pinch from, you know?

Then what you do, say you've robbed some old Levi jeans, you match them up with a proper Levi tag and *bang* – people think they're new. Even flogging them at half price **[snaps fingers]** you're getting money for *nowt*.

And this was your idea? You were both doing this, you and Doug?

Not likely. I just suggested it to him one day, off hand, like. I felt sorry for him because he was always getting collared. I didn't think he'd actually do it.

So you didn't personally steal anything?

You'd never catch me doing owt that greasy. *Literally* the only time I ever helped him was that one night down the Labour Club. He had too much gear. He needed to get it all tagged up. He was practically begging me, because everything he did was sloppy-as. It was the drink.

And you split the money?

I didn't need the money, son. Like I said, I did it for him. [**Pause**]. I should've had my fucking head read.

How so?

The golden rule – I told him – the golden rule was you *never* tagged something that wasn't brand name. That jumper, I was like, sling it, it looks homemade. But did he listen? Did he fuck. And of course, it ended up in my half of the gear, didn't it?

When was this exactly?

When? A couple of days before New Year, 1993. It was… ah, what's her name? Morris Clarke's wife [**makes thumb-and-index-finger spectacles**], Mrs Magoo, sitting with the *acting society*.

Acting society?

Something to do with the weirdos from Peel House, over on the blocks. They put plays on and whatnot. Prancing about in the rec. hall, playing make believe. Thought their shit didn't stink. Fucking bollocks.

You're not a fan of the arts?

Did I say that? You think I'm thick?

No, I didn't...I mean, I believe where you come from shapes you as an artist, not, ah, precludes you from becoming one. Take Una Cruickshank [2] *for example.*

Never heard of her.[3] Look, I know what real art is, right?

---

[2] **Una Cruickshank (1947-?), the Burn Estate's most celebrated daughter. Presumably left for London at some point during the mid-1960s and is now being hailed as '*one of the most singular, mind-altering artists of her – or any – generation*' (Stephan Santerre, *In The Frame*, Vol. 114 issue 5, p.55-60).**

Una spent her working life in complete obscurity and it wasn't until 1988, during the private re-development of ex-Hackney Council housing stock, that her life's work was discovered: 1,409 paintings, all covered in an inch of dust and stacked neatly in an otherwise empty bedsit. Although mostly of fog-shrouded riverbanks (*Willow Trees #1-137* etc.), in several canvases figures can be discerned – the most famous of these being the untitled work commonly known as *The Green Girl*, the stark, abstract *Talitha* (which modern X-ray techniques estimate to be comprised of upwards of *two hundred layers* of black paint), and finally *Jean Healy Sleeping in the Reeds*.

Jean Healy is my mother.

As for Una herself...her fate is unknown.

Like my mother, Una grew up on Loom Street, a street that no longer exists. It was razed as part of the Rowan-Tree housing association's 'regeneration'. Sometimes, at night, I go and stand by the building site's perimeter fence and look out across where their houses once stood. In their places are new cement foundations, portakabins, diggers. I wriggle my fingers through the chain-link diamonds, striving to be even an inch closer to where they had lived their lives. Which is to say, not very close at all.

[3] **How I first came to hear of Una is pertinent. Several years before I embarked on tracking Doug's last movements, I was in the library flicking somewhat aimlessly through the stacks, killing time before I had to go home. I came upon an edition of art journal *In the Frame*, the one I quote in the footnote above. I had never seen Una's work before. An entire page was given over to a reproduction**

And it sure as shite isn't a load of snobby bitches in wigs. So we went down the Labour Club to sell the gear, and I knew that lot wouldn't be interested, so I left them to it, started showing people at the next table. One of them pulled out the jumper. Like I said, I didn't even know it was in there. They started taking the piss out of it, and Morris Clarke's wife saw and was like, That belongs to my daughter. How did you get this? And I was like, I don't know what you're on about. See, the line we used was we had a mate in the catalogue warehouses who got all the surplus stock for next to nowt, but she wasn't having it. Kept going, How did you get this? How did you *get* this? And now people were starting to look over. All her friends giving me the evils.

Then she grabbed it and turned the bit over, and of course, the name-tag's still on where she'd sewn her fucking daughter's name. I still remember the orange stitching. Corina Clarke.

---

of *The Green Girl* and when I saw it, a chill of recognition washed over me, though exactly what I was recognising was still obscure to me, as I had not then heard of the myth of Peg Powler. Transfixed by Una's work, I devoured Stephan Santerre's article. Imagine how shocked I was to learn that Una had been a resident of the Burn Estate, a fact he himself had learned from correspondence with one of Una's childhood friends.

Yet it wasn't until writing this document that I discovered that childhood friend had been my mother. I received the letters which begin this book (*Day of the Dark*) in mysterious circumstances, and when I read them I was floored. Stephan Santerre – the influential art critic who had championed Una's work ever since its discovery – was the same Stephan my mother had been corresponding with during the final year of her life in 1991!

I immediately contacted Stephan's London offices, only to hear that he had recently passed away due to complications following a kidney transplant.

Wait, Corina? I know her.

Good for you. I fucking didn't. I'd never met her in my life, but they thought I'd been up to no good. You know what I mean. Morris Clarke's wife was like, *This man's trying to sell me my own daughter's clothes!* She grabbed my bags, and we had a bit of a tug of war 'til they split and all the gear flumped out, knocking drinks and ashtrays. Doug was flogging some jeans to some bloke, and the bloke went in the pocket and found an old bus ticket or something. Doug hadn't checked them properly. The bloke started kicking off, and then the whole place went up.

Doug legged it, left me standing there like a fucking plum. I mean, what choice did I have? I legged it too – *whoosh* – straight out the fire doors.

Like I said, that was the only time I'd ever helped him, but you know what a place like that's like for gossip. It didn't take long for word to get round.

I imagine people weren't best pleased.

I mean, haway – you're buying clothes out of bin bags in a Labour Club, and you expect *what* exactly? That was that estate all over – always looking for a hand out, always wanting something for nowt. Always ready to play the martyr. Small lives, you know?

Not that I cared, like. Still, I did think it wise to keep my head down for a bit because there was this one bloke, this local psycho.

What was his name, out of curiosity, this, ah, psycho?

Vincent.

Why was he…?

Why? There's always one like him. Always.

Could you elaborate?

You want me to try and explain a man like that? I don't know…It's like in the nature programmes on telly – here's one animal, but then along comes a bigger one and rips its throat out, just because that's how it is. Then the bigger one's off doing something else, and it's already forgotten about the thing it's just killed, even though there's still blood all over its face.

[Silence].

That didn't make sense. Tape over that bit or something.

Wait a minute. Why would Vincent be after you?

Fuck knows. Doug'd probably sold him gear in the past, but because I was with him the night he got found out, Vincent might think I'd been in on it all along.

What exactly did Doug sell Vincent?

Gear. I don't know. Shirts, coats – *gear*. I told you, I wasn't –

A dress?

Eh?

A black dress. Surely you must be able to remember selling a black dress to someone like Vincent?

I don't know what you're on about.

No, it makes sense now. It must have been you two. He let you both in through the back gate, into the kitchen, didn't he? It was late, past midnight. I could hear you rustling through the bags. He picked out the black dress, gave you less than your asking price, and you left the way you came in.

How the fuck would you know that?

Well…well, because I was listening on the landing. Because, ah, I'm Vincent's son.

[Ian stands up, startled].

He can't do nowt to me. He's in jail. I seen it in the paper.

He is yes, but he's getting out soon. And, ah, I've been to see him. When I said I was coming to interview you he, ah, got quite het up. He still remembers how you swindled him.

I told you, that was Doug's game, not mine.

He doesn't see it like that, and he has been pumping, ah, pumping iron. If you help me today, I promise I'll keep quiet about your whereabouts, about everything…or if you'd prefer, I could talk to my dad. I could tell him what you told me – it was all Doug's idea. You had nothing to do with it. My father and I are really close. He, ah, listens to me.

I'm not scared of him.

Of course.

I'm not. And I don't need nowt from you neither.

I know that too…It's just, I've come all this way and…

You alright lad?

[**Muffled sound of dropped mp3**] *Sorry, yes…just a little sweaty, that's all. It's, ah, stuffy in here, isn't it?*

[**Sitting back down**] I'm alright.

So the dress. He gave Mam it for her birthday. She loved it. She thought it was from Selfridges.

[**Sigh**] The tag was.

And the dress?

Spastic Society, I think.

We…she was buried in it.

I don't know what to tell you.

Just tell me about New Year's Eve.

Well, a couple of days later I went round Doug's to make sure he was keeping his head down. His place was always a tip, full of bits from the houses. That was something else he did. When a house went empty, people stripped it for the lead, slate, the copper in the walls…timber was worth something, too. There was a lot of that going on. Another greasy business you wouldn't catch me doing. When were you last there?

The estate? I'm still there.

Christ. What's it like?

Like I said, it transferred to a housing association and they're in the middle of knocking it down. Only about half the old estate's left.

What about the precinct? Fat Gary's?

Still there for now. Gary died though, not long ago. He had a heart attack behind the counter.

He was never out that shop, was he? His fat ghost'll be haunting them new houses. What about the bakers?

Gone.

The Laundrette?

Gone.

Yvettes'? She did a lush fry-up.

Hanging on. She's the only one left, now the hairdresser's closed, though I think that was after your time. Anyway, so you went round Doug's…

And he was shitfaced, as per. **[Whistles through teeth]**. I used to think I could rub off on him, like. Be a good influence. But it's never simple with people like that. You try your best, but they resist.

You're saying he didn't want to be helped?

I'm saying part of him got off on it. I was his audience. He needed me to see what he was doing to himself. He was adamant he was going down Fat Gary's to get more drink, but I was like, We need to keep our heads down 'til we figure out the lay of the land, you know, regarding what'd happened in the Labour Club.

You mean with Corina's jumper?

Think about it. It was New Year's Eve, and Fat Gary's was the only off licence on the estate. *Everyone* would be down there at some point. Everyone we didn't want to see. Plus it was right around the corner from your old house.

Still my house. I still live there.

I was like, Use your head. But he kept saying, *I'm a man.* Just that, *I'm a man.* I was like, Nobody's disputing that. Just chill the fuck out. But that's what it's like with pissheads, isn't it? Everything's measured in how much drink they've got left. Balls to everything else. He wouldn't shut up, so in the end we went down.

313

Please, ah, please don't take this the wrong way, but why would you agree to that after everything you've just said about people being after you?

I told you why. Who else was going to look after him?

So what happened then?

There was a gang of lads on the precinct, rotten little scunners. They seen us, and you know what it's like – once you're seen, there's nowt to be done but keep going. They were like, *Go in the shop for us*, and I was like, Jog on dickheads. They knew I meant business, so they started going on at Doug. He didn't say owt, so one of them punched him in the back of the head. A quick jab – *whack*. I was like, If yous don't do one *right now*, I'll bray yous all into next fucking week. So they did one.

We got in Gary's, and Doug was shaking. He was like, I did it again. I was like, Did what? Bottled it, he said. He could never stand up for himself. This 'other him' took over, he said.

Then he started crying.

What did you do?

What did I do? I just let him get on with it. That's the last thing you need if you're crying, another bloke seeing you do it. You must have gone in there all the time. He was sound, Gary, wasn't he?

He was always nice to me, yes. He used to order me in magazines special.

I'll bet. I've never seen that many jazz mags.

Not that kind of magazines.

You never looked at the top shelf?

[Silence].

Are you blushing? There's no shame in it. Anyway, Fat Gary and his missus were watching the whole thing. Oh, what was her name again?

Something Irish. Sian? Sian.

Whatever it was, she was looking at us with that face she had [**pulls face of pinched disdain**]. Doug got a big bottle of cider with his filthy pennies, and you could see her getting edgy. But Gary was sound as usual, chatting away, like [**eerily accurate impersonation of Gary**]: *Oh, we're not doing anything for New Years, oh, we used to go down her brother's in wherever-it-is, 'til he became one of them Hari Krishnas, and* they *celebrate New Year in fucking August or something, so now we just watch Big Ben on the telly and dah-de-dah.* You know how he was. And Doug just started necking his cider right there at the counter.

Them teenagers were still on the precinct. They were like, We'll see yous again, and I was like, Whatever. But Doug couldn't hack it. He made us go the other way, towards yours. He stopped outside your house, mumbling stuff. I had to drag him away. Was it your place that had Christmas lights all over the roof?

No, that was Mrs Zimmerman from further along. She got so old she started leaving them up all year round. After Mam died, we didn't do any of that. We didn't even have a tree.

I can't remember when we saw old Bundy, if it was before or after what happened outside Doug's place. Let's say it was before. Bundy was coming up the road. He'd been on the building site.

He lived in a shed on the allotment, didn't he? Dad used to give him tins of food.

He was a worse pisshead than Doug, so I didn't believe him when he said about the bomb.

Exactly what did he say?

Just that they'd dug up a bomb. Like I said, I thought he was talking bollocks because he was blotto.

Perhaps I could talk to him.

Bundy? No chance. He can't still be there. You can't be a pisshead living in a fucking shed for thirty year and not be dead. I guarantee it.

Interview with Fredrick Bunden. Burn Estate Allotment. 4th May 2016 [4]

[Unintelligible noise] – *say? OK, we're recording.*

I said there's a tap outside, son.[5]

---

[4] The allotment is located on the west edge of the estate and all but abandoned now, choked by Japanese knotweed – or 'Parson's Prick' as my father used to call it. Sheds and shacks in various states of collapse; their boards warped and rotted, their caved roofs receiving the silent white sky. Forgotten trowels rust into the earth they once tended, while shreds of cassette tape flutter from listing bamboo canes, tattered battle-flags from a war long since lost.

Fred Bunden's shed is a casualty of this war. The entire exhausted edifice leans as if resting against an invisible lamppost. In the distant past, someone – perhaps Fred himself – had begun painting the shed's outer walls, only to have seemingly given up after several Pollock-esque slashes. Immediately outside the threshold is a heavily stained deckchair and a perforated oil drum containing dozens of charred beer cans.

Fred was not expecting me, but I couldn't fault his hospitality. He readily agreed to be recorded. He was also hammered.

[5] I was dirty and sweaty by the time I paid my visit to Fred because earlier that morning, I'd finally got around to taking Ludwig's head down off the wall. I wrapped it in a blanket and carried it up to the allotment, to my father's plot, in a sports holdall.

It was strange being at the allotment again after all these years. Dad had worked this patch of earth for as long as I could remember, having taken over from his own father, Trevor, after his death at the age of 48 – one of nine men killed in the Upton Hill blast furnace disaster of 1972. The allotment formed part of my earliest memories: Dad crouching down to me, snapping a peapod open under my nose – I can still smell the loam – before putting the sweet, cool pea on my tongue.

Now the plot had gone to seed. I tried to recall how Dad had arranged it. Over by the shed had been the potatoes, carrots, and

317

I'm fine. Thank you for agreeing to speak with me. I was told you might still be living here.

Cheers bonny lad. I've got everything I need here. You've got the bed…a table there. There's the telly and a DVD. I get the 'leccy from that there [**Fredrick motions to what appears to be a dozen or so car batteries nesting amid a tangle of dangerous-looking cables**]. One of the lads rigged it. I don't have it on all the time though, 'cause it's a drain. Got a little fridge too. Are you hungry? [**Opens fridge. A pungent smell emanates**].

Oh, no thank you.

Got yoghurts.

I'm fine.

---

turnips. Beetroots, too, though I never liked those. Down the middle had been sweet peas and strawberries? Cabbages along the far side? I wasn't sure. One corner of the plot, though, had always been reserved for a special purpose. Down past the rhubarb barrels were the graves. Ten in total, with a different variety of rose growing on each. Dad's dogs.

They were waiting for me, the graves, like graves always seem to be waiting for someone. At the end of the row was a relatively new mound, which I guessed contained the rest of Ludwig. The rose Dad had planted on it was not yet in bloom, and I didn't want to disturb the plant itself, so I found a spade in the shed and dug a fresh hole. I lowered Ludwig's head down in the blanket. It stared blindly up at me. I could see myself reflected in its glass-eyes, standing at the edge of the grave like a mournful apparition. On a whim, I slipped a 50p coin into Ludwig's mouth, the way the Romans used to do. Then I filled in the hole.

Anyway, that was why I was dirty.

I've got corned beef. I've–

Honestly, no. How long have you been living here?

Before my brother married that heifer from the Isle of Man, I know that. He came in here and I said to him, I said, She's a wrong 'un. Just look at her *hands*. Big as boiled hams. And I was right – she cleaned him out…she…I think she shacked up with an ombudsman after him. God help that poor bastard…

I'd like to ask you about the bomb you found. The one that went off where the Moorside houses are now.

[Cracks open a can of lager] Boom!

Boom, yes. What can you remember? How did you find it?

Weren't me. It was what's-his-name? Len Carmichael's lad. Dean? Dan? Dean did.

On the building site? What were you doing there?

You see these shelves? Built with timber from them houses. Big companies don't miss it.

You were stealing?

Haway. I was down Carlin thirty year, on the pig iron. [6]

---

[6] Carlin How forge: once part of the Skinningrove Iron Company, one of the many Iron and Steel Works to the southeast of Middlesbrough, and not far from Upton Hill, where my

319

The sand was so hot you had to wear wooden clogs lest your shoes caught fire. I've grafted my whole life. I've paid my stamp. **[Opens fridge again]**, I think I've got some… no, I had that last night. There's some haggis Harry's wife did me, but that's my tea. She's a star, she is. She makes it from scratch, gets all the lungs and oats and that. She boils it in a proper sheep's stomach. Beautiful.

I'm fine, really. So what did Dean do?

She looks out for me. They both do. That's not how people are anymore. That's not—

You were telling me about Dean Carmichael? He found the bomb, you said?

Dean? Head in the clouds, that one. He must've gone off and started digging. Head in the clouds, Len's lad. He must have went off.

---

grandfather Trevor Barr was killed. Carlin How shut down in 1971, just another victim of the Teesside steel industry, the corpse of which has been torn apart by companies with names reminiscent of ancient, vengeful Gods: *Koninklijke Hoovogorens, Corus, Tata*, and, most recently, *Shaviriya*. Eventually only one blast furnace – Redcar – remained ablaze.

But then, in October 2015, Shaviriya went into liquidation and Redcar was 'mothballed' indefinitely. 3,000 jobs gone. And so it came to be that the flame which had lit this corner of the world for over a century was extinguished for good, and Ironopolis – that once great citadel to which we had all been subjects – finally fell.

The explosion happened next to the well. Is that where Dean found the bomb?

The well, aye. You're from around there, then? You know the well?

I've had dealings with it, yes.

Len went to fetch him. Dean was digging it out and Len, he knew what it was straight off. Len was into all that. He watched the documentaries. All round here got bombed, you know. All the places like St. Esther got bombed. It was an UXO, Len said. A big bastard.

Pardon? UXO?

That's just what Len said.[7] You'll have to ask him.[8] It's a daft word, but it got stuck in my head. UXOUXOUXO [laughs]. It's canny saying it.

What did you do then?

Do you like cowboy films? I've got a DVD here where they string him up by his tits.

---

[7] From Wikipedia: '*Unexploded ordnance (or UXOs/UXBs, sometimes acronymized as UO) are explosive weapons (bombs, shells, grenades, land mines, naval mines, etc.) that did not explode when they were employed and still pose a risk of detonation, potentially many decades after they were used or discarded.*'

[8] Despite my best efforts, I could find no trace of Len or Dean Carmichael.

*Westerns aren't my cup of tea. If it's not too much trouble, I'd
like to keep talking about the bomb.*

I can't remember. It was yonks ago…I used to know all the
lads, but it was yonks ago and they've all moved on. Or dead.

Dean's father, Len, he said it was a big one…

Aye, and we were off like rockets!

Didn't anyone call the police or the, ah, bomb squad?

Nowt to do with us, was it?

*So after you left the building site, do you remember meeting
two men called Douglas and Ian? Or Pav, as he's known? They
used to live around here.*

Who's that?

*Douglas and Ian? Ian was short, dark. Doug was tall and
blonde. They might have sold you some clothes?*

Clothes? People give me what I need.

*So you don't remember talking to them? They said they saw
you.*

I used to know all the lads. Good lads, like Harry. There
used to be good folk up here. What's-her-name grew
marrows *this big*. She'd give me them and I'd pack them
with brown sugar for the marrow rum. But now there's

322

scunners causing trouble up here, kicking hell out of the raised beds. That's why I come here in the first place, to keep away from that.

Ian said you were the one who told him about the bomb.

UXOUXOUXO [**opens fridge**] Harry's wife makes her own haggis from scratch. She gets the lungs and…[9]

Ian. Cont.

Anyway, so you saw Bundy, then what?

We got back to Doug's and your Curley was waiting.

Curley my uncle Curley?

Vincent had sent him round to take us over your dad's garage.

Why?

Do I have to spell it out?

I…it's just your story goes from one thing to another. People coming and going without any–

---

[9] There followed several more cycles of haggis / Westerns / nostalgia / overweight women from the Isle of Man, before I was politely able to make my escape. Fredrick Bunden would be the first – though not the last – instance of my pursuit of the truth being hamstrung by time, memory failure, and, as I later came to realise, outright lies.

This is what *happened*. What do you want to hear? Then Curley came round for a cup of tea? Doug knocked the drink on the head, then we all had a wank? This is real life, not some shitty play like what Morris Clarke's wife used to do.

But how am I supposed to make sense of it?

That's your problem.

But I [pause]. *Fine. So Curley took you to my dad's garage and–*

I didn't say that, did I? I said your dad *told* him to, but Curley had other ideas. He gave us a choice. If we handed over the money from selling the gear, he'd tell Vincent he couldn't find us. I said we didn't have any money – which was true – and he was like, then you better get it. He said if we thought about doing one, he'd go and see my lass.

Who was your girlfriend?

Wife now. Paula.

How long have you been married?

Twenty year this September, but I don't wear a ring. Fat fingers.

That's your China anniversary. Congratulations.

Is that what it is? Anyway, I was like, You leave her out of this. I don't give a *fuck* who your brother is. Took Curley by surprise, that, me standing up to him, so he went for Doug instead. He got his cider and tipped it all over him, then he grabbed his knackers and *twisted*. We had 'til tomorrow, he said.

Did Doug know Paula?

Look, I know this all comes across like me and him were thick as thieves, but he was just some bloke who hung round the scrapyard sometimes. He wasn't part of my life.

Did he ever have a girlfriend?

Doug? As far as I know, he was never with anyone the whole time I knew him, though he did let something slip once. He was blotto at the scrap yard, and babbling about all kinds of weird shite, and at some point he said he'd been engaged to a Sarah-someone. I actually met her once, briefly.

You met her? When? What was she like?

I'm getting to that. It isn't pretty. You're writing that down?

Do you have her surname?

Nah. That was all he said. It must've been before the drink ruined him, though, because there was no way the Doug I knew was getting with a woman. The way he lived, man. There was hardly owt in his flat – a knackered settee with foam coming out, a telly and a video and the bits of scrap he'd pulled out the houses. It stunk too, his flat, like when you've left the washing too long before hanging it up. Imagine being a lass and going back and seeing that?

And then there was his toilet.

His toilet?

Taped up tight with a whole roll of gaffer tape. Right round the lid again and again and again. You had to piss in the sink, and there was a bucket for shitting.

Why?

Stuff comes up, he said. I was like, gaffer tape won't do nowt if your pipes are backing up, but all he'd say was *stuff comes up*. This is what I'm on about – he needed help, but by that point I was sick of it being me having to give it to him. After Curley went, Doug was sprawled on the floor, dripping in cider, and I lost my rag. I was like, What's the matter with you? Where's your fucking pride? I thought you were a *man*? And that's when he got the knife.

He attacked you?

I saw this thing on telly once, about the Vietnam War. There was this look what the soldiers got [**Ian slackens mouth, defocuses eyes**]. He looked like that, like his eyes were just burn holes in his face. I grabbed him and this happened [**shows me the palm of his right hand, the pale ridge of scar tissue scoring his head, heart, and life lines**].

Oh my God.

I don't hold a grudge. He was fucked. He didn't know what he was doing. He was like, It's all Vincent's fault. Vincent's going to get what's coming to him. Are you alright?

Yes, it's just…you know.

I was trying to calm him down. I was like, You're not doing this. You're no murderer. But then I remembered that he already kind of was.

What do you mean, he already kind of was?

There was a girl. He was driving and crashed and the girl in the other car died.

When? What was her name?

Fuck knows. It's probably in the papers somewhere.[10]

And he never talked about it?

Would you? I'd want to forget something like that.

---

[10] Problem is, it isn't. Teesside University Library has an online newspaper archive; the crash didn't make the nationals, and there is only a partial collection of local dailies spanning the years 1999 to present, which is no good to me as the accident would have happened in the mid-1980s. The local papers themselves don't keep archives, and only offer a back-copy service for the previous year.

But that's not how it works. Even if he could somehow erase it, it would leave a hole in him. A lacuna. And that's worse.

A lacuna? Speak English, man.

I'm sorry. I, ah, I just think it's important.

Listen, having a knife waved in your face very quickly helps you realise what is and isn't important. So I went into the kitchen to sort my hand and when I came out he was halfway up the street. He might've been a pisshead, but he could *run*. At that point, the sane thing for me to have done would've been to ring the police, but I ended up going after him.

Because you were looking after him, right?

[**Narrows eyes**] Do you want to hear this or not?

Yes, sorry.

By the time I'd caught up he was banging on your door. I bet you got a fright.

He obviously wasn't expecting me to open it, so we both sort of stood there. You were hiding behind a car.

I wasn't hiding. I was keeping an eye out.

So I invited him in and—

You *invited* him? I thought he must have threatened you or something.

You've got to invite in anyone who knocks on New Year's Eve. That's the rule.

You're as crackers as he was. I thought, any second now, Vincent's going to launch him through the window.

Dad was walking Chopin [11] so it was just me. I was listening to my tapes in the back room. Do you like Kate Bush?

Don't know her.

Oh, you should listen. Try 'Never for Ever,' that's her best one. Then 'Hounds of Love' then 'Lionheart,' though most wouldn't agree there. If you want, I could make you a copy?

I'm alright, ta.

I like Joni Mitchell too, but not as much.

Never heard of her. I just listen to whatever's on the radio. I never liked all of that *duh duh duh* stuff. That heavy metal stuff.

---

[11] After Rachmaninoff (see footnote (FN).15), there was Chopin, a bullmastiff which Dad pronounced *Chopin'* – as in *with an axe*. Dad got him a couple of years before Mam died and, out of all of his dogs, I hated Chopin the most. It howled longer and louder than any dog before or since, ate its own faeces, and spent hours lapping at its rocket-red penis, this enormous, twitching, mucous-covered lipstick that frequently pearled with grey-yellow semen. Even its name was an aberration; completely at odds as the beast was to the sensual, moonlit melodies of its namesake.

I've heard every Kate Bush song a million times but I never get bored. I think of songs like friends, something that'll be with me for the rest of my life.

Don't have many friends, do you? Listen, I've left my wallet in the house, so…

Oh…same again?

[I leave the table. Ambient pub noise. Then, under his breath, Ian absent-mindedly whistles a tune I recognise.[12] He stops before I return a minute or two later].

Cheers. So what happened in there? I never got the chance to ask Doug before, you know.

He told me he used to work for Dad. He asked me if I'd ever finished my jigsaw, which I still don't understand.[13] He was very drunk. We went into the living room. I had some crisps and peanuts and scotch eggs out. I offered him a drink, meaning pop, but he wanted a real drink. Dad had some whisky in the cabinet, and we just sat there. I'm not good with people, but we managed to talk a little.

About?

---

[12] **The song is 'The Infant Kiss', from Kate Bush's album *The Sensual World*. Not her best, not her worst.**

[13] **Having not yet read Doug's journals at that point. See Doug's entry for 3/5/1986.**

330

He asked about my leg. I had an accident when I was younger, at the well over by the waterworks. Did you know it?

Yeah, of course.

He said he used to drink up there. He said someone had spoken to him from the bottom of it.

See, that's the drink rotting his head.

Yes. Probably.

Probably? Are you sure that's just lemonade you're supping?

That's when I saw the end of the knife sticking through his coat pocket. He saw me see, and he said, Your dad's not who you think he is. So I said, Then who is he? But Dad came back before he could answer. I assume he didn't run into you.

I was round the back, in the alley.

Chopin started howling and Doug panicked. He sort of lurched into Dad's backroom, which was off limits. He was trapped, panicked. He stumbled into the mantelpiece and knocked Mam's urn over. The ashes exploded up in a big grey cloud. It's OK, you can laugh.

[**Chuckling**] Sorry, it's not funny.

It's sort of funny.

I've always wondered why he came out covered in dust. Your dad must've shit a brick.

He just sort of froze. *I don't think he could quite process what he was seeing – this drunkard coughing up his dead wife. Doug ran into the kitchen. Chopin was howling his head off, and Dad said 'Kill' and let go of the lead.*

From The Journals of Douglas Ward [14]

2/5/1986

In the group today Karen handed out these journals. Told us they were Tools Of Examination to record thoughts & feelings & shite. Said if we could write down the events what put us in here, we might see Common Threads. Common Threads meaning bits of our personality or how we act what is bad & happens over & over. Our Lives Are Not A Series Of Random Unconnected Events. Her words. Think she believes it too.

---

[14] Doug's first entry from his first journal. I possess seven such journals, spanning the years 1986-1993. The first couple are ruled hardback notebooks, reasonably legible and diligently kept. However, by the early 1990s, his handwriting had deteriorated dramatically – scrawled across the cheapest, rough-pulp notepaper. Months go by without an entry. Pages violently torn out. Strange stains and markings. The final journal consists of only a handful of mostly indecipherable entries written in a child's colouring book, the kind sold in wholesalers for a handful of coppers.

I have copied entries in full, in accordance with this document's opening pledge to transparency. I've kept Doug's stylistic habit of randomly omitting articles. As much as possible, I feel it important to let his voice rather than mine tell his story. The only alterations I made were in the name of comprehension: grammar, spelling etc.

But will try coz it's late & my nightmares & Mellish's snoring won't let me sleep.

Mellish is my pad mate. Foul Manc bastard. Everything about him stinks: Breath. Clothes. Farts he lets rip loud enough to knock me awake the rare times I drop off. "The BeeGees" he says. BeeGees = Bubble Guts. One of his jokes. Cunt. He's in here coz his wife let milk boil over on hob so he smashed her head so hard off the side her eye-socket shattered. Blind now in that eye, he says. Smiling like he's remembering a happy childhood.

Mellish doesn't go to Karen's sessions. Man seems at peace with himself. He has no journal to write in, unlike me.

But I don't know where to start. Starting is the hardest part. Common Threads, she said.

3/5/1986
Here's a start. Vincent's door was the colour red of the kind of blood that comes with stitches. He had only one house back then, not two. He hadn't knocked through yet.

Baz Stark had introduced us. Me & Baz both played Sunday League for the Anchor & Hope. Baz a predictable winger, always turning inside on left foot. Open book for a decent defender. Baz said this bloke Vincent was looking for someone who knew his way round a motor. Said I should give him a bell. I needed work so I did. Vincent invited me over & I went on the bus. My first time on estate.

His living room was full of Chintz. Dado rails & doilies. His smiling wife with tea & biscuits. Wagon Wheels. Pink wafers. A dog barking outside [15] & his weird kid at the table doing

---

[15] **Rachmaninoff. A snarling German Shepherd the size of a**

333

a jigsaw, but not putting it together. Just pushing the bits about like toy cars.

Vincent in the other chair with those eyes. Starkey tells me you're a good mechanic.

I suppose.

You suppose?

No, yes.

Teacup in his hand looked like a child thing. A dollhouse thing. His bairn kept dropping bits of jigsaw. He was really getting on my tits, the kid. Just being near him got on my tits.

Vincent said, I know enough good mechanics. I'm looking for loyalty.

I'm loyal.

Not like that cunt out there — meaning his dog — that's beast loyalty. I need the other kind. Comprende?

I said I did but I didn't.

Vincent thought for a bit then leaned over. Clamped his big skull-crusher hand on my knee. You'll do for me, he said.

His kid dropped a shower of pieces onto the carpet & Vincent snapped. Start with the fucking <u>corners</u> you little shite.

---

supermarket chest-freezer. He was the first dog Dad named after a composer. I think he got the names from the sleeve of Mam's LP *Eleven Classical Classics*, a record I never once heard played. Rachmaninoff's thing was destroying cardboard. I was a teenager at the time, and every week the night before bin day, Dad would pick through the rubbish while the dog watched patiently; nothing but an occasional sweep of the tail to hint at any internal psychosis. Then Dad tossed armfuls of cereal boxes, frozen-pizza boxes, fish-finger boxes into the yard and Rachmaninoff would lose whatever passed for its mind – head snapping back and forth, jaws, teeth, claws, tearing, grinding, mincing all into drool-soaked confetti. Dad would cheer as he watched, pleased by the crazed relentlessness of his pet.

& that was how I got my start at Barr Auto & MOTs.
That was how I fucked my life.

5/5/1986

So I started working at garage & at first everything was sound. Cars came in broken & went out fixed & that was down to me. *I'd* done that. It's daft, but it felt like I was making a difference & I was grateful to Vincent. I had no qualifications or nowt, but he'd taken me on. I thought he was a mate.

People warned me. They'd heard stories about him, but I'd say that wasn't how it was. Me & him were equals. But even then, before anything happened, that wasn't really how I felt. There was a nature programme on in the day room a few weeks back, about sharks. These suckfish things that live on them. Eating their parasites. Picking dead meat out their teeth. I couldn't watch it.

There was him, his brother Curley & me at the garage. I did most of the bread & butter graft. The oil changes, brake pads, clutch cables & that, while they sat in the office with a man called Beech. Beech gave me the creeps.[16] Cunt was

---

[16] I received a jolt upon first reading this name. Only last Christmas, I'd woken in the middle of the night, in need of relieving my bladder, and, stepping onto the landing, I smelled cigar smoke, heard voices. Dad downstairs with another man:

'Aye,' said the other man, 'she reckons she's got a system.'

'Christ,' Dad said.

'She owes me thousands.'

'She should stick to cutting hair.'

'I don't mind. She'll be emptying my Santa sack one way or the other.'

Dad chuckled. 'You're a sick cunt, Beech.'

At which point, I creaked a floorboard, and the conversation stopped.

always sweating. Always smirking at you like you were both in on something, only you weren't. I avoided him. Kept my head in the engines & said nowt.

Then, after a few months, Vincent invited me down the Labour Club. I felt nervous. Good nervous. Like on a date. A lass on a date. He even paid for the drinks. Then a few pints in, he popped the question. In an off-hand way, like: Oh, you know, there's this bloke. Friend of a friend in Leeds who's got something for me to pick up. I'd go myself, but I've got a short notice job on at the garage. So hows about it?

I asked what it was, this thing he needed picking up.

Just a bag, he said. That's all. Drive up, get a bag, drive back. Another tonne in your wages. Two quid a mile. Not even Ayton Senna got that.

Did I agree straight away? Or um & ah? Don't remember now. All I do remember is the balancing act: the fear that Vincent wouldn't like me, weighed against the fear he would.

So I drove over. A bloke in a pub in Morley handed over a bag without looking at me. I drove back with it on passenger seat. Didn't look inside. Vincent didn't look at me when he took it.

I started noticing things in garage. Just a weird feeling at first. Like an energy when I opened up in the mornings. A smell, too. Weird metallic smell. Maybe a new stain on the floor. I asked Vincent about it once & he'd said it was from night before, after I'd gone home. Mate of his had driven round short notice with his motor leaking sump oil all over the show. I'd said fair enough, even as I was looking at his hands. Pink & clean even under the nails.

Not long after that I found a tooth in one of the mechanics pit. Long & yellow. An animal tooth.

& now yes, Karen, I can see how sackless I was. Only a mug wouldn't have put it together. But by that point I'd fallen

in love & people in love deserve everything they fucking well get.

Pen running out. Will pick up later.

11/5/1986
When I was little, Mam used to say there were good people & bad people & she knew which was which coz she could 'see it in them.' As a bairn I wondered what it was she saw exactly. No lie, I started examining myself in mirrors. But what was I looking for? Maybe I didn't have it, this goodness? Or maybe I'd lost it already? It had faded away? Fell out like milk teeth?

Years later, when I was grown up, I went out to Dunes nightclub in Redcar with Baz Stark & his lass & her friends, & Sarah was there. Sarah. She was wearing a green dress with green shoes. Green eyeshadow. Blonde hair over one eye. A vision floating in dry ice that I asked to dance. She said yes & as we danced, I tried wrapping my head round why I was alive & so close to someone that beautiful & I knew I'd regret it forever if I didn't try to kiss her. So I did. She held the back of my head & kissed me back!

If my life was mountains, that would be the one with the flag in it.

I took her out the estate one Sunday. Planned a walk down a nice bit of the Tees. Egglescliffe way. Willow trees & no scunners. We swung arms, walked slow. She was telling me a story I was only half-listening to, one her folks had scared her with when she was a lass. About a woman what lived in the water & drowned kids or something. But I was too nervous to properly listen, what with the ring in my pocket. Expensive one from Allott's Jewellers in town, bought with Vincent's bag money.

In the end I made a hash of it. Stopped her mid-sentence. Got the ring the out. Blurted words.

She looked into my eyes, then nodded. Just a nod. But I didn't think about that at the time. Didn't think about anything. Not about those black sports bags, or the weird smells in the pit. The occasional clumps of fur I found. Or that me & Sarah had only known each other two months. All I thought was that I had it in me after all. That goodness.

When I told Vincent the next morning he smiled & splashed whisky in my mug. Said, Welcome to the club.

13/5/1986

That very same night he rang me up. Said he had a short notice job on. Right now. Needed me. I rode my bike over. Front doors chained but light coming through the planks. Went round the unlocked side door to his office, which was empty except for Vincent's clothes folded nice & neat on his desk beside his boots. The whiskey bottle sticking out of one like a foot severed at the ankle. I followed noises onto garage floor, saying Vincent's name like some twat in a horror film whose guts are about to go up the bricks.

Vincent was in Y-fronts & heavy leather apron. Blacksmith apron. Hair yanked back in a ponytail. Welding goggles like insect eyes. When I was close enough to see myself in them, he grinned.

You've passed your probation, he said. You've kept your head down, grafted. Plus I've been keeping my ear to the ground & you haven't been shooting your mouth off neither. That's good. Means it's time you took on more responsibility.

Why are you dressed like that?

Haway over here, he said. I'll show you.

& I should've ran. Anybody else would've ran coz running wasn't the coward's way. What I did was the coward's way.

I went with him to one of the mechanic's pits. I'd been down it earlier that day but now it seemed deeper. A greyhound was looking up at us.

Name's Frieda, Vincent said. Steel Cup winner a few year back. But she's been stopped a few too many times. [17]

Suddenly he had a tyre-iron in his fist.

Frieda trembled & shook. Ears flat.

No good to anyone anymore, he said. But isn't that true for us all eventually?

He looked at me with those eyes.

I said I didn't want to be involved.

But you already are, he said. Them bags you've been picking up – what did you think they're about? He held the tyre-iron out to me, said there was another apron on the hook if I didn't fancy getting messy.

I took the tyre-iron from Vincent & hung the apron over my head. The ladder into the pit felt twice its normal length. Frieda knew what was on the cards. She started whining. Circling & pissing. When I looked up, Vincent was there. We don't have all night, he said. There's six more coming in the van. Chop chop.

All the way down that ladder I thought, this isn't me. I'm not doing this. I can't do this.

Follow through with your swing, Vincent said. Demonstrated

---

[17] 'Stopping' a dog involves the administration of pharmaceuticals to artificially lower a dog's 'grade' – i.e. its category of competition – in order to lengthen its odds. Lengthened odds mean that once the dog is taken off the drugs and regains its true performance levels, it is highly probable to win. 'Stopping' is a common and highly illegal practice that will, over time, destroy an animal's internal organs.

by extending arm like a fishing cast — swish. Do it right &
she won't feel a thing.

Frieda wagged her tail. I edged forward, iron raised & stopped.

I can take her home, I said. I've not got many friends so I
can just take her home with me.

Vincent's voice low & powerful. You don't want me coming
down there.

So I got close & hit her. Felt it go in her head. Freida folded
over herself with no sound & Vincent laughed. Came round
& hauled me out with one hand. In the light, there was no
blood on me at all.

Vincent's little brown teeth. Well done, son. Well done.

& do you know what I felt? Gratitude!

Hanging on the wall was a long pole with a hook on the
end that I'd never been able to figure out in all the time I'd
worked there. Vincent swung it down into Frieda's side. Wet
crack of ribs. Hauled her up dripping with dead eyes open.
The hole I'd done in her head somehow not serious-looking.
Vincent crouched beside her & sliced her ear off. [18]

I think I puked. Vincent dragged Frieda onto plastic sheet
in corner & soon we heard an engine outside. Beech &
Curley. Six more greyhounds, spinning in circles. Panting.
Panicked. Spooked. Shit cloud wafting out of van's back doors
when they swung them open. Me & Vincent did them all, a
pit each. Curley threw them down alive, hooked them out not.
He turned the radio on & I swear down they played 'Hounds
of Love'. Beech didn't help. He stayed in the office, boozing.

Behind the garage was a field that Vincent said he'd won
in a poker game years back, off the bloke who owns the

---

[18] English greyhounds have their I.D tattooed on the inside of
the right ear. Irish dogs have I.Ds in both.

scrapyard. I'd always wondered why Vincent had never done anything with it. But he had. Out back was a mini digger, the kind water companies use for pulling up streets to get at the pipes. Vincent got in & dug a trench. Beech & Curley watched from doorway as I pulled all seven dogs in, Frieda last. When Vincent dumped the earth back the field was a field again. The lights of the estate & blocks twinkled in the distance. How long had he been doing this? I went inside, got changed. Vincent handed me a cup of whisky & envelope with £100 in. Told me to put it towards honeymoon.

When I turned up for work the next morning, the pits were already scrubbed & it was all just a bad dream. Vincent stuck his head out the office. Put the kettle on, sunshine, he said. Managed to get through that day by thinking of Sarah. How she'd seen the good in me & after my shift, I went to her. She always smelled so good, but that night when I breathed her in all I could smell were ears. Ears curling in a furnace.

Karen keeps telling me the past is the past. It's out of my hands. Only my future can be changed. That I should use that as A Jumping Off Point. But has Karen ever done something so inhumanly fucked that it stops being what you did & becomes what you _are_?

15/5/1986

To this day I don't know why I got stopped. I wasn't speeding. Wasn't drunk. In films, it's always a 'broken taillight' but with me it's a mystery. Some copper sense maybe, what told him the sports bag on the passenger seat I kept glancing at was fishy. Or the way the vinyl steering wheel creaked under my white-knuckle fists after they pulled me onto hard shoulder.

Whatever it was, when copper leaned in & said 'What's

in the bag?' I freaked & dropped into gear & stamped the accelerator with his head still in car. His ear came off without a sound. Blood-spray as I swerved into traffic felt nice almost. Warm. Then I was in two places at once. Metal tearing.

Then I was gone.

Woke up in the car pointing back the way I'd came. Broken glass & steel. Ambulances & police. Blue lights in daytime. I didn't know where I was. In front of me, firemen were cutting a woman out of a silver car crumpled like a foil ashtray. She was young. Black hair all over her face. Mouth hanging with blood. Not moving.

I felt wind on my face. Windscreen gone. Felt my weak tooth, the one I'd had a root canal on as a kid, banging in time with my heart. Steering wheel bent around my chest. Hard to breathe. The bag still on the passenger seat, its fake leather peeling. I wished it gone. Thought about reaching over but my arm wouldn't work. Nowt worked. A cloud of pain forming somewhere below my head. An ear stuck to the dashboard with crusting red. A jokeshop rubber one.

Black out.

Came to in a hospital with coppers standing over me. You're in deep shite, they said. An officer disfigured. The ear couldn't be re-attached. He was getting married later that month, they said, in the Bahamas. Sunglasses weather. Plus a woman was dead. 22 years old, just passed her test, just graduated university. Whole life ahead of her, they said. Then there was the matter of that sports bag. The EPO inside. Anabolic Steroids. Phenobarbitone – that was the controlled one – What was I doing with all that? Who was that for? As they talked I willed the pain to come & take me away.

One day I opened my eyes & Vincent was sitting in the chair. I wanted to run bare-arsed out of bed with tubes in my arms. He had a bottle of Lucozade. From Beech, he said. Sends his condolences. Hopes I'll be back on my feet soon. Vincent's hand crept into mine, the one with drip sticking out of my veins the same cold blue as his eyes. He said, Remember when we talked about the two kinds of loyalty? Man & beast? Remember you said you were the first kind? Well, I'm going to hold you to that coz you...

I woke up & the chair was empty. Copper stationed at top of ward as always. Impossible for Vincent to have been there. Morphine hallucinations. But if so, how come I could still feel his hand squeezing mine? Squeezing as if to say: You remember what happens to beasts on my watch, don't you?

Ian. Cont.

When I heard everything kicking off, I got on the wheelie bins and looked over your back wall. Doug running into the yard.

Chopin crashed into the kitchen table. Lucky for Doug that he did, really.

I was like, Get on the kennel!

No, you missed a bit. First, he ran to the back gate but it was locked. I had the key in my pocket. Then he got on the kennel.

So what?

So it's important to record the truth, no matter how inconsequential. Otherwise we're just swapping fictions.

Well, whatever happened, he ended up on the kennel and the dog – you might not have seen this – but the fucker got hold of Doug's trouser leg and shredded it. Still, he managed to get up on the wall. Then he slipped. Fell right on top of me, the twat.

Dad was screaming, You're dead! You're effing dead!'

I thought he'd come through the gate.

Like I said, the keys were in my coat. The back-gate key and the washhouse key were on the same ring. We kept the pop in the washhouse, locked, and I always forget to put it back on the hook after I'd been in. Dad hated when I did that. Where did you two go?

Mine. I lived on the blocks, so I thought it was less likely anyone would find us. *Please* tell me they've knocked those things down?

The blocks? No, they're still there. They're due to be demolished in a few months actually. They're a bit run down now.

Now? They were fucked even when I was there! I remember the council tried fixing them up back in the early 90s, but they didn't have the money, so this housing association said they would. We'd have got new kitchens, new windows, the lot, but what did everyone do? Voted fucking *no*. Made out like it was some grand cause, but really they just liked living like that. What's that look for?

No, nothing… it's just, ah, maybe it's not that simple? Housing associations are perceived as being profit-first, but there's this vicious circle of deprivation and depression that's–

Blah, blah, blah. I don't know why you use big words when small ones do the job. It's the misery, mate. They're addicted to it. They wanted the audience, just like Doug did. I'm telling you. I lived there.

I live there too.

You're from the estate, not the blocks.

It's the same place, we're the same people. We don't go looking for chaos and misery.

But that's just it – in the blocks, you didn't have to go *looking*, it found *you*. Pre-fabs, man. The walls worked loose over time, like fucking teeth. All these sounds and smells mixing – people arguing and shagging and tellies and radios going, and some cunt's rancid soup stink, all day, all night, forever. Sometimes I'd be having a shite, and I could swear someone was whispering in my ear. Coming out of the fucking *taps*. I felt like I was losing my mind.[19]

---

[19] I decided against telling Ian about the snatches of conversations I'd heard taking place in my own house ever since I was a child: the 1am comings-and-goings of people I never saw. Nor did I describe the months and years following my mother's death; how, in my bedroom, Dad's weeping reached me from the other end of the house, transmitted to me night after night through the walls and wires.

Then surely you can appreciate, ah, how some lose the drive to escape a place like that?

[**Pause**] There's always a choice. Either start listening to those voices, or don't. I didn't. I wasn't going to get dragged down by all that shite. Or by Doug. That's why by the time we got back to mine, I'd made my decision. I was going to sell my collection and get the fuck out.

Collection?

Look at me. What do you see?

[**Pause**] *I don't know what you want me to say.*

What am I wearing?

A tracksuit top?

Pfft. This is an Ellesse Trasimeno. Look under the table.

Cords and trainers?

Lois Jumbo Cords and Stan Smiths.[20] So what's that make me?

Sorry, I'm a little slow…

---

[20] His corduroys had what looked like white paint splattered on them; his trainers had holes in the toes. They reminded me of the old pairs I'd had as a child explicitly for playing in. 'Knocking around shoes' Mam called them.

A casual.

Casual clothes?

A *casual*. That's the style. Back then, you either wore your brother's hand-me-downs, or some old hippy shite, or else you were a skinhead or some other daft thing. But being a casual was about looking smart and showing respect for yourself. It was about the brands, you know? Sergio Tacchini, Fila, Ellesse.

Lots of shops sell that, don't they? Everyone wears that kind of thing now.

And why's that, eh? Because we made it popular and it got – what's the word? – *mass marketed*. Anyone can get a pair of Samba now, stitched by some Indian kid on 10p a week, but back in the day it was all quality European gear. There was only a handful of shops – I'm talking three or four – what sold it.

You had limited runs, serial numbers. Some guy walking down the street in a pair of size eight Baltics was literally the only guy in the country walking down the street in a pair of size eight Baltics.[21] Think about that.

Like, it's just copies now. Kids don't know the history. The stuff I had, though, was pure history. My thing was Adidas trainers.

---

[21] **Adidas 'Baltic Cup', released in the 1970s (cannot ascertain exact year). Blue suede upper with yellow leather stripes and chocolate gum sole. Streamline shape, similar to that of the Adidas 'Spezial', originally designed for indoor sports and, apparently, extremely rare.**

This is all new to me. How popular was it?

There was always a violent side, scraping at the football and shite like that. But then this acid house malarkey came along – *boom, boom, boom* music – and a lot of them drifted into that. Drugs and that. To be honest, I don't know which was worse. I was only ever about the trainers, me. There was a shop in Newcastle called *Kaspar Kirsch*, on Jesmond Road. It was a German lad what ran it, and he got everything straight from the continent.

Kaspar had been on at me for years to sell him my collection, and I'd always said no. But after the jumper business, and Curley, and what happened round your gaff, I was like, what's really important here? So I decided to sell to Kaspar. I'd use the money to set me and Paula up somewhere far away. I still had his number – Kaspar's – so I rang him up, told him I was ready, but it had to be that night. Kaspar said he'd take everything off my hands if I could get up to him. He couldn't go anywhere because his missus had just had an operation or something. So I rang Tubby to get a lend of his van.

Sorry, Tubby? You mentioned him earlier.

He owned the scrap yard off the roundabout before the dual carriageway.

I used to ride my bike past there sometimes. The big tyre walls and barbed wire? It seemed post-apocalyptic, the outpost in the radioactive desert, like something out of Sunabouza.

I don't know what that is.

Oh, ah, it's a manga.

Mang-what?

Like a Japanese comic. Anyway, I still remember that sign on the gate.

The Doberman with the toothpick? *Go ahead, make my day?* It's the only scrap yard I've ever been in that didn't actually have a dog. Tubby was shit scared of them. He kept rabbits. Did you ever go inside?

Never. It's a building site now.

Sounds like everything's a building site now. His office was made from random bits that'd come in over the years, and he was always adding to it. He had like five grandfather clocks and a sideboard full of boiled rat skulls, arranged by size. French windows and guttering everywhere.

Was he fat, Tubby?

Have you seen them statues in Chineses?

Buddha?

I don't know, but he was spitting dabs of one. He probably spent as much time in the Chineses, too.[22] When I got made redundant from Littlefairs, I did a bit of driving for

---

[22] According to people in the Burn Estate Labour Club, Tubby died of heart disease in the early 2000s. I couldn't locate the other people mentioned in the following section of Ian's story.

him. Anyway, Tubby said I could have the van, so we went over to get it.

Wouldn't it have been better to leave Doug in the flat?

Tried. He wouldn't stay there. He didn't like being anywhere on his own when the toilet wasn't taped up.

I just wanted to get the van and go, but Tubby invited us in. There were two other fuckers with him, playing cards. One was this bloke called Grimes. I knew him, he was always round Tubby's. Do you know them warehouses where the industrial park was, just past Peelaw Bank? He owned some of them and he flogged all kinds of weird shite. Like blow up dolls and that, the perv.

I can't remember the other bloke's name, this horrible looking fucker with a greasy comb-over. He kept giving Doug weird looks, and all I'm thinking is, Doug don't flip out. Then the bloke was like, I know you. You were in the nick with me.

Doug had been to prison? Because of the girl?

The girl, yeah, and for what they found in his car after the crash.

What was in his car?

Drugs with weird names. I don't know what – like I said, this is just what he told me that same night he mentioned being engaged. He was passing out and didn't make any sense.

Why did he have weird drugs?

He wouldn't say and I didn't push it.

But you were friends. You seemed to have spent so much time together and yet you never really communicated?

He was a fucking drunk! That's what drunks do – they drink and drink and drink 'til the milk bottles start piling up outside and the windows fill with flies and the smell gets bad enough that the neighbours ring the council. And are you, son of the Great Vincent Barr, are you *seriously* telling me you don't have an inkling?

[Pause] *I think I've drank too much lemonade. Excuse me.*

[Several minutes pass in which I do not urinate. Ambient pub noise. Ian remains quiet. I return].

You alright? You were in there a while.

I have a small bladder. Please continue.

I've forgot where I was.

Tubby's scrapyard, a greasy comb-over.

Oh yeah, so he was like, you were in the nick. But Doug didn't flip like I thought, he kind of went green instead. I got the keys off Tubby and got him the fuck out.

Weren't you ever curious to know more about Doug?

Knowing people gets you nowt but grief. All I wanted was to get the trainers to Kaspar.

How many pairs did you have?

Eighty-six. Worth over ten grand easy.

Wow. That much?

[Tuts] Why not just do that for everything, eh? Boil everything down to nowt? Shoes – they're just bits of leather you wear on your feet. Fucking, *history* – it's just a load of bollocks what happened. It's reductionist – see, I know big words too. I feel sorry for people what think like that.

I didn't mean to upset you.

I'm not upset. It's just ignorance, that's all.

Then tell me what got you interested.

Why? What's your passion, eh?

[Ambient pub noise].

Come on, what?

WWE wrestling.

[Chuckling] What, the big lads in spandex?

The big lads in spandex, yes.

How old are you, again?

I'm forty-three.

[Whistles through teeth] But it's not real, is it?

How do we define real? The story-lines might be fiction, but the pain isn't.

Cool your jets, man. You want to know? Fine. In Easington Colliery,[23] where I grew up, my brother Richie was the fucking king. He was six year older than me and down the pits with my dad. Richie and his mates were the first casuals round Easington. They used to go to the football, the away games, and it was the Liverpool fans what started it off in the late 70s – 77, 78. They picked up the gear when they went over for the European Cup. Richie and them started taking notice and dressing like that too. This was before the strikes, mind. People still had some coin.

Richie was the first casual I ever seen. One Saturday he was going through Newcastle on the lash, and he came downstairs wearing a pair of brand-spanking new Tobaccos, done up with the laces tucked in. Fucking *lush*. You were going on about art before, well, to me, that's it.[24] Richie

---

[23] **Easington Colliery. Former mining town in County Durham. In 1951, a pit explosion killed 83 men. 1,400 jobs were lost when the mine was closed in 1993.**

[24] **Adidas Tobaccos, 1978. Brushed light-brown suede uppers, chocolate leather stripes and gum sole. Shape borrowed from 1970s 'City Series'. The 2012 re-issue featured a tan leather upper, white rubber sole and chocolate heel. Tobacco insignia on tongue. Having seen pictures of both, I think I prefer the re-issue.**

looked sharp as *glass* in his Lois jeans and Farah top. He looked taller and stronger than everyone.

I was fourteen, fifteen, and my mind was fucking blown.

That's a nice memory.

It put me into competition. I wanted to look like that, too, but I soon found out how dear it was. It was all import, you see, and only a few people were bringing it in. That place I was telling you about in Newcastle, *Kaspar Kirsch*, I went with Richie once when he bought a top – a Fila Settanta I think it was – for like £25. That was serious money in them days.

I was jealous-as. I was still in school, still only had a paper round. So I saved up and saved up and finally I went through *Kaspar Kirsch* to get a Settanta of my own. I couldn't wait to get back and start swanning around Easington in it…but when Richie and his mates clocked me, they took the piss. They'd stopped wearing Fila *last month*. That was how fast it changed.

I think I've had this shirt a decade.

But that's also the buzz. It wasn't a code you cracked once, you had to keep cracking it. No half-arsing. Richie was always a step ahead, always had one eye on the next thing, and I sharp realised I had no chance of keeping up until I had proper money. I left school and got a job in the warehouses at Littlefairs Sweets, over in Chester-Le-Street. I could start showing him who was boss then.

You didn't want to follow your dad and brother down the pit?

[Shakes head].

Why not?

Fucking mug's game, mate. Like, I'd see Dad and Richie after a shift, their red eyes and faces filthy. Always hacking up black shite. Fuck that.

Did he say anything, your dad?

About me not going down? Not much. Richie was his favourite anyway. The pit was this world that I wasn't part of.

I know how that feels.

You got a brother?

I'm an only child. [25] *I meant about feeling like you and your father are from different worlds.*

---

[25] This happened after Mam's death, but before the N.Y.E incident with Douglas. I woke in the middle of the night from fog-shrouded dreams to see my father's silhouette hulking on the edge of my bed. Streetlight struggled through the curtains and, in my discombobulation, I thought my subconscious had switched gears on me, that I was simply in another layer of dream, but then the silhouette put a bottle to its lips and said 'I know you're awake, boy.'

I didn't stir. Through one cracked eye, I saw him drag knuckles across his mouth. 'I come from men,' he slurred. 'My dad was one of five brothers and my mam – your grandma Doris – she was the only lass of seven. When they got together, they had four sons – Curley, Eddie, Kit and me...'

Silence crashed when he stopped speaking. My scarred leg itched.

'...So when your mam got pregnant, I knew you were a boy. I thought, here we go, the first of many. And that's when I changed. That was when I wanted a girl.' He rolled the bottle against his forehead. It was almost empty. 'Because men are crude. We are, we're supposed to be. But there's a gentleness to a girl. Your mother's gentleness. I wanted to see if I was capable of that.'

In the weeks leading up to this encounter, my father and I's already-fraught relationship had taken an additional turn into strange territory. I'd long since mastered the art of staying out of his way, but whenever our paths did cross – if, say, he came into the kitchen for another bottle while I was microwaving a pizza – I now felt him watching me. This was as unusual as it was unsettling, as an unspoken rule stipulating that our respective gazes be averted when we did meet had been firmly in place for over a decade. Yet now I found myself being inspected as if I were a forged bank note held up to the light of my father's new-found and inexplicable scrutiny. I thought, What have I done now? How could I have possibly disappointed you further?

But Dad wasn't finished: 'So after you were born, we started trying for a girl, but Jean wasn't getting pregnant. Still, I wasn't worried, like. Time we had. And anyway, I already had you, the son who was going to one day take the reins...' He finished the bottle and sighed. 'But then you got older and I forgot all about girls because I needed another son.' He leaned closer, bed springs creaking, his sheer size blocking out what little light there was. His wiry beard scratched my cheek and I could smell the caustic sourness of his breath. 'But there were no more boys either. There was just you, and...' He didn't finish this next. He withdrew to the edge of the bed. 'And what does it matter now?'

He clomped downstairs. A minute later I heard a glass smash.

Sleep was impossible. I lay there and tried to understand what had happened. By degrees, the birds began their dawn chorus and daylight filtered into the room. That was when I noticed the rusty stains on my sheets where Dad had been sitting. Blood, by the look of it, and quite a lot of it.

But whose?

I wasn't arsed. I passed my HGV and started on the lorries, started earning a decent wage. I got to go all over the country and the first thing I'd do whenever I had a few hours lay-over was check out the gear. There was *Nik Naks* in Soho, which was good, and *Walsh's* in Liverpool. That was Mecca. It all started at *Walsh's*.

Like, with the amount of away-games he went to, you'd think Richie would've at least once had a look in, but I guess he preferred knocking heads together in a car park. He liked a ruction, you know? All that *firm* shite. It got to the point where it was his gear that was old hat, and he didn't like that one bit. But by then the strike was on.

I was twelve or thirteen. I remember watching it on telly.

Easington was a warzone. Dad and Richie went out on the pickets every day and it just dragged on and on. Then, when winter rolled round, there was no coal to heat the fucking houses. Funny, eh? People did whatever it took. Everything that could burn, burned. They sawed down trees, the fences, the allotment sheds. Even the telephone poles. I'm not joking. No fucker could afford a telephone anyway. Dad and Richie used to get up at 3am to get to the coast and rake for seacoal.[26] They'd sell it door to door or swap it for food.

And you didn't help?

Wasn't my fight, was it? I knew what Dad was thinking –

---

[26] **Coal fragments washed back onto the beach after being dumped out to sea along with the slag.**

you're not one of us. I gave Mam what she needed for the house, and he despised me for it.

Maybe he didn't?

He did. Richie hated me too because I bought his gear off him. I offered him a fiver for his Tobaccos and he was so skint he had no choice.

Then, one day, I was over in Liverpool, in *Walsh's*, and they were just sitting on the counter – Adidas Atlantis, the rarest of the rare.

They're good?

Good? Only 100 pairs ever made. Ultramarine leather, white stripes, gold sole.[27] And they were right there, in front of me. I was in love. Have you ever been in love?

I don't know.[28]

---

[27] **See the final pages of this document – *Recorded Telephone Conversation with Kaspar Kirsch*.**

[28] **My longest (read: only) relationship was with a woman called Jennifer. Like me, she worked part-time at the library. I was thirty, thirty-one, she a mature student doing some kind of finance course at the university. One night at the staff Christmas dinner the year I was made redundant, she had a little too much to drink and kissed me at the bus stop. I liked Jennifer well enough, but when she broke it off a few months later claiming that I was 'stunted', I mostly felt relieved. I never took Jennifer back to Vivienne Avenue. As far as I know, Dad never knew she existed.**

This footnote bears no impact on the rest of the story. I suppose I just want to include for posterity that I was once capable of inspiring desire.

I gave Walsh a week's pay there and then. Richie's eyes were hanging out of his head when he saw, and if he didn't hate me before, he did now. And, sure enough, back I come from work one night, and they were gone. I was like, Where are they Richie? And he was like, Where's what? That was him all over, still entitled. So I was like, You're *nowt*, mate. Freezing your arse off on that fucking picket – if you think that's achieving owt, then you're thicker than you look.

Did he give them back?

After I broke his nose he did. He went running to Dad like a bairn – big, hard Richie – so I told Dad to fuck off too. They could all fuck off, I'd had enough. There was a job going at the Middlesbrough depot, so I applied the next day.

How are things between you now?

Last I heard, Richie was in Sunderland at the Nissan factory. I think he's got a bairn. I don't talk to Mam much, and Dad's dead. I didn't even go to the funeral.

Do you miss him?

What's it matter? He's dead.

You're still allowed to miss him. I miss mine.

You can still see yours.

No…I can't. He died, too. A month ago.

So you fucking lied to me.

I thought there'd be a higher likelihood of you staying if you thought he was still a threat.

I already *told* you I wasn't scared of him.

You could have, ah, left. Why didn't you?

Because you needed my help! Because I was trying to do you a favour! You came in here with your tape, scribbling in your little book. A forty-three-year-old wrestling fan. Mate, I *pitied* you.

I didn't ask you about your dad. I didn't ask for your life story. You offered those.

Think what you want.

I'm sorry I lied to you. I hate lying, I can't even do it properly. I start sweating and I get all, ah, tongue-tied. This whole deception has taken years of my life, but look — now neither of us need put on an act.

Who's putting on an act? You don't know me. Nobody knows me. I can walk anytime.

You're free to do that. I'd like it if you didn't, though.

[Pause]No…I said I'd help you, so I'll help. I'm a man of my word, unlike some.

I deserved that. And thank you.

So how did he die, your dad?

It was a heart attack. They found him in his cell. I suppose he had it coming, what with his lifestyle. What about yours?

Same as most miners – lungs. I read about your dad in the paper not long ago, about them greyhounds. They said he'd been at it for decades. I mean, did he ever say why?

He wouldn't tell anyone anything.

Not even you?

Not even me. In a roundabout way, that's why I'm here, to try and get answers.

So I'm not the only one with communication issues?

Touché.

I didn't know Vincent like Doug did. I just knew of him. Bits and pieces.

But if I get enough pieces, maybe I can start putting them together.

Like a jigsaw.

I've never been very good at them. I just want to know who my father was. Wouldn't you?

I always knew who my dad was.

[Pause] *Do you still collect trainers?*

The stuff's all changed now. There's still some new runs coming out, but I'm more about the Old School.

Did you sell the Atlantis' to Kaspar too?

Had to. It was for Paula. It's called taking control of your life, and it's what people lacked back in Easington, and on that estate.

So you and Doug got Tubby's van and went back to yours…

Loaded up and set off. Doug was passed out in the passenger seat, or at least I thought he was…until he jumped out of the fucking moving van.

What?

He jumped out. I thought he'd be lying in the road with his brain coming out, but he was looking up at one of them posh houses out of the estate.

Moorside. [29]

---

[29] Moorside. The houses to the east of the estate, built on the site of the old waterworks and the notorious St. Esther slums. Rowan-Tree began a three-phase regeneration of the land in the late 1980s, finally completing it in 1994. In many ways, Moorside foreshadowed what lay in store for the Burn Estate a generation later. Sarah's house was located in the first phase.

It was big. Two garages and a front garden and a whatjimicallit? A sundial. There was a party going on inside. Doug was like, this is Sarah's house.

The Sarah?

The Sarah. I suppose I'd half-thought he'd made her up. He rang the bell and a young lass with a baseball bat and Dracula teeth answered.

Telephone Conversation with Mrs Sarah Overgaard, 25th August 2016 [30]

Thank you for talking with me Sarah.

---

[30] I resorted to walking around Moorside and knocking on the door of every house with a sundial in the front garden, putting out of my mind the possibility that the detail hadn't simply been a story-telling flourish on Ian's part. Surprisingly, however, there were sundials aplenty.

Sarah's house – old house, I should say – was the sixth I visited. A Mr. Rolfe answered the door. He told me that the Overgaard's – that being Sarah's surname – had moved away several years earlier. Improvising (badly), I explained that I was a childhood friend of Sarah's, who was looking to reconnect in the scant window provided by my hectic business trip to the UK (I was a rare shoe dealer). I fully expected Mr. Rolfe to tell me to sling my proverbial hook, but instead he obligingly provided me with Sarah's current telephone number, explaining that Sarah gave it to him when he and his wife had moved in, should they have any future questions regarding the idiosyncrasies of the house.

I was grateful to Mr Rolfe for his assistance, but couldn't help thinking he should be more careful giving out such sensitive information willy-nilly. After all, there are a lot of weirdos out there.

I almost didn't. This is very strange, you know.

Believe me, I understand. I don't want to take up much of your time, but as I've explained, I'm interested in the New Year's Eve party you threw in 1993. I'm trying to get an idea of Douglas' final movements and I realise it's something of an ask, but anything you can remember would be of enormous help.

Were you two friends?

I only met him once, but perhaps we could have been. How did you first meet?

God, I don't even remember. He was just around. One of his friends was seeing one of my friends, or something like that. It was all a long, long time ago. When he showed up that night, I hadn't heard from him in years.

How was it to see him again?

All of a sudden he was just *there*, in my living room, and at first I thought it was someone dressed up as, well…as a homeless person. He looked terrible and his clothes were filthy. Everybody was looking at him. He was never comfortable with people looking at him.

The first thing he said to me was that his tooth hurt. I was so confused – the whole scene was really confusing – that I ended up grabbing him and locking us both in the bathroom. My husband Toby was like, *Who the hell's that?* but I just needed a minute.

Must have been a shock.

That's an understatement. I got Doug to open his mouth, and it looked like an abscess. Have you ever had one?

No.

It's agony. I gave him some painkillers. I didn't know what to say. I went to unlock the door but he stopped me, and that's when I realised the situation I'd put myself in. See, he'd sent me awful letters from prison. Threats. I'd had to get the police involved.

Do you still have any of these letters?

I threw them away.

What did he say then, in the bathroom?

He just came out with it. He wanted to know if I'd ever really loved him.

And what did you say?

There was nothing *to* say. It was all such a long time ago. We'd both been so young.

How did he take it?

How did he take it? Well…

Doug. Cont.

8/6/1986

I've been going to the poetry class on Thursdays. Hardly anybody goes coz they all reckon it's for fannies, but it gets me out of association & helps me build confidence in my words. Coz I need words in here. Sarah's got to know how I feel.

I swore I'd write her every day & I won't break that promise (37 letters down, max 1,058 to go). Have just finished tonight's in fact. In it I describe the house we'll get when I get out. Somewhere nice, away from the estate, with windows that don't pool condensation. Proper garden for bairns when we have bairns. A place to put down roots. I wrote 8 pages, both sides, on spiral notepaper from canteen. Blue biro smears across my left-hand words.

I write at night with torch. My pen clicks. Clicking pisses Mellish off, the blancmangey whore. His fat upside-down head lowering from top bunk. He says: You tryna wake the dead or summat?

Waking the dead is the last thing I want.

Waiting for Sarah's replies does my head in, but it's a blessing in a way. Every day's the same in here: same mushy peas on Sundays. Egg & chip Tuesdays. I spend my days bagging nickel hooks & handles for bedroom furniture & at night, after bang-up, Mellish'll lumber down off his bunk to drop his guts in the pad shit bucket. All that white bread, he says, straining. Here comes the Beegees. I wrap pillow round head to stop his shit particles rotting in my lungs. Then, when he's snoring, I wank off to favourite memories: the weekend me & Sarah only got out of bed for the pizza man, the time she sucked me off on the back of the 551. I jizz silently in keks. Rank, but I don't want it on sheets.

I tell Sarah none of this.

But through it all, I think: <u>her letter might come tomorrow</u>… & if it doesn't, well at least I can look forward to day after. Then there's the days they do come, man. Just seeing my name in her joined-up writing's enough to burst me out of all this concrete like a fucking Exocet. Hers is proper grown-up writing. I's that look like 9s. Zeds that look like 3s. What I do is, I don't open it straight away but put it under my pillow while I get through the day. Savour it. Let the secret of it drop like a screen between me & the rest of the cunts in here. I wait 'til I can't take any more & then & only then will I go to it, to her. Careful not to tear envelope, slip out the folded paper. Hold something she's held. Her letters always so short compared to mine. 2 pages max, where I can write 10 easy without even telling her half the shite going on in here.

Thought: coz her writing's a lot smaller & better than mine, it's probably that we write the same amount, it just looks less. Going to count the one I've yet to send against the last one of hers'. Result:

Me: 2,252 words.

Her: 500 dead.

So guess not.

<u>19/6/1986</u>

Her letter came today. She's got new lockers at work. Tall ones, like in American High School films. She's worried she's getting a cold-sore. Her auntie Wendy came for the weekend & won a pressure cooker at the bingo.

Ends with this:

Will write soon, Sarah x.

Not <u>love</u>, Sarah x.

Not <u>I love you</u>, Sarah x.

Have just finished writing back. Filled 13 pages with memories of us before all this. Like the day at the river, when I asked her to marry me.

I put:

> Know that I love you more than
> anything on this Earth.

Which might be too much, but it's near the bottom of the page & I've written on both sides. Scribbling it out would be like showing her the scribble of my mind. Scribble of my heart. So I leave it in.

Plus it's how I really feel. Why shouldn't a man say those things to the girl who's already agreed to marry him?

<u>22/6/1986</u>

Maybe she just forgot to write 'love'? Was in a hurry to catch the postman & just forgot?

<u>23/6/1986</u>

No. Who's ever been in hurry to catch postman? Only happens in films, that. Plus love is the only word that matters. Swear down, if all she put in her letters was I LOVE YOU DOUG – just that on a blank page & sent it every day, then I could hack this place. This pad. This shite in my head getting worse & worse like telly static being turned up.

So why doesn't she?

GUILT, that's why.

Last year this Christian Aid bloke on the high street rattled his bucket at her, so to get shot of him she said she already donated regularly to charity. Bucket bloke asked who to & she panicked & blurted out donkeys. First thing that popped into her head, she said later. I creased up. Couldn't breathe. But it was no joke for her. The lie went bad inside her until one day she cracked & started donating for real: a £5 standing order for old seaside mules too knackered to go up & down the beach anymore.

Coz that's the kind of person she is. Lies twist her guts up. So maybe she can't write 'love' coz she feels no love?

Was thinking about all this on the landing on way to work. Lost in own head & not watching where I was going & smacked right into him. Si Cullen from Hemlington. Said I was sorry, but he didn't look happy.

Screw your fucking head on Doug.

26/4/1986

Got her letter today. Savoured it. Opened it. Stomach dropped. Suffered through a sleepless night before I could ring her house. Her mam answered, said she was out.

Out where?

Work.

On a Sunday?

It's them new Continental shift patterns.

Her letter says she can't visit next week.

Do you have any idea what these Continental shifts are like?

But this is the third one she's missed. I can't rearrange — all the slots are full.

Murder, they are.

But—

369

She said, I read in the paper it costs the taxpayer over a billion a year to keep the likes of you. Then she hung up.

Her mam doesn't like me. I remember first time Sarah had me back for tea & her mam asked what I did & I said mechanic. She looked down her nose at me & said "I suppose that explains the muck on my settee."

Thought: try & see not speaking to Sarah as a blessing. Lets me get a grip. Don't write back straight away either. Play it cool. Show her I'm independent, have a life of my own. Yes, even in prison. Important not to become one of the people I'm in here with. The Obsessives & Fuckups doing 5-year stretches for crawling through women's bathroom windows at night & that.

<u>29/4/1986</u>
STUPID!! SO FUCKING STUPID!!!! It's all there in black & white! <u>CLUES!!</u> I missed them first time round coz of length of time between her letters. But read them all in one go & BOOM! Clear as fucking day!

Like this innocent little sentence from February. She writes:

I haven't been up to much this week.

At first you think, ah well, slow week, fair enough. But THINK about it. What does "not been up to much" MEAN? Even in here, where the tedium can <u>melt</u> your fucking face: wake up, slop out, work, bang-up, repeat — even in here there are experiences & details to be teased out. My head is bursting with thoughts & feelings all the time! I write her 10 fucking pages a day! Does she seriously expect me to believe her life is emptier than mine? No, she's being hazy on purpose coz she doesn't WANT to tell what she's thinking & doing, coz what she's thinking & doing doesn't involve me.

Now this one:

Me and Andrea went shopping.

When a lass says "went shopping" it means "went clothes shopping." But what clothes? Why does she need new clothes? She has plenty of clothes. Did she buy a new dress? New shoes? New knickers & bra? Why does she need new knickers & bra?

Or this:

It was Becky's birthday on Saturday
so we all went out to Dunes.

This one's the worst. <u>WE</u> all went out. Who's WE? Who's she with at nights while I'm lying awake listening to Mellish's arse? Who's buying her Tequila Sunrises? Whose hot breath in her ear? Whose arm round her? Whose fat cock pressed against her thigh? But can't write any of this to her. Would look like I'm being controlling. Paranoid. Possessive. The shite that sends women into the arms of other men, who are also all those things only hide it better.

Next visiting day after this one is 1st August. Factory Fortnight. She's got no excuse for missing that one.

She'll be there. I know it. I can talk to her about the secret meanings in her letters. Get some things straight. She'll come. She will.

2/7/1986

Pad too hot, so braved day room during association. Whenever I'm surrounded by "populous" I feel myself shrinking. The other me takes over, the one who took Vincent's tyre iron. The one who killed that girl. I want to hate this other me.

Cartoons on telly. Cats & dogs clouting each other with frying pans. Kept eyes glued to screen. Tried to ignore Si Cullen watching me.

Si sat down beside me. He said, Ask me why my nana can't juggle oranges.

I pretended like I thought he was talking to someone else.

<u>Ask</u> me why my Nana can't juggle oranges.

Si's grinning mate hanging off his shoulder. Ask him the fucking question.

So I did. I asked Si why his Nana couldn't juggle oranges.

His eyes vicious in his caveman skull. Lips peeling back. Rows & rows of fucked teeth.

My Nana's <u>dead</u>, he said.

You sick bastard, his mate said. That woman raised him like he was her own.

Other me apologising: Sorry, sorry, so so sorry.

Si stood up, blocked out telly. Said, one day soon I'm gonna learn you respect.

Need to get out of here. Need to get out. Need Sarah. Sarah Sarah Sarah Sarah Sarah Sarah Sarah where are you?

6/7/1986

Her letter came today. ¾ page long. She's been to see something called Fright Night at the Ritzy (didn't say who she saw it with, but who goes to pictures on their own?). Sign off:

Sarah x

Been lying here for hours trying to write reply but nowt coming out. Nothing but a fizzling in my head like the round black bombs in cartoons. Crackling fuse, inching down...

14/7/1986

Hottest day of the year the papers say. Sweat dripping on notebook, pages curling, turning armpit yellow. Wyndham [31] steams & groans. The stink of this place: B.O, arse, spunk, smoke, bleach – almost visible, a brown fog on the landings. Cataracts of shite. Walk into the day room & get slammed by hot farts of men with too many spam fritters in diet. Uniforms made from rayon shite that doesn't breathe. Sweat rash all over my chest & back, coming together like armies on a map. Angry red cock & balls & itchy pubes. One of the cooks – big lad from Hexham in for counterfeit notes – fainted in the kitchens this morning. Took a whole vat of cauliflower cheese with him.

Still haven't replied to her last letter. She can make me crawl out of my skin with one casual reference to Fright Night. How the fuck do I combat that? No, Doug, that's wrong. How do I turn it into love?

Si stared me out the whole time in dining hall today. I kept my face buried in my liver & onions. Panicked when I got up to empty my tray & he followed. Saw screw in hall who I knew loved his football so I talked him up about Middlesbrough's chances of bankruptcy. Thank fuck I'd read the papers so could fake an interest. Kept conversation going until Si melted away. Not wise to be seen talking to screws,

[31] **Wyndham Hall.** Former Cat. C prison near Masham, on the edge of the Yorkshire Dales. Opened 1882, closed 1997.

but even less wise to find yourself alone with that fucking loon.

Just have to get to August. Just need to see her face. A fortnight. That's nowt. People don't eat for months & not die. People hold their breath underwater for 10 minutes & not die. Human beings can be incredible. Remember that: <u>Human Beings Can Be Incredible</u>.

<u>1/8/1986</u>

Heat unbearable. Weeks of it now. People reaching end of ropes. But today, finally, Sarah is visiting. I shave with blunt razor. Sweat rash wrapped round throat. Had been keeping it at bay with athlete's foot cream, but ran out. Nowt I can do about it now, though thought of Sarah seeing it makes me ashamed.

Can't write now. Too wound up. Almost time. Will pick up later.

That didn't go well.

First thing I noticed was her scarf. A silky thing with Japanese-y fish sewn into it. New? Looked new. Expensive. She sat down across from me at plastic anti-riot table. Hands in lap. She smiled, but could only look at me in short bursts. Me, I just gawped. She was more beautiful than ever & all the things I'd planned to say were annihilated.

How are you getting on? she said.

Oh, you know, I said. When I should've been screaming "I'm fucking dying in here without you."

Then, in a quiet voice I didn't like, she apologised for not visiting. That her letters were taking longer. There were these crazy new shifts at work &—

Continental, I said. Murder.

374

Around us, the other tables were getting on like houses on fire. Even Mellish was there with his half-blind wife who'd come over from Manchester on the coach. Room filled with chat & laughter & then there was us, in the corner. An interview where we both knew the job was going to the other bloke.

I told her she'd caught the sun.

You think? I've been working on my tan. Sick of being a milk bottle (image of her on Redcar Esplanade in one of the many new bikinis she's been buying. Shrugging a shoulder strap for some cunt's oily fingers...).

Sarah fidgeted with her engagement ring. Slipped it up & down her finger.

It's sweltering in here, I said. Why don't you take that scarf off?

Summer cold, she said.

A scarf won't help. You look fine.

Better not. I'm just getting over it.

I tried to sound casual. In control. Like I wasn't locked in a concrete box. It's a nice scarf. Where'd you get it?

This? Had it yonks. Andrea gave it to me, I think.

Flat out bald-as-fuck lie. I'm in prison. I know one when I hear it.

The ring went up & down on her brown finger & shouldn't there be a band of untanned flesh – however faint – where that ring – everlasting symbol of my love – had protected it from the sun? Something inside me cracked.

Screws called time. Visitors stood, hugged, shuffled out dabbing eyes. I told Sarah I loved her. Staring at her as I said it. Not wanting to, but needing to.

I love you too, she said.

& I wanted to throw it all in her face. But didn't. Not brave enough. Never brave enough.

375

Past lights out now. Don't know how much longer I can write. Hand is killing & torch batteries dying. Need to buy more, but canteen will take days. Already starting to tell myself her ring finger was optical illusion. Something I've cooked up in my hot-house head.

Thought: what kind of man am I?

11/8/1986
Weather finally broke. Black clouds swallowed the sky & rain so hard the sewers backed up & swamped shower block with turds. It's showing no sign of stopping. Thunder & silent flashes of lightning scorching backs of my eyes. Still got no batteries, so am writing this by afterimage. Mellish, though, snores through.

Storm reminds me of the Day of the Dark.[32] We were in the playground when the sky went black & the rain like a

---

[32] Typed 'Day of the Dark Teesside' into Google and returned the front page of the Evening Gazette from 3rd July 1968. Headline: MIDNIGHT AT MIDDAY.

Intrigued, I then read a Gazette article written in 2010: THE GREAT DARKNESS REMEMBERED: *It was over 40 years ago that The Darkness fell on Teesside. Green fork lightning, tropical rains, and hailstones bigger than golf-balls fell on the terrified people of Middlesbrough, many of whom got on their knees and prayed.*

One local recalled: *I thought it was the Rapture.*

The phenomenon, according to the article, was caused by a freak collision of nature and man: two huge weather fronts – one cool from the north, one humid from the south – clashing over Teesside, scooping up heavy pollution from the iron, steel and coal industries (of which there were still significant amounts in those days), stacking swirling vortex upon swirling vortex to form a jet-black maelstrom some seven miles thick, completely blotting out the sun.

cliff moving closer, lit from the inside by forks of green lightning. The bell rang & we scrambled to get inside & in the panic I fell & smashed teeth off floor. Shovelled up by a dinner-nanny into assembly hall where we sang hymns as the roof peeled off. Mrs Mearns, our teacher, warbling "Cross Over The Road My Friend" with one fist round the crucifix at her neck. Then the lights went out & the wind screamed & the thunder shook in my cracked tooth.

Mam still drummed her Bible shite into me in them days. Genesis 6:17: <u>For behold, I will bring a flood of waters upon the earth to destroy all flesh in which is the breath of life under heaven. Everything that is on the earth shall die.</u> But I didn't want to die. There were so many things I hadn't had a chance to do yet. Like I wanted to be a footballer. I wanted a moustache. I wanted to find my dad & ask him how come he'd left. So there, in the assembly hall, my mouth pissing blood, I said the only prayer I've ever meant: Please, if you let me live I'll believe in you forever.

So what happened? The storm eased off & the sun came out. When Mr Plant the headmaster was sure it was safe, he sent us all home early. Picking our way around fallen trees, sloshing through puddles bigger than ponds.

Mam was chain-smoking on the front step when I got back. She took one look at me & dragged me to the dentist where I spent the rest of the day getting drilled.

Now I find myself here, in this pad, delivered into adulthood by way of my broken promise to God, having achieved none of my youthful dreams. Not even the moustache. So no prayers this time. Bring on the flood.

15/8/1986

Her letters have stopped.

    I need to be alone. Need to be alone, but there is no space. Snide, edgy bastards everywhere. No end to the farts & eyeballs. All month the vulture-shadow of a question circling: that scarf. <u>What was under that scarf</u>? Hickies are the only answer I can come up with. Loads & loads of hickies. Proper blackberry suckmarks [**scribble**].[33]

    Sarah's mam answers every time I call. Continental shifts, she says. Continental shifts. Nowt you can do about these Continental shifts. Her voice in my ear like an oncoming stroke. I need to get her on side. Make her understand the agony of love slipping through grasp. But always there's some cunt behind me, waiting for the phone, tapping foot. The lad from Hexham, pink bits dangling from his cauliflower cheese burns, reeking of chip pans.

18/8/1986

Rang own mam today. It rang & rang & rang, but I knew she was there. She never liked answering, even when I was a kid. She'd stare at the thing like it was from Neptune, waiting for the other end to hang up. But I wouldn't. When she finally picked up, her voice sounded like 750,000 menthol Superkings.

    What do you want?

    Good question. What <u>did</u> I want? I wanted her to make it all better, like mams are supposed to. As simple & as impossible as that.

    She sparked a lighter on her end. I'll pray for you, she said.

    Not once has she visited me in here. Not once. This, a woman

---

[33] Holding the page up to the light, I managed to make out: '[...suckmarks] *going all the way down her neck to her [–]'*. I suppose Doug didn't want to follow that thought any further.

who goes to church every Sunday to raise money for little swollen-bellied African bairns, but who can't find it in her fucking tar-packed heart to get on a bus & see her only child as he rots behind bars. Instead, she sends me a few quid canteen money for pens & batteries. Guilt money, like Sarah's donkeys.

So I say how Christian of you & hang up.

19/8/1986

I don't care who she's with. Or where she is. Or who she is. Don't care who's sucking on her neck coz there are parts of me she doesn't know. I am a man.

20/8/1986

Heart smashed.

21/8/1986

2 litres of Scrumpy Jack, cold out the fridge. Condensation trembling like chipped diamond.

22/8/1986

Tonight, as he had a horrific, splattering shite on the bucket not five feet away from me, Mellish said Si was looking to "do me in".

But I've never done anything to him, I said. My voice sounded all floaty & small.

He reckons you're in with — hhnnnuuugggghhhh — someone on the outside who he isn't a fan of.

Vincent.

That's the fella. Apparently, this Vincent's rubbed him up the wrong way a few times.

Vincent isn't my mate. Tell him that, will you?

Mellish chuckled in shitty dark. I ain't getting involved. This

Si was in the Falklands from what I hear. He's <u>seen</u> stuff. Exocets & that.

I started saying again how I hated Vincent more than Si, but Mellish's exploding guts drowned me out & anyway, is it true? Do I hate Vincent? Karen says this diary is for honesty, so that's what I'll do. That night when I got to walk into the Labour Club with him & everybody saw us together I felt like his [scribble for several lines][34]

23/8/1986
I rang him.

Vincent didn't interrupt while I explained. Waited till I finished to say he hadn't heard anything about Sarah carrying on with anyone.

Please, I said. You know everything.

Silence down his end.

Speak to me! Surprised myself with that. Desperation making me brave. Or maybe it was all the concrete & steel between us.

He sighed. Just let it go.

Let what go? Who's she with?

Some lad. Dunno who.

Some lad? What lad? What's his name?

Never seen him before. Think he comes from up Thornaby-way. Anyway, not from round here. That's all I know. I've got better things to do.

Find out who he is.

Pause. Then: Look, I'm going to tell you this once more — Let. It. Go. What good's it going to do you? The outside can twist your head when you're inside. Trust me, I know.

---

[34] No amount of sunlight would reveal what this had once said.

I want you to sort him for me.

Silence again. Telephone crackle.

Coz that's what you do, isn't it, sort people? I want you to take him down the pit.

Careful, he said. Careful what you're saying here.

But I was ready to chew through guts. You <u>owe</u> me. I kept my mouth shut too like you wanted. I'm in here coz of you.

No, he said. You're in there coz you're <u>weak</u>.

Then line went dead.

<u>25/8/1986</u>
Her letter came:

Dear Doug,

I feel horrible for doing it like this, but I don't think things are going to work out…

More paragraphs after that, but I can't process. Something about how I'll always be "special" to her. Always be her "friend". Some shite about the right person being "out there" for me, somewhere, waiting for fate to bring us together. Her words. She's sent the engagement ring to my mam.

Letter ends: "Sarah." Not even a kiss.

No mention of a lad from Thornaby.

I wrote back saying I know about him. Saying I still had eyes in her world. Said I hoped he gives her AIDS & that I'd be out in time to watch her die.

<u>28/8/1986</u>
Told Mellish I was going to talk to screws about Si & his meaty little mouth puckered like an arsehole. Was I barmy

or summat? Nobody likes a grass, he said. *Grasses got what they deserved. I had to fight my own battles. Deal with Si face to face. Man to man.*

What if I can? What if I can break him in front of everyone while he's playing day room dominoes? Then get out & go round Vincent's & make him beg? Make him go, Please, please – I'll do anything, just don't hurt me. Leave him on his knees on the hearth rug, crying in front of his wife & sackless bairn?

Sarah will regret it then. Will regret leaving a man who handles himself like that.

She hasn't responded to my last letter. I send another.

31/8/1986
WHAT'S HIS NAME? How can she be with somebody with no name? Is it normal name like Steven or Karl? Or foreign? Pierre? What's he look like, this Pierre? What would his skull feel like if I brought a tyre-iron down on it?

30/9/1986
Used to be important to keep track of time. What day it was. How many days in month etc. For sake of head. Structure important in a place like this. But not me. Not anymore.

Still no letter. I write again. 11 pages this time. Last of notepad.

13/10/1986
Dragged into governor's office. Cunt sat there flanked by coppers. One copper showed me pages in sealed plastic bag, like on telly: a letter I'd written to Sarah. Seeing it in plastic made it different somehow. Words I don't remember writing. Bad words.

She wasn't pressing charges, copper said. This time. Then they took away my letter & phone privileges.

15/10/1986

Mellish has been shipped out! His wife's arthritis was so bad she couldn't make the coach trips anymore so he put in a request. Ticket back across the Pennines. Bet she's thrilled. As a goodbye present he dropped one last shite in the bucket for me to slop out. I hope his van goes off a cliff.

So last few nights I've been alone in pad. Moved onto top bunk. Finally: the peace I thought I craved, but after bang-up I still can't sleep. Can never sleep. Will never sleep again.

18/10/1986

Mellish, wherever you & your rotten arse are, I take back everything I ever said about you. You are a <u>saint</u> next to Lester, my new padmate. Lester's in his mid-60s with 1 green tooth sticking out of top gum that you could open beans with. Flaky glop in the folds of his neck fat & the Cunt. Never. Shuts. Up. He starts gabbing right after bang-up & keeps going till his diabetes knocks him out. He told me my fortune within 10 minutes of meeting him. He rubbed his hairy, stretch-marked gut like crystal ball & said: 'You will meet a tall, dark stranger tonight...in the showers. Hur Hur Hur.' Laughing like if slime from beginning of time could laugh.

Came back from dinner tonight & he was on top bunk, thumbing through a fishing magazine. My stuff on bottom again. Air smelling of dead eggs.

& what did I do about it?

Guess.

Hur Hur Hur.

27/10/1986

Does Pierre have wheels? Takes her out for drives at the weekend? To the beach? The moors? Does he have a tartan picnic blanket? Lowers her onto tartan picnic blanket in tall grass?

30/10/1986

Don't want to admit it, but writing in this thing is all I've got left. When my pen is moving I can forget. But the problem is I have nobody to write to & nowt to write about. No further need to untangle past, coz future's dead. So I record what's around me & at the moment, what's around me is Lester.

I fucking despise Lester, but after bang-up there's no getting away from him. Still, every now & again he'll say something interesting. Like tonight.

It's best to shower as late as you can. It means all the hot water's gone, but also less people. Less chance of bumping naked into someone you don't want to bump naked into. So it was getting on to bang up when I got back to the pad & found Lester stretched out on my old bunk with the contents of my poetry folder across his disgusting guts. Cunt flapped a page at me.

What the bleeding hell's this? he said. Chocolate from the Marathon bar he was eating smeared all over the page.

I was annoyed, but not as much as I made out. I know Lester noses through my stuff when I'm not there, which is why I leave the poems in the drawer where he can see them. Decoy for this journal, which goes in mattress slit.

I told him we sometimes got photocopies in the poetry class to take away & study for imagery & rhyme & that.

Lester wrinkled his nose. & this is considered good poetry, is it?

The poem was the Betjeman one about the bombs.[35]

You don't like it? I said.

Squire knows nuffink about bombs.

& you do?

Lester sucked his fingers clean. Too right, he said. I was in the Blitz.

I thought of the cartoon bomb fizzling inside me.

Let me <u>tell</u> you about the Blitz, he said.

He was 15, he said, when it started. 7th September, 1940. He lived in Poplar, that's East London, right behind West India Docks with his Mam, Dad, 4 brothers & sisters. Their neighbour was an old bloke with a shelter in his back garden, who let Lester & family join him during air-raids. While the city split apart around them, Lester would feel the perv's bony old hand creeping up his thigh. Every night the docks got bombed. Week long firestorms that cracked your skin from a mile away. After the sugar warehouses were put out, they'd go down & chip lumps off the 6-inch layer of toffee tarmacking the ground.

What him & his mates used to do mornings after a raid was pick through the rubble looking for treasure: prising coins out of gas metres, sifting bricks for miracle bottles of unshattered plonk. Once they'd even found snaps of someone's missus in the all-together.

Had to scrap a few lads for them, Lester said, his fat arse forcing the mattress through bunk slats above my head. Nice big udders on her, if I remember. Mind you, you'd swing if you were caught. People looked down on that kind of thing. You heard stories. Ghouls what tinsnipped fingers off bodies to get the rings. Stripped them naked for clothes. But that wasn't us, Lester said. We weren't grave robbers.

---

[35] **John Betjeman's 'Slough' (1937).**

385

I kept silent.

Then, one night, Jerry hit all the houses along Ricardo Street & in the morning Lester & his shithead friends went over to see what they could find. What they found was ruins: mountains of brick & timber pocked with guttering fires. Charred fragments that had been sucked up into inferno now floating down through greasy brown dragnets of smoke. Back walls blown off houses so you could see all the different wallpapers inside. Armchair balanced over thin-air. Books lying open like shot birds. The street was deserted, seemed they'd even beat the corpse-strippers to the punch that morning. They scrambled the sloughing heaps of masonry in search of loot & that's when they saw it. Lying in the smithereens. The bomb.

Lester shifted on his bunk & released jazz-trumpet fart. Thing was bigger than I was, he said. Massive. So guess what we did?

What they did was start bouncing bricks off it, coz they thought it was a dud. Then the police came & whistles blew & they scarpered & soon the whole place was closed off. What was left of the neighbourhood gathered to gawk.

Would've thought people would've been sick to the back teeth of bombs, Lester said.

Lester & Co. hid in the crowd as the bomb squad went down into the crater & then KABOOM! A red mushroom cloud raining bricks. Some poor fucker next to him laid out cold.

We didn't know at the time, Lester said, but there's no such thing as a dud bomb. Only dud timers. All it took was a knock to start them up again & there was us, lobbing bricks off it. Mugs.

When the dust cleared nothing was left. The crater itself

now a crater. The bomb disposal men a pink mist drifting over Isle of Dogs.

In the dark, his voice thick with sleep & diabetes, Lester said: I mean, that was just <u>one bomb</u>…& we were dropping <u>tens of thousands</u> of 'em on each other every day. That's when I realised there was no surviving this war, that I was just waiting to die. Waiting for the bomb with my name on it to whistle through the flack & spotlights & end me.

It did something to me, he said. I stopped caring. Maybe it's the reason I did all the things I later done.

I wanted to say he did those things coz he's a fat, evil cunt. But I didn't & besides, he was already snoring.

<u>2/11/1986</u>
Did this in poetry class tonight. Needs work. Used "mist" twice in 2nd bit & can't think of a word in the kiss line.

Reoccurring Nightmare

Beyond the reeds & willow trees
Past the river's watery sound
The Tees that here is not the Tees
(Where she'd once seen the good in me)
His field & what's buried in the ground
The fog rolls over all my crimes
Them rotting horrors make no sound
Jaws & Claws & Skulls & Spines
Waiting, waiting to be found.

My naked body knows this cold
& that she's out there in the mist
I smell her rank perfume of mould

Squint through the mist to there behold
The (something?) of her icy [36]

<u>4/11/1986</u>
Back in Wyndham now, but signed off work on account of broken rib, broken nose, cracked tooth. Same tooth I done on Day of the Dark. Same one from crash, the day I became a murderer. A fat bluebottle's banging itself against tiny window opening as I write. Thing inches from rest of the world & too stupid to know.

Been in hospital last 3 days. Beds lining scuffed walls, silent human-lumps in some. Far-off squeak of soles. For a second after I first woke up, it was déjà vu. It was after the accident again & somewhere above or below me Emily [37] was bleeding

---

[36] The 'kiss' to which I assume he was referring. However, he never managed to write it. The rest of the page is rumpled and torn, save for the same kind of rusty smears my father left that night on my duvet (see FN.25).

[37] I believe this to be the first of several references to the young woman killed in the car accident. Getting hold of the crown court records (which, given the seriousness of Doug's charges, it surely had to have been) proved impossible. Moreover, without a surname, any hope of finding Emily in the Births, Marriages and Deaths annals – an obituary, even – was similarly doomed. Another option was to trace her through the newspapers, but as stated in FN.10 the nationals hadn't deemed this young woman's death newsworthy, and the local archives are incomplete.

In a last-ditch effort, I got back in touch with Sarah Overgaard to see if she had a contact address for Douglas' mother. I was secretly fantasising that Mrs Ward was the kind of diligent mother that kept pristine news-cutting scrapbooks of her son's case, someone who, at the very least, would know Emily's surname.

But Frances Ward, Sarah informed me, had died years earlier. All of which means that there is a hole in this story – yet another one – where Emily X, 22, her whole life ahead of her, should be.

out on an operating table. But then I was chained to bed with a screw watching & my face felt like burst sausage casing & I remembered.

Had been lying on bunk writing poem when a shadow fell over page. Looked up expecting Lester, but it was Si & friends, shutting pad door behind them. My day dreams of man-to-man with him shrivelled & exposed me as the coward I've always known myself to be. Real-life beatings don't last long. Si punched me square in teeth. Fireworks, blackness.

My last thought before waking up in hospital: What's his name?

[Irregular, yellow-brown stain on page. A fragment of silver wing adhering].

Bluebottle ran out of time.

4am: Tooth agony. Darkness. Everyone else sleeps. Just me awake. Just me alone. Jus

5/11/1986
Dentist showed me tiny x-ray plate no bigger than stick of Juicy Fruit. Saw my jaw how it really is, under the meat. Same as the ones that rolled up out of ground when I was in Vincent's digger.

I look at part of my own skull, ghost-blue in the x-ray. We are all bones below. I know that better than most. How fragile, too. How easy to cave in. My own. Sarah's.

Vincent's.

3rd root canal on same tooth. The gas made me feel like cheddar under grill. Dentist told me tooth was stable for now, but for how long? Multiple root canals were a risky business.

It could hold a year, 5, 20. Could go tomorrow. A ticking timebomb. His words.

Sarah. Cont.

How did he take it? Well…he just sat there, on the side of my bath. I had been going to break up with him anyway, even before the accident. I didn't like who he'd become. He'd go into these moods. He started drinking, and whenever I asked him what the matter was, he'd snap. He was working too much for that horrible man…oh, what was his name…?

Vincent?

Vincent! that was it, Vincent. He'd ring up and I'd say to Doug, no, let it ring, but he never would. Vincent made him work all hours, right through the night sometimes. Whoever heard of a garage doing that?

Short notice jobs, perhaps?

All I know was that Doug changed. When he went to prison, he started sending me a letter a day, literally – this was before they got nasty – pages and pages of how he loved me, how we were going to be together forever. And his mother would be ringing me up at all hours in floods of tears, stewing in the guilt she felt at never visiting him. She couldn't bear it, she said, to see her son in a place like that. She'd read me the Bible down the phone, the parts about how she'd failed as a mother, then the contradicting parts about how it was all *his* fault – *thy son shalt not besmirch thy mother*, or whatever – I've never read the Bible – and she'd want me to tell her what bit trumped what.

Yikes.

I felt like *I* was in prison. I should've never said yes to marrying him, but I was nineteen. I hadn't wanted to disappoint him. I didn't think you *could* say no. Do you know what? When he got sent to prison, I was relieved. What kind of person does that make me?

Probably a normal one.

[Silence].

Did you tell him any of that in the bathroom?

No.

Why?

How could it have helped either of us? Plus, by that point, my husband was threatening to call the police, so I opened the door and let him in. God, I shouldn't laugh, but he was dressed as Morrisey, you know with the quiff? And he was waving these tulips about. Ridiculous, really.

You were green, weren't you? Were you a zombie?

Oh yeah…my oldest, Fiona, she'd had chickenpox earlier that year and missed her School's Halloween party. She loved The Munsters and had had her heart set on going as Eddie Munster, so when New Year came round she begged us to have a fancy dress party. I ended up being Herman because Toby's allergic to the makeup. Actually, thinking about it, I don't know why I couldn't have just been the mother. How do you know about that, anyway?

I talked to the other person there with Doug that night.

Oh, him. He was pretty sheepish. Our friend kept him in the corner. When Doug came back down, they both left quietly. And that's it, I never saw Doug again. I don't know what else to tell you.

You've been more than helpful.

Actually, wait. There is something else. What's your address?

[I tell her] *Why?*

I'm sending you something.

What?

You'll see when they get to you.[38]

---

[38] **A week later I received a package. Seven journals (see FN.14) and a note:** *Doug left these to me in his will. They've been under the stairs for 25 years. I don't know why I brought them with me when we moved. I've never opened them. They're yours now. Sarah.*

So we went in [to Sarah's house] and she had green makeup all over her face. She dragged him off, left me with all these dressed up dickheads. Some cunt pretending to be Winston Churchill, trying to intimidate me by saying he was in the Navy and knew Taekwondo. I was *this close* to kicking off, so everyone backed off. Left me to help myself to a sausage roll while the husband had a fucking eppy on the landing.

Doug looked shattered when we got back in the van. I was like, Doug, enough. I've got my own life, a woman what loves me. I don't need this shite. I need to deliver these shoes. But he wouldn't get back in the van, started necking a bottle of wine he'd somehow swiped from the party.

I hope, by now, I've managed to get across how much of a nightmare he was. Still, I sort of regret leaving him, because of what happened after. But if you hang around people like that long enough, it starts rubbing off on you. This doom mongering that life doesn't mean owt.

You think our lives have some sort of cosmic order?

You don't?

I'd like to believe.

Then believe. What's stopping you?

Evidence to the contrary.

Listen, I'll tell you a story. After I took the job at the Middlesbrough depot, I got a flat on the estate. I didn't know anyone. No mates, nowt. On weekends I might go to a Boro game, maybe, but otherwise I'd just sit around the flat. I suppose you could say I was lonely.

I know.

[**Gives me a strange look**] So one day I woke up and the only thought in my mind, crystal clear, even before I'd opened my eyes was *today I'm going to roast a chicken.* Fuck knows why, I'd never roasted a chicken in my life. All I'd been eating since I left home was beans on toast and pot noodles. I couldn't cook. Still can't, actually. That's Paula's thing. But all the same, I got on the bus to the supermarket and got a chicken, all the veg, gravy, the lot. Are you still with me?

Not entirely.

So I got back and started chopping the veg, making the stuffing and roasties, but when I went to put the chicken in, I realised I'd forgotten the fucking tinfoil. You have to cover the chicken otherwise it goes dry, doesn't it?

Mam did the same. Her roasts were wonderful.

My mam's too. Anyway, I couldn't be arsed going all the way back to the supermarket, so I popped over to Fat Gary's.

He always had stuff like that.

Good old Fat Gary. He had two rolls of foil left, remember that – two rolls. So I bought one, and for whatever reason I decided to walk back along Bathurst, past the electricity transformer. Now, I *never* did that because it was the long way, but for some reason that day, I did. And I was just walking past, minding my own business, when I heard a voice *hey, hey over here*. I couldn't see anybody. I reckoned someone was having me on, but then the voice went *in here* – meaning over the wall, inside. There was the high wall, wasn't there? With the glass on the top and the gate bit? So I looked through the gate, but still couldn't see anyone. I was like, fuck this, but then he came out from behind the transformer, this naked bloke.

Pardon?

A naked ginger bloke from behind the thing with his hands over his cock and balls.

What was he doing?

He wanted to buy my trousers off me, but I didn't see a wallet on him. I think he'd been crying.

Did you give him your trousers?

I chucked him the tinfoil. He kind of scuttled out like a crab to get it, then scuttled back round the thing. I could hear him ripping and scrunching, then he came out wearing this massive silver space nappy **[laughs in a somewhat forced manner]**.

When was this?

Oh, yonks ago.

But when exactly? What year?

It would've been…86, 87. 1986. What's up with your face?

Nothing. Please go on. What happened then?

He climbed over the gate and wrapped the rest of the tinfoil round his head and poked some eyeholes and a nose hole. We had this moment of, like, just looking at each other. Then he ran off. Weird, eh? Are you alright? You're sweating again.

Sorry. I'm just thinking.

But that's not the end of the story. I still had to roast my chicken, didn't I? I went back to Fat Gary's to get the last roll of foil, and I was just paying when Paula walked in. When I saw her my heart just…stopped. I've got a picture, if you want to see?

I'd like that.

[He takes out the wallet he'd earlier claimed to have forgotten and hands me a small, cut-to-fit photograph which is surely now much older than the woman it depicts. She has equine features, straight dark hair, green eyes. A small but prominent port-wine birthmark on her temple, shaped like a boomerang or a torn-off fingernail].

She's beautiful.

I didn't know I could feel like that, you know, about anyone…

[Ian gets up suddenly and leaves. I'm unsure as to whether he is going to come back. I wait, still holding the picture of Paula. The edges are so worn that they feel like linen. Ian returns ten minutes later].

Are you alright?

Me? Yeah. Just having a slash. Too much beer. Just… **[Removes Paula from my fingers].**

Do you still want to go on?

It was a slash, not open-heart surgery. Right, OK, so Paula needed tinfoil too, and Fat Gary, he was like, sorry, this customer – meaning me – he's just got the last one. But I handed it over to her without a word. We pretty much got together there and then, and I never did roast that chicken.

If you don't mind me asking, how exactly did you do that, get together? What did you say to each other? I'm not…I just struggle with the mechanics of it.

When it hits you hard like that, you don't need to think. It was like I'd always known her. That sounds like some shite you'd hear in a film, but there you go.

It sounds really nice. I guess I'm just never able to get a concrete answer.

There *is* no concrete answer, that's the point. The world had already set it in motion. Like, if whatever happened to that naked bloke hadn't happened, then he wouldn't have been naked. And if he hadn't have been naked, I'd never have met Paula. You see? You have to be *open* to it, that's what I'm saying. And Doug wasn't. That's what done him in in the end. More so than the booze, even.

What happened to that naked man must have been traumatic. Would you consider sparing him from it, if it meant that you wouldn't have met your wife?

Not a chance.

So after Sarah's, you parted ways?

Aye. I drove off. I was at a crossroads, metaphorically like. The estate had already got him, but it hadn't got me, and do you know how I knew? **[Pause]** No, I'm asking you. Do you know how I knew?

How did you know?

Because Paula was mine.

Did you sell the shoes to Kaspar?

Every single pair, even the Atlantis. Kaspar's eyes popped out. After, my plan was to drop the van back round

Tubby's, take Paula to a hotel in town, and then figure out where to go from there. I was nearly home – just up Crane Street, past the building site – when the bomb went off. The whole van lifted off the road. Where were you when it happened?

In bed, but not sleeping. There was a strange feeling immediately before, like when you go through a tunnel and your ears pop.

All the windows blew out on Crane Street.

My first thought was it was a natural disaster. Pompeii or something…

Gas leak, I thought. I didn't know it was a bomb 'til I saw the telly the next day, but even then, they never said owt about anyone being killed. It was like a week after, one of his fingers was found in someone's gutter and they got his prints off it. Then more bits started turning up. They only said it was Doug about a month later, when it was in the paper.[39]

You hadn't wondered where he was?

It was normal for me to not see him. I keep telling you, I

---

[39] Again, this didn't make the national papers, but at this point what's one more loose end to contend with? Bundy, Geordie, Ian – see FN.9, see effing-FN.579 blah blah blah. What if everyone's having me on? What if I'm trying to reconstruct something that never was? What if I long ago lost my effing marbles?? Jesus, Alan! What are you *doing*???

had my own life to lead.

I guess he wouldn't have felt any pain.

He was in enough as it was.

So what did you do then, that night, after the explosion?

What did I do? Got the van back to Tubby, rang Paula at work and told her I was coming to get her. And that was that, we never looked back.

And she agreed? Just like that?

We loved each other. What's more important than that?

What about her job?

What about it? She worked in an old people's home. That's the good thing about old people: wherever you go, there'll always be some.

Do you ever regret leaving?

Not once.

Do you miss Doug?

[Pause] Some people are just marked. I did what I could for him, but at the end of the day, some people are just marked.

Thank you for speaking to me.

[Tilts mild slightly in my direction].

Right, ah, well, like I said, I'm trying to find a man who used to live round here. His name is, ah, was Doug. That's all I know, really. I don't have a second name.

---

[40] My meeting with Geordie was a direct consequence of a conversation I'd had with Corina Clarke, local hairstylist and possible woman of my dreams. She told me of her worries over the troubling and bizarre aspects of her brother Jim's disappearance. Her exact words: "*Something awful's gone on, I know it, but I'm never going to know what.*" I sympathised as I, too, laboured under my own familial enigmas.

Thus, I found my thoughts returning again and again to my mother's tiny urn, and to Doug's N.Y.E visit. It had been Doug who spoke of the voice coming from the bottom of the well. Doug who had told me '*Your dad's not who you think he is.*' As soon as he'd said this, I realised that I had been thinking it my whole life. I wanted to find Doug, ask him to expand on what he'd meant. Perhaps I could even write it down, attempt to finally make sense of things?

To this end, Geordie was the first person I spoke to in the compilation of this document. I found him in the Labour Club after having no luck in coaxing Doug's memory from any of the other patrons. He was sitting alone near the piebald dartboard, nursing a creamy half-pint of mild. Age-wise, I judged Geordie to be in his mid-seventies but he had, he informed me, just turned sixty-two.

His voice crackled-and-popped like a warped vinyl record, delivered in self-contained bursts that gave the impression, somehow, of being part of a pre-recorded monologue on which the needle was being lifted and lowered by unseen forces.

I remember him. He was a lost lad.

Lost? What do you mean?

Plenty of them round here.

Did you know him well?

[Shakes head] I'd just see him about when I was out with Claudette.

Claudette?

My dog. I'd take her out at night, so we'd meet less dogs. Claudette didn't like other dogs because she didn't think she was one. That's when I'd see him, Doug, out and about.

Would you happen to know where he is now? I'd like to speak to him if I could.

He's dead.

Excuse me? When? How?

When that bomb went off, he was there.

The New Year bomb from 1993?

Aye. There's still thousands of them right under our feet. All sorts just waiting to be dug up.

You're saying Doug was responsible?

402

That's what I heard. I saw him the night it happened. Some lads were knocking him about. Horrible lads. Round here's always been bad for that. When they went, that's when me and Claudette went over. He was blotto, and I couldn't understand owt he was saying. I think he was afraid of her.

Claudette? What kind of dog was she?

A greyhound. She was beautiful. I was on the river one day, and there was a black bag on the bank. It was making a noise and when I opened it, it was full of dead pups. Claudette was the only one still alive. She was such a beautiful dog, and soft as shite. That's what I tried to tell him, Doug, but he wasn't making any sense.

Did you stay with him? Where did he go?

I got him on his feet and let him get on. He went off in the direction of the building site, and I don't know what else he done after, before he blew himself up.

Did he have friends? Anyone he went around with?

There was one bloke. This stocky lad. Shifty.

Do you have a name? Anything?

[Shakes head].

OK, well, thank you very much Mr Coombes, it's been lovely speaking to you.

You know, people used to call Claudette the Street Sweeper. If there was a plastic bottle on the floor, she'd carry it miles in her gob until we found a bin. Then she'd see another one and she'd have that too. Sometimes she'd have four or five bottles at once. Have you ever seen a dog do that?

She sounds nice. I lost my dog recently.[41]

Aye, she was the best dog ever. Another thing she used to do was…[42]

Doug Cont.

---

[41] Ludwig, by the way, was the only dog I ever felt anything for. His instant-coffee eyes peered out at a world in which he never seemed to quite know his place. He was also the only one of Dad's dogs not to have had that choke-chain streak of combustible violence, the prerequisite of all his earlier beasts, though Dad still span yarns about Ludwig's savagery. The castrated would-be burglar being a tale he was particularly fond of telling. Appearances had to be upheld, I suppose.

Because of this, I'd worried Ludwig wouldn't cut mustard in the Barr household but, surprisingly, Dad took to his lumbering placidity. It was a new development. My entire life, the house had shook with the boom of huge dogs. In fact, Chopin's (see FN.11) machine-like barks had probably been the last thing my mother heard as she departed this world. So in that respect, perhaps Dad's love for Ludwig stemmed from the fact that he was the first dog to ever give him silence enough to grieve. To just close his eyes and wrestle his loss.

[42] Numerous Claudette-related anecdotes followed. Before I left the Labour Club I emptied my bladder. It was in the urinal that I met the gentleman who put me on the trail of Ian Pavel (see FN.1).

2/3/1987

Not written in this for while coz I'm back at Mams. Old room. She's given all my stuff to "poor African babbies what needed it." I want to ask her why Jesus allows these poor African babbies to die shrivelling in the sun with flies in their eyes, while she can watch it happen on her colour telly, sitting in her nice comfy armchair with a tin of Quality Street.

First thing I did was get pissed & it was fucking glorious. Have been wrecked ever since. Mam doesn't like it, but I'll be gone soon. Council given me a flat on estate. I told those cunts I didn't want to go back coz there's people I don't want to see but do they give a fuck?

12/4/1987

Burn Estate's gone downhill. Whole streets boarded up. Nasty scunners on BMXs. This wind blowing through the place what makes you feel like Last Cunt on Earth. What happened? Here's my flat, 7B Campbell Road: cig-burned settee with foam puking out. Single bed, jizz-stained mattress. Wardrobe with no hangers & half-picked-off Gary Mabbutt footy sticker on inside of door.

This must be what Karen meant by My Future.

I made it Karen. I made it.

20/5/87

Had to get out today. Can't take flat anymore. Took my drink up field. I like how the streets fall away & tarmac crumbles & the knotweed rolls back the world. Crickets sing but you never see them. Dragonflies cut up the air. Close my eyes & I'm not even on estate. I'm nowhere.

There's a hole. A well. Don't know what's down it or how deep it goes but I talk into it & listen for echoes that never

405

come. Only a silence filled with ghosts of other sounds & a fear that any second the silence will break. I piss down hole. Chuck my empties down.

Last night I waited in alley opposite Sarah's house. Her mam closed the curtains at 9 but I stayed there all night [**unintelligible scrawl**] can't stop imagining her with Pierre. Fucking him, holding herself open like the magazines. Other times they're just holding hands & that's worse.

So was lying next to hole thinking about this when I heard a voice. Opened my eyes & sun was down. Orange across rooftops. One or two stars. Cold. I'd nodded off. Must have dreamed it. I got up slow like an old man. My cider was on rim & was about to pick it up when someone said my name. Coming from the hole. From _in_ the hole. A voice from far away: Come. Down. Here.

Other me did what it said. Leaned over into nothing.

Come. Down. Here. With. Me.

I can't, I whispered. I'm Scared.

Shhh…

I put a foot on rim. But the thought of falling…

No, I said. You come up.

The hole said nowt. I looked down. Heard metal thuds from below, getting louder. Something climbing up to me & then I woke up & it was early morning. My hand down my keks. Rolled over & puked. Cider bottle still on rim where I left it. Downed last bit & looked down well.

Nowt there.

Checked my pockets. Nobody had been through them. £17 of giro. Enough to keep me going as long as I didn't eat much. I don't eat much.

*I watch films when I'm not stripping houses. I'll watch anything, not fussy. Watched one recently about [**unintelligible**] chased round desert by bondage blokes in monster trucks. Another where two dickheads make a robot woman what won't shag them. Tonight I watched Frankenstein. Flat head. Trapped under beam in burning windmill. Credits roll. Got no sympathy for him. That's what you get if you expect love.*

In my viewing I've noticed one kind of scene in particular popping up again & again. Always starts with something weird. Like hero realising he's got mind powers in alley & floats up through lines of washing on brainwaves. Or speccy kid fucks up flick-knife punks with secret ninja moves learned off old Jap fella. Or cartoon where mouse chases cats down street.

In all these scenes there's a pisshead. Wrapped in rags, fingerless gloves, slumped by bins with brown bag bottle. From the shadows he sees what happens & in every film he does the same thing: looks slantways at bottle then tips it into the gutter.

Two things wrong with this.

1: No serious drinker would EVER pour out booze. <u>EVER</u>. Whatever awful shite's going on around you, you never let go of the bottle coz it's the only thing floating you on the sea of your nightmare.

2: Drinkers never doubt their eyes. What you see is REAL. Shadow men in corners of your eye: <u>REAL</u>. Wriggly things under the wallpaper: <u>REAL</u>. The booze gives you the right kind of eyes to see what's always been there.

& what's there is the truth. I know, coz Emily showed me.

*

Saw the family moving out of the first house on Loom Street when I was coming back from Fat Gary's with the Scotch blend. Had to act fast. Once word gets round a house is empty it's a race to strip it before new people move in or council puts shutters up.

But I needed Ian's help. At first he held out, like usual. Like it was beneath him. But things have changed in his world & [scribble] He thinks I don't know, but I do. The cunt's brought it on himself. The way he treated her, I'm surprised she took as long as she did.

We waited till it got dark & broke in round back. Nobody hanging around. Good sign. Sent Ian into kitchen to get at pipework under sink. I went upstairs. Boiler duty, bathroom fittings, taps & that. Only had torch to see with. Beam spazzing up walls. Floorboards creaking. Place empty just a few hours & already dead. Mildew stink of the Dead. Went into bedroom that must've belonged to a little lass coz the walls pink. Found a dolly in there, face down. People always leave things when they leave. Small things what have a power I don't understand. Scrunched up sock. Hairpin. Old shopping list. Things what make me go tight inside. I left dolly where it was & went in bathroom.

Shone torch on two eyes looking back at me.

My muscles went to glass. The eyes were just above toilet rim, the closed lid resting on top of her head. Sharp fingernails clicking porcelain. Then she started coming out & I saw her. Thin nose. Liquorice-shred lips. Shatterteeth. Green skin. She opened her mouth wide & that's when I knew it was Emily. I wanted to sink with her into total dark. Just the two of us forever. I caressed torch on/off button like I would the skin of a lover. If I had a lover.

Emily smiled. Her tongue a black thing rolling over teeth

to lick lips & I knew she was dead. I'd seen her dead in car, mouth hanging with blood & then Ian screaming downstairs & I dropped the [torch and it (?)] bounced & I was on knees scrambling for it & pointed it back at toilet but Emily gone. Shut lid black against white. My dick harder than in years. Reached out to open lid but stopped. No guts. Weak. Vincent was right.

Ian came up with hand wrapped in shirt. The thing in wall he wanted was caught on something else in wall so when he'd yanked it with no gloves he sliced palm open like a muppet mouth. Mouth hanging with blood. Said he was going to A&E, left me alone again. Water trickling down toilet bowl. Soft plink of water on tiles. That just happened. Repeat: that just happened. I downed last of Scotch Blend. Tasted like shite. But then, everything I drink tastes like shite.

[undated] [43]

Saw her tonight. Sarah. [In town(?)] with husband. Two bairns. Young girls. Bobble hats. Duffle coats. Holding hands. He said something in her ear. She laughed [clouds of white(?)]. Only two people on earth who'll ever know what's funny [scribble] Shop windows lit up with Christmas & she walked right past me. Why not? I'm invisible now. Watched them melt into crowd & that's when tooth started up.

Ian got caught in Brit[ish] Hea[r]t [Foundation(?)]. Took to police. Fuck him. I got drink [and] got home.

---

[43] The final entry is almost certainly written in run up to N.Y.E 1993, thus putting several years between the penultimate entry and this. It is written in a colouring book across a picture of a pig-tailed girl frolicking in a swimming pool. Someone (Doug?) has haphazardly coloured the girl green.

Tooth screaming. Never been this bad. That prison dentist said it could go in 10 years [or could go(?)] tomorrow. Ticking timebomb. His words.

Interview with Paula Yardley. 10th December, 2016 [44]

[44] Many tortured months into the creation of this very document, I received a package of letters (see F.N 3), the contents of which I've still not entirely digested therefore won't – not even sure if *could* – get into here. Sufficed to say, they compelled me to pay a visit to Sober Hall, a residential home in High Leven, to see a man by the name of Henry Szarka. I knew this to be Henry's whereabouts as on more than one occasion the ladies in Corina's salon had discussed him fondly. Henry was a well-known figure on the estate. For many years he drove the mobile library of which I, as a child, had been a frequent patron.

I made no appointment at Sober Hall and when I got there I was told by the lady at reception that Mr Szarka was currently recuperating in hospital after a flare up of emphysema. However, he would, she was sure, be back in a week or so and be up to receiving visitors. Apparently, he didn't get many of those.

As I was leaving, I passed the manager's office just as a woman was emerging. She was tall, early fifties, with striking green eyes and a port-wine boomerang (or torn-off fingernail) on her left temple. I took a closer look at the sign on the door: PAULA YARDLY, DIRECTOR. I thought, no it couldn't be...could it?

A week later I called her. Posing as a family friend, I arranged a meeting to discuss Henry's health ahead of paying a visit to the man himself. I decided to secretly record the conversation.

I've since struggled to find ethical justification for doing so, ultimately concluding there to be none. What I am doing is selfish, pure and simple: the digging into of other people's scar tissue in order to account for my own. In fact, this entire document is a monument to that impulse. Thus, like all self-servers, I've had to resort to a kind of 'moral squinting' in order to substantiate my actions. In my case, I sense that out there, beyond my meagre ken, the answers I seek are actually threads of the Total Understanding which we all, to varying degrees, feel the tug of not possessing in its entirety. Without meaning to, I keep coming back to the

So, Paula, how is he?

Well, he's on oxygen and a steroid nebulizer. His dementia's being managed with medication, but his condition has deteriorated extremely rapidly of late. He's convinced there's someone in his toilet, for example. You'd be best off speaking to his doctor. Still, he's a character. Still very popular with the other residents, the ladies especially. It must be the hair.

I don't want to impose too much today. I really only want to say hello.

_____

imagery of threads: threads that are woven, threads that guide. Perhaps our only hope of personal comprehension is to follow our own thread as it entwines with others, to persist in such entanglements until such time we are able, with luck, to step back and see our contribution to the tapestry as a whole.

Didn't my own situation bear out this theory? To wit: I receive a letter mentioning a Henry Szarka, resident of the care home managed by Paula Yardly, the wife of Ian, the man who knew Doug, Doug who had perhaps come closer to the truth of my father than anyone; the self-same Doug whose broken thread I was already hard at work trying to follow! Coincidental? I let myself be seduced by Ian's idea that maybe the world had set things in motion, and that it was my job to be open to it. My reasoning, then, followed that the secret recording of my conversation with Paula – and, by extension, the writing of this very document – was defensible on the grounds that not only would it afford me my own personal piece of mind, but might, in some wild way I couldn't possibly fathom, also one day afford others theirs. Who was to say this document would not guide someone else to a vantage point from which they, too, could see the pattern they weaved on the loom? In short, wasn't I just doing my bit?

But alas, being engaged in such highfalutin metaphysics meant that I forgot to charge the MP3 recorder that morning before leaving the house...

I'm sure he'll appreciate a visitor.

May I ask you something else?

Yes?

This is a little odd, but I think I know your husband.

Really?

From the Burn Estate, years ago.

Burn Estate? My husband's from Edinburgh.

I'm talking about...your husband's Ian, right?

My husband's Caleb. Who did you say you were again?

Alan Barr. I was speaking to Ian – Ian Pavel – earlier this year, and he led me to believe that the two of you...were married?

Ian? Haven't seen or heard from him these past 25 years.

Why would he tell me that?

You tell me **[laughs]**. So how was he?

He seemed...I thought he seemed alright. We mostly talked about his friend Doug.

Oh God. Him.

You knew him?

I wanted nothing to do with him, or the dirty little schemes they cooked up.

I got the impression Ian was doing fine. He said he was running a business.

Let me guess, the trainers?

The rare trainers, yes. He sold his collection so the two of you could make a fresh start.

Ah, the collection! Hundreds of pairs in a lock up somewhere, right? He tried that guff on me as well, but I only ever saw the same three or four pairs, and those he'd pinched off his brother Richie. I remember him – Richie – ringing up *my* house, demanding I get him to give them back. I thought he was talking about cigarettes but –

Tobacco?

Right, the stupid names. **[Sighs]**. Ian lied about everything, even the littlest things. I don't know if he even realised he was doing it. He had this feeling like he should be someone – some version of himself – only he never knew what it was. He was so insecure. None of his family were speaking to him. He didn't have any friends, except Doug.

If it's not too personal, may I ask how long you were together?

[Doing mental calculations] God, two years nearly. I

finally woke up once he got sacked and started pestering me for money. Banging on my door at three in the morning drunk. I can't believe I was ever with him at all... Excuse me, Mr Barr, fun as this trip down memory lane has been, I have work to do.

Yes, of course. Thank you for speaking to me and I'm sorry for the mix up.

If you see him again, tell him to stop saying we're married, will you?

I will.

Also, before you visit Henry, I should ask, how do you feel about birds of prey? Owls, hawks, that kind of thing?

I, ah...why?

Because th–

[mp3 battery dies].

Ian. Cont.

Well, I think I've got everything I need for now. Thanks for speaking with me.

I've got plenty more stories for you. Some really good ones.

I should get back before dark. Perhaps another time? Give my regards to Paula.

Yep. Are you sure you won't stay for one more?

I don't think I can drink any more lemonade.

Yeah, well, I should probably be getting back too, before the missus wonders where I am. I've got a batch of pristine München [45] coming in what needs the paperwork doing. They've been sitting in some lock-up in Dusseldorf for years. I'll be able to retire on these if I play my cards right.

OK. Well, good luck.

You know, I don't think about Doug much now. Maybe that's a bad thing, but life doesn't stop, does it? So this has been good. Remembering him makes me thankful for everything I've got.

I'll be in touch if I need anything else. Could I have your number?

[**Ian gives me his digits** [46]] Hey, one more thing.

Yes?

About this remuneration…

---

[45] **1970s. Originally red or blue. Cult status.**

[46] **Later, after my conversation with Paula, I tried reaching Ian on this number. It was not recognised.**

Recorded telephone conversation with Kaspar Kirsch, 13th April 2016 [47]

Hello, Kaspar? My name's Alan Barr and I believe you used to run a shop on Jesmond Road?

I did, but I'm not in that business anymore, sorry.

I realise that, I was just wondering if you could point me in the right direction? I'm looking for a pair of Adidas Atlantis.

What?

Adidas Atlantis. Ultramarine leather with white–

They don't exist.

…white stripes, gold sole? Only 100 pairs ever made? A friend led me to believe you once purchased a pair.

This friend is having you on, trust me.

Are you sure?

---

[47] *Kaspar Kirsch* was not in business anymore, though several online articles and 'casual' forums reassured me it had at least once done so. I then entered 'Kirsch' into an online telephone directory and returned one 'K.Kirsch.' The man I was after.

A thought: since beginning this document, I've come to realise just how much everything hinges on the name we happen to be born into. How different would this all have turned out had the names of those involved been other than what they were? If I had not been born Barr?

Who is this? Rudy, is that you? [48]

It's Alan Barr, sir. I was told you came into possession of a pair on New Year's Eve, 1993. They were part of a larger collection sold to you by a man called Ian Pavel.

Who?

Ian Pavel.

[**Laughs**] Come on Rudy, enough of this horseshit.

[**Hangs up**].

---

[48] **???**

THE FINAL LEFT

Henry Szarka of Sober Hall

Take a right, Paula Yardley had said, past reception and the day room, then make another right and follow the corridor all the way to the end. One final left, and Henry's room was at the far end. I couldn't miss it.

Garlands of disconsolate tinsel drooped from the ceiling panels. On the walls, separating the whiteboard staff-rotas, framed old-timey advertisements echoed across the gulf of decades: *Bovril: Puts BEEF into You*, *Lux WON'T Shrink Woollies*, *Lucozade: Replaces Lost Energy – Invaluable in Sickness and in Health*. The smell of boiled lunch drifted wraith-like, infused with the tang of disinfectant and, fainter still – the bass note – whatever lingering human mishap that had required disinfecting. I walked carefully so that my soles wouldn't squeak, avoiding the joins in the sea-green linoleum flooring.

The girl behind reception was too busy to notice me. Whatever she was looking for was evidently not among the sheaves of paper she was rifling. She spat a scissor-snick curse under her breath: 'For *effs* sake.' With her head lowered, the flakes in her parting betrayed need for medicated shampoo. I left her to it, and pressed on.

Since receiving my mother's letters a month earlier, I'd attempted in all seriousness to conceal from myself the fact that I was afraid of coming here, of seeing the man at the end of the final left. In this endeavour, of course, I'd failed, as one cannot dupe oneself, merely shame oneself in the attempt. Therefore, in preparation for today, I'd dredged my memory for Henry-shaped fragments, tried tapping into the boy I'd once been as I waited for him on the kerb with my finished library books in my armpit. But I'd failed there, too. If only I'd known then what I knew now, I could have paid more attention. Instead, there was nothing but

421

the dashed boundary around the man, a 'cut here' line along a bag of oven chips.

Preoccupied as I was with such thoughts, I almost walked past the day room without giving it a glance, but at the last moment I happened to look up and promptly stopped dead. The room was full of birds of prey, a dozen at least: barn owls, kites, kestrels – I've leafed through my fair share of twitcher tomes – peregrines and sparrowhawks; all bob-and-weave on the arms of residents wearing heavy, medieval–looking leather gauntlets. The residents themselves were frowsy. Tatterdemalion nightwear and boil-washed undershirts, clear plastic tubes disappearing up nostrils. The birds turned their heads towards me in that eerie way birds do, their petulant tar-drop eyes glaring, and it was several moments more before the residents themselves – their senses not as serrated as the killers on their arms – followed suit.

Are you afraid of birds of prey? Paula had asked earlier while I secretly recorded her, but who, after truly considering such a question – after taking into account the blinding speed and merciless talons of such creatures – who could sincerely claim they weren't?

The elderly lady nearest me sat in a high-backed, throne-like chair and her eyebrows were drawn on. 'I've got a sparrowhawk,' she said, 'isn't he handsome?' The sparrowhawk itself eyed me with prehistoric coldness. Its perma-scowling beak sent a familiar trickle of unease down my spine.

'Handsome, yes,' I said.

A younger woman in the middle of the room looked over and said, 'Please, no sudden movements. You don't want to spook them,' though I was unclear as to whether she was referring to the birds or the residents. She tacked her way towards me, through the clutter of chairs, past several other bird handlers wearing the same black polo shirt she was. Some of them crouched by the sides of chairs, murmuring comforting words to the residents. The birds themselves, as far as I could tell, seemed above it all.

The younger woman reached me. 'Didn't they tell you we were here today?' she asked.

I shook my head. 'Well, actually, the manager said something just now...'

She was blonde – natural, I thought – fortyish. Pretty. Embroidered in yellow thread above her left breast: KIMBERLY. She was not, I noticed, wearing a ring. 'We come into places like this a lot,' she said. 'It helps them, you know? Brings them out of themselves. There's been studies.'

I scanned the room, remembering descriptions of Henry. Paula: *He's still very popular with the other residents, the ladies especially. It must be the hair.* And my mother's letter: *His hair was still ducks-arsed, but now had a touch of grey at the temples.* There would be more than a touch now, but regardless, I could see no corresponding head of hair in the day room. Nothing before me but wisps, tufts, straggles, and at least one toupee.

The old woman lifted the sparrowhawk on her arm and addressed Kimberly. 'He looks like a Gus. They mate for life, don't they?'

Kimberly's practised smile just about reached her eyes. 'No, they don't.' She turned to me. 'So, who're you visiting?'

Gus glared at me. I'd only ever seen a sparrowhawk once before, when I was a child, and only then for about three seconds. The bird was stunning up close: his striped chest feathers exquisite; his irises the same cadmium-yellow as his razor-tipped feet. The same colour as Kimberly's stitched name.

'My Dad,' I said. 'But he must be in his room.'

Kimberly nodded sympathetically. 'You should get him to participate. These birds do wonders. There's been studies.'

'This one's giving me the eye,' I said, meaning Gus. He didn't look like a Gus to me.

'I'm sure he likes you.' Unusual parts of me tingled when she smiled at me.

'Can he fly?' I asked.

'Oh aye. In the wild they'd be swooping down to feed on small mammals, but we've trained these ones. They're really very docile.'

I saw myself reflected in the tranquil murder of Gus' dilated pupil, and remembered the death I'd witnessed all those years ago at my father's bird-table – the black lightning-bolt leaving naught but free-falling down and viscera in its wake – and I thought, *Is that so?*

Kimberly's polo top was hanging out at one side. As she tucked it into her jeans, I caught a glimpse of delicate pink flesh. My surge of longing collapsed instantly into self-flagellation. *You think she's interested in YOU, limpy? Haven't you enough to contend with today? Do you really need to add rejection to the list?* Recently, I'll admit, I'd been getting worse. What had started as the surreptitious checking of ring fingers, the glancing at of women in search of the tell-tale signs of loneliness in and around the eyes, had gradually been incorporated into a full-blown Science of Yearning which included – but was not limited to – ascertaining potential romantic compatibility with women

424

on the bus via the contents of their shopping bags. I was becoming, in a word, strange.

So that Kimberly wouldn't be able to read any of this madness on my face, I turned back to the day room. A line of something I'd read came back to me: *These predatory birds are evil.* Where had I read that? Whose words? It didn't matter. I said goodbye to Kimberly and left the Day Room, walking with a stiff-legged gait I hoped concealed from her the worst of my limp.

My clammy palms squeaked the wooden guiderail running along both walls of the deserted corridor. Outside the windows, the day was dying; jaundiced clouds distending under their own weight, sleet splattering the panes and gathering on the sills. I walked on, each step removing me incrementally from the warmth and light of the day room, from Kimberly's smooth unattainability. I fell into daydream: Kimberly and I at a party, the host's breathless question: *So how did the two of you meet?* Kimberly smiles at me as if to say: *Do you want to tell him, or shall I?* Then I say: *Well, I was paying a visit to an old folk's home to see my Dad – or maybe he's not, but that's a different story – and there she was with a sparrowhawk. We just hit it off –* I snake my arm around her waist, our hip bones clinking like champagne flutes – *and the rest, as they say, is history.*

When I was younger, my Grandad Ronnie would ask me if I was courting. He'd say things like, *I saw you canoodling with some lass round the back of the shops,* or *Who you smooching this week?* It made him laugh to see me squirm, and Mam would slap his arm, *Knock it off! He's going red!* But in truth I didn't mind. His playfulness implied that regardless of how late a bloomer I was, he had confidence that I *would* eventually align myself with the broad curve of human experience. With Dad, however, it was different. He never said a word regarding my lack of success with the opposite sex, and I detected within his silence a whole howling world of expectant consternation. Like most other boys my age, I thought a lot about girls, but I began to do so increasingly through the lens of my father's disappointment. To even entertain the idea of, say, asking a girl to Wimpey, or to the Ritzy, was to also envisage Dad's chagrin at then having what he'd always suspected of me confirmed when I was inevitably turned down. In the end I never asked anyone, though I became increasingly desperate to do so. It wouldn't have mattered whether I even liked her – I'd have gone out with anyone if it meant he left me alone.

I reached the end of the corridor and turned right. Nobody was around. Laminated posters were on every door, each including the name of that room's resident and a montage of pictures I imagined represented pastimes that person enjoyed. For example, Elizabeth Treelaw's poster displayed stock-images of ballroom dancers, while Spitfires and Messerschmitts dogfought to the death in the cobalt-blue skies taped to Cliff Wood's door. Cakes decorated Dorothy Volk's door, which was open enough for me to see that her room was utterly devoid of possessions – the mattress stripped, the plastic bed rails lowered in the massing gloom. Don't jump to conclusions, Alan. Perhaps Dorothy was in the day room with the others, affording staff the opportunity to give her place the once over? Perhaps Dorothy was the lady with the sparrowhawk I'd talked to? Sweet, happy Dorothy with the drawn-on eyebrows, who wasn't at all cooling on a slab somewhere?

The second corridor was the same as the first. At the junction, a mop and steel bucket leaned against the wall. The bucket itself was rusted and had evidently been in use for some time. It appealed to me, the bucket. We had a plastic one at home that felt perpetually on the verge of cracking whenever I attempted to wring the mop out into it. The kitchen floor had always been my chore, a battle I'd been losing since I was head-high to the mop itself. Too many large dogs, you see, and when it rained they'd pad into the kitchen to shake out their coats. Dad never took off his boots, either. The trails he left on the lino were Arthur Murray-numbered footprints to a dance the rhythms of which would always elude me.

For a moment, I wished myself to be the mop bucket. Things would be so much easier if I were the mop bucket. I'd have but one expectation made of me – a simple task with a definitive end.

'I'd be the greatest mop bucket the world has ever know,' I said aloud as I turned the final left.

There was a window at the end of the corridor. Pitch dark outside, sleet on the cusp of snow proper, and as I approached I saw myself reflected in the glass. Behold Alan Barr: those horrible NHS specs, that stubby button nose. Balding from front to back...and how had I let myself get so *fat*? Certainly, a case could be made that my lack of exercise was due to mobility issues arising from my boyhood injuries, but that would negate the influence of a certain brand of microwavable mini-pizzas unappetisingly named *Pizzips!*. These delicacies came in such flavours as Texan BBQ, Pork Pileup, and Tandoori Chicken. I probably partook three to four times a week, and had done so for more years than I cared to count.

I turned from my reflected bloat. Henry's poster was embellished with black-and-white photographs of Teddy Boys: young men in the sort of ostentatiously tight-fitting suits I associated with Victorian Mourning – all ornate lapels, cravats, and drainpipe trousers, their hair slicked into outrageous edifices. Eyes brooding through curtains of cigarette smoke. Women whirling in centrifugal dresses. Rock 'n' Roll-possessed greasers wrestling huge guitars, caterwauling into chromed microphones. The names of some of those singers came to me: Chuck Berry, Eddie Cochran, Gene Vincent. Elvis too, of course, before the deep-fried paranoia took hold. And my mother's favourite, Marty Wilde. I had memories of her playing his record for me – the reverential way she held the disc in its musty cardboard sleeve, which was unadorned save for a handwritten price in an old-fashioned currency I didn't understand. The LP itself didn't sit quite flush for the needle, which somehow complimented Wilde's metallic yip-yelped croon. The song itself was beautiful. It wasn't until I played it again years after her death that I realised he had been singing about suicide.

Outside Henry's door, I braced myself and knocked.

No answer. Maybe he was sleeping? Zonked out on medication? Or, you know…

These predatory birds are evil.

I put a hand to my breast pocket, felt the letter there above the thump of my punch-bagged heart, and let myself in.

Henry Szarka sat in the chair by the window, sucking on an oxygen tank. He wore a grey velvet-cuffed drape coat over an A-Bomb-white shirt and a dude-rancher's choker – a silver bull skull cinched by two rawhide tongs. On his feet were scarlet-suede brothel creepers, the soles at least three inches thick, and his *hair*…Paula had been right, his hair was magnificent. The same mercurial silver-grey as his suit, it jutted majestically out over the precipice of his forehead like a brylcreemed Hindenburg seconds before the fireball. A tube ran from the gauge at the top of his oxygen tank to a clear plastic mask he pressed to his face with a hand, I noticed, tattooed with the faded ghosts of swallows. He had to be almost eighty, and looked it.

Henry's eyes flicked between me and the other door in the room, which I assumed was the bathroom. The oxygen mask fogged when he spoke. 'Who – *wheeze* – you?'

'I'm Alan.' I was shaking. Why was I shaking? Why hadn't I practised this? The door closed behind me.

'No – *wheeze* – leave it open!'

I wedged the rubber stopper under the door. 'Are you OK?'

'You've got to – *wheeze* – help me.'

'Do you want a carer?' I reached for the emergency cord dangling near the radiator.

'No! – *wheeze* – *you*.' His hand rose and fell on his immaculately tailored chest. What would I do if he keeled over? I'd skimmed a first-aid manual once, but if ever there was a subject beyond the realm of books, it was CPR.

'Henry, try to calm down. I'm Alan Barr. You were a friend of my mother's, Jean.'

'I don't know – *wheeze* – no Jean,' he said.

'Jean Barr? From Loom Street? You used to lend her books?'

His eyes narrowed. 'Loom Street? I knew a – *wheeze* – lass from Loom Street once.'

'Yes, well, I'm sorry to have to tell you that she passed

away some years ago now. But that's, ah, that's by the by. The reason I'm here today is that before she died, she, ah, well, she was corresponding with someone. Actually… anyway…' – *Damn it, Alan!* – 'Anyway, those letters were recently sent to me…' Was he even listening to me? He kept glancing nervously at the bathroom door. But I couldn't falter now. If I did, I'd never get it out. I marshalled myself.

'Well, Henry, to cut a long story short, her final letter appears to suggest that you…that you might perhaps be–'

'I remember.' Henry said in a viscous voice. 'We'd take her up the old – *wheeze* – waterworks and – *wheeze* – oh…'

'I beg your pardon?'

'*Wheeze* – I know what you're thinking but – *wheeze* – it weren't like that. She came of her – *wheeze* – of her own – *wheeze*–'

'Who did? Who are you talking about?'

'*Accord*,' he said. 'Her mam was – *wheeze* – crackers. She wanted – *wheeze* – it.' He closed his eyes. 'She did.'

I unfolded the last letter my mother ever wrote, dated New Year's Eve 1991. Henry took it from me with a palsied hand.

'I'm talking about *Jean Barr*,' I said. 'This letter suggests…well, read for yourself.'

As his eyes hobbled across my mother's words, I took the opportunity to scrutinise him closer, to try and detect myself in him, but even on the threshold of octogenarianism, Henry still trumped me in several physical categories. His features, shrunken and crumpled as they may have been – except for his ears, they were still rather large – remained pleasing, as if Father Time had decided to season his good looks, rather than eradicate them entirely. He also dressed better in the extreme winter

430

of his life than I had at even the Summer Equinox of mine. And then there was the hair; thick enough to stand a garden trowel in, whereas all I still had going for me in that department were a few wisps of ashen candyfloss. However, there *was* something off about him. Now that I was closer to the man, I became aware of a smell; something at once naggingly familiar and not entirely unpleasant, but which danced just beyond identification.

'Remember?' I said. 'It was during The Day of the Dark? You drove to Loom Street and my mother came to see you in…in your van?'

The letter fell from his hand. 'I did terrible – *wheeze* – things in that van.'

A groan came from the bathroom. Henry's face elongated in terror. He sucked on the mask at a frenzied rate.

'It's just the pipes,' I said. 'It happens in winter.'

Diamante beads of sweat sluiced the deep crease between his eyebrows. He held the oxygen mask to his mouth like a trembling CB receiver. 'That's no – *wheeze* – pipes. There's something down there. A – *wheeze* – dead – *wheeze* – woman. She talks to me at – *wheeze* – night.'

My testicles retracted. What had Doug written in his journals? *Liquorice-shred lips? Shatterteeth?* 'A woman?'

'*Wheeze.* Aye.'

'What does she…say?'

Pointing at the closed bathroom door, he said, 'She says I've to come clean. *Wheeze.* Says she'll take me down there with her – *wheeze* – if I don't.'

'It's just the pipes, Henry. Nobody is talking to you. You're just unwell.' As much for my own sake as for his, I attempted the soothing tone of the bird handlers in the day room.

431

He embarked on a bout of splattering coughs that sounded like the time I'd dropped an entire family-size microwavable lasagne on the kitchen floor. The paisley handkerchief with which he managed to catch the majority of his emitted foulness was already stiff with goo. At the window, bona-fide snow heaped on the ledge, burying us both. I watched it fall as Henry recovered himself.

'I know I'm ill,' he said finally. 'That's – *wheeze* – why you've got to – *wheeze* – hear me out.'

This was the part where I left, I thought. Where I dismissed what Henry was saying as the garbled nonsense of a dying mind; where I forgot about why I was receiving letters from my long-departed mother, and let go the nagging questions that had brought me to this room. Where I reported this conversation to Paula and then found Kimberly and asked her to have a cup of tea with me. This was that part. But I didn't. Instead, I sat on the edge of Henry's hydraulic bed and said, 'OK Henry, what do you want to say?'

He lowered the mask and each word seemed to sit more heavily on his chest than the last. 'There was a lass – *wheeze* – long time ago now. She'd come in the van. *Wheeze*. She'd leave things in the pages – *wheeze* – for me. Love hearts and that. Said she – *wheeze* – loved me. Gave me – *wheeze* – eyes. You know?'

'No…no, I don't.'

'So I started – *wheeze* – following her. But it wasn't like that. Not – *wheeze* – bad. She knew I was. She – *wheeze* – let me.' A tear as thick and clear as superglue oozed down his cheek. 'One night I seen her – *wheeze* – on her own. Little – *wheeze* – white school socks and–'

'Wait. How *old* was she?'

'*Wheeze*. School age. I seen her on her own so I–'

'What was she called?'

Another long, whistling drag of oxygen. 'Betty,' he said.

'And what did you…?'

'I parked up and waited and then – *wheeze* – then I don't know.'

'What do you mean *I don't know*?'

'I don't know. *Wheeze*. Then – *wheeze* – then she was in the back of the van. I had it – *wheeze* – down a lane. Nobody could – *wheeze* – see. She wanted to. They look like bairns but – *wheeze* – they're not.'

'Yes,' I said, 'they are.'

Faintly, from some distance, I thought I heard the squawking of a bird.

'I drove to the burn,' Henry said. 'Into the – *wheeze* – trees. Then…I…don't know.'

'Did you let her go?'

'Don't – *wheeze* – know.'

'So you took a little girl, only you don't remember what you did? Or what happened after? What *do* you remember?'

'That there were others. *Wheeze*. Other ones. I never got caught.'

Maybe I was too close to this? I was liable to end up in here with him if I didn't start employing more objectivity. 'Henry, I don't know what to do with what you're telling me.'

The bird squawked again, closer now. When I turned to the door, Henry said, 'Lily whatshername.'

'Excuse me?'

'Lily whatshername. Lily – *wheeze* – Butler.'

'What about Lily Butler?'

This time he pointed to his own toiling chest.

'Henry, I'm sorry but I don't believe you. Lily disappeared just over a year ago and you're…well, frankly, you're not a well man.'

He showed me the tobacco-brown nubs of his teeth. The teeth of my father. 'Afore this' – he tipped the oxygen mask – 'I was still my own – *wheeze* – boss. Still had my gaff. She wasn't planned. I was just – *wheeze* – out in the woods – *wheeze* – walking. And she was there. Bonny lass – *wheeze* – all on her lonesome. Once I saw her it all – *wheeze* – came back. The feeling. The *urge*. I thought – *wheeze* – she's your last – *wheeze* – hoorah. I said – *wheeze* – *Hey, I've got some canny new computer games – wheeze – in the van. Do you want first dibs afore I put them – wheeze – out?*'

'You *still* had that van?'

So much talking was taking its toll. He nodded weakly. 'It's parked outside. They – *wheeze* – gave it to me.'

'Impossible.'

He didn't answer, just breathed fitfully, eyes half-closed.

'Why not tell the police?' I said. 'Why tell me?'

He shook his head. 'She says – *wheeze* – says I'm to tell you.'

'The woman in the toilet said that?'

'*Wheeze.* Aye.'

'But why me?'

He shook his head again. The toilet kept up a gentle tinkling from the other side of the bathroom door, and I thought: *Her tongue a black thing rolling over teeth to lick lips & I knew she was dead.* I picked up my mother's letter. 'I think my coming here was a mistake. You should rest.'

His wet eyes rolled in his head. 'Don't leave me alone. *Wheeze* – please.'

'Henry, Mr. Szarka – am I saying that right? – I really do have to be going.'

A string of brown drool clung to the mask when he took it from his face again. 'She waited – *wheeze* – for me to get done with the bairns. Just drifted around the shelves.'

I stopped at the threshold of the room.

'Day of the Dark, like you said. So dark we – *wheeze* – couldn't see. Had to get the van – *wheeze* – panel beat after.' He made a feeble fist. 'Hailstones as big as – *wheeze* – this. She seemed so…'

'She seemed so what?'

'Sad,' he said.

From the corridor came further squawking and, now, yelling.

'And then what?' I said. 'What else?'

He wept. His frail body wracked within his immaculate clothes. 'I don't know.'

I slipped Mam's letter back into my pocket. 'I'll ask a member of staff to come down. I'll leave the door open.'

And when I left, it came to me what he smelled of. Hotdog water. He smelled exactly like hotdog water.

Reversing Paula's directions, I took a right and closed in on the subsequent left. I decided that, just to be safe, I should tell Paula what Henry had said. It was the responsible thing to do, although, if I'm being completely honest, I was also eager to hear a health professional reaffirm to me the extent of Henry's illness, for her to advise chalking up the horror of his words to the disintegration of his mind. Because I could feel said horror spreading within me, soaking like the crudest of oils into the whitest of carpets.

Something was wrong up ahead. A puddle of grey water

was expanding from around the corner. The mop bucket I'd seen earlier was knocked over, the mop itself splayed melodramatically across the linoleum floor. Several tawny feathers lay scattered here and there. I stooped awkwardly to pick one up, fondled it between my fingers in that way television detectives do clues, but it was utterly without smell when I ran it experimentally under my nose.

From the direction of the day room a man cried, 'Grab him for Christ's sake!'

'*You* grab him! He's closer to you!' A woman – Kimberly? – yelled back. This was followed by a long, rusty peal which sawed at the upper registers of my hearing. Something heavy broke and someone screamed.

What the *eff* was going on? I slid along the wall until I was afforded a view of the day room corridor. Several bird handlers – Kimberly among them – carried drooping nets, ducking the feathered bedlam slamming repeatedly and violently into the ceiling panels. The bird held some poor creature in its claws. Another bird? No, it was too small and furry for that. I was wondering whether Sober Hall had, say, a pet gerbil, when the elderly gentleman emerged from the day room. He had the hangdog features of a late-career James Stewart, and shook against the matrix of his zimmerframe. Three vivid claw marks raked down his bald head.

Gus the sparrowhawk gripped the wig firmly in its talons, beat its powerful wings amid the tinsel, and screeched.

The old woman on whose arm the bird had earlier perched tottered into view. 'Gus! You bring that back right now! Where are your manners!'

'Bastard came out of nowhere,' James Stewart said.

'People, please!' Paula stepped over the smashed computer monitor on the floor by the reception desk. She was doing a 'shooing' motion I associated with herding sheep. 'Everyone, back in the day room!'

'Bastards used to play holy-hell with our homing pigeons,' James said as he was ushered out of sight. 'So we'd pop 'em with air rifles.'

'They're just acting on instinct,' Kimberly said.

'So were we,' said James.

'Leanne!' Paula yelled from inside the day room. 'First aid!'

Against the ceiling, Gus let go of the wig. It seemed, for an instant, suspended in aether, before he snatched it again and rocketed into a strip-light housing, which dislodged and shattered to the floor to a chorus of terror and delight from the residents.

'Leanne!' Paula roared.

I slid fully into the corridor and my movement caught Kimberly's eye. She looked directly at me and in that moment I forgot about the maelstrom above, the waning Teddy Boy behind, the dead woman below.

Her lips formed silent words: *Don't move.*

She rocked the neck of her bird-net in her palm like a baseline tennis player awaiting service. One of her colleagues – Alex, according to his polo shirt – a young man with neck tattoos, was positioned further down the hall. Another fellow, chinless beneath his ginger goatee, lurked by the entrance to the day room. Behind him, Paula crossed her arms nervously, and behind *her* rubbernecked several residents clearly having a blast.

I edged towards them.

'*What are you doing?*' Kimberly hissed. '*I said don't move!*'

I gave her a goofy, Fonz-like thumbs up which I instantly regretted.

'On the count of three,' her goateed colleague said, 'One, two…*three!*' They swooped their nets in near-synchronicity. Gus shrieked.

The rims of their nets clashed. 'Watch what you're doing!' Kimberly yelled.

'It's not me, it's Alex!' goatee yelled back.

'Shut up!' Alex said, but it was too late. The nets misaligned in such a way as to offer an inviting opening which Gus did not need to be asked twice to take. Wig still in his death grip, he burst free of the nets and headed straight at me.

Now, it's been my experience that in situations such as these, time takes on qualities adverse to those it is commonly supposed to demonstrate. Time did not, for example, *slow down* when, at age fifteen, I regained consciousness while sliding into a well to my death. It did not afford to me one endless, molasses moment in which to deliberate a favourable course of action. For it to have done so would be to suggest that time itself was in some way benevolent – which I don't believe it is – or, perhaps, marginally less fantastically, that I am in possession of the supposed assets (heroism, *nouse* etc.) that allows certain people in certain circumstances to seemingly *bend* time to their personal will. This is also hokum. Then as now, my panic served only to blur any precious remaining seconds I had into a white-noise of paroxysmal motor function, enabling possible such unfathomable actions as…

I don't think I'll ever know why I made a grab for the wig. All I remember is bursting through the skin of my terror to meet Gus' black-gold eyes zeroing in on me. From the day room, I distinctly heard James Stewart call for me to 'show that bastard who's boss'.

So I did. Or more accurately, I tried. As Gus streaked down, I jumped (what in my world passes for a 'jump') to snatch the toupee from the bird's grasp, but my fingertips merely brushed the wig's sandy softness before I landed heavily on my heels, my vertebrae impacting like cars in a pile-up. A grenade of pain exploded at the base of my skull, and then Gus was on me and the world filled with black klaxons of panic, wingbeats, screaming.

Something enveloped me briefly, and suddenly Gus was struggling in Kimberly's net.

'Oh my God, are you OK?' she said.

All I could think to do was my Fonz thumbs-up. Only this time my thumb was slick with blood.

'Leanne!' Paula bellowed.

When I was a child, my Dad built a bird table for the front yard. He poured little piles of seed on it, hung fatballs off hooks screwed into the sides. The fatballs he made himself by dumping birdseed into bacon grease, hand rolling it into balls, and skewering the whole congealing mess with lengths of wire. He'd sit in his chair in the front room for hours, watching and recording visitations, scoring pencil lines into a little leather-bound notebook balanced on his right knee. He taught me the names of the birds that flew in to feed. There were a lot of sparrows, but I didn't much care for them; their dull browns and greys didn't fire my imagination like the regal hues of blue and great-tits did. The crazy paint-by-numbers plumage of the goldfinch; the starling's midnight-rainbow gorgeousness. I loved the way pied wagtails jerked across the seed as if individual frames of their animation had been removed. Dad taught me their calls, too. His whistle was a delicate, crystal tremor and he'd smile at my spluttering emulations. No, he'd say, pursing his lips – press your tongue against your gnashers like *this*. Some of my happiest times with my father were at that window.

I recall one particular day. In my head it's Saturday morning, although I might be making that up, and I'm eight, maybe less. The two of us sitting in the front room as birds flit around the table outside. Nothing out of the ordinary – a drab procession of sparrows – when suddenly, out of the literal blue, a black streak slits the air and pounces. Dad is on his feet in a flash, notebook falling forgotten to the floor.

He hammers on the single pane glass with such force I'm sure it'll shatter. 'Get away! Go on, fuck off!'

But he's too late – it's already over. The blur shoots back into the sky, leaving nothing but a handful of feathers on the now-bloodied birdseed. Seconds have elapsed.

Dad goes outside, his head in the sky, shielding his eyes from the sun. I lean down to pick up his notebook. It's a dog-eared thing which, judging by the tiny pencilled dates inside, he's been keeping longer than he's been keeping me.

He comes back in and stands at the window, rolling up his sleeves. 'Sparrowhawk bastard,' he mutters.

Sparrowhawk bastard. I've never forgotten that. At the time, it was a mystery quite why a sparrow – after all such a tiny, fragile creature sacrificed to the natural order of things – should enrage him so. Indeed, the conundrum would only deepen as I got older because, I thought, hadn't I once been a tiny, fragile creature, too?

*

'Lucky boy,' Ranjit said, 'Looks worse that it is. No stitches.'

Ranjit – for that was how he'd introduced himself upon the ambulance's arrival – was a large medic with latex-gloved hands and soft eyes. I sat in one of the day room thrones, trying to be stoic while he disinfected my talon wounds with stinging iodine swabs. Sitting over from me, James Stewart underwent a similar procedure, and was midway through telling his health professional the protracted and non-sequential tale of how he and his boyhood friends used to 'pop those flying swine right out of the sky'. He held the remains of his hairpiece in milky, misshapen, blue-veined hands that resembled the calcium deposits found deep in underground cave systems. When our eyes met, the conviction gripped me that I had somehow slipped through a tear in the Space/Time Continuum, and was in fact sitting opposite myself some three decades hence.

Ranjit said, 'I feel like I'm in here at least a couple of times a month, but it's usually the normal care-home stuff, you get me? But hawk attacks? This is a new one.'

The bird handlers were carrying away the final cages. Some of the birds inside stared out darkly from behind the bars, while others slept – or feigned sleep – their heads tucked beneath wings. They were so still on their perches that if I hadn't just been the gory climax of an airborne toupee-snatch, I would have sworn them to be the work of a taxidermist. Through the large day room windows, I watched as they were loaded into a white transit van emblazoned with the logo: **CLEVELAND BIRD SANCTUARY**. I saw Gus go in. He seemed profoundly disinterested, and I envied him. The wounds he had left here today were, for him, already forgotten. He suffered no guilt, thus made no mistakes. Caged though he may be, his future was unshackled by his past.

'A few more minutes and you'll be ready to rock and roll,' Ranjit said, and I thought of Marty Wilde, and then of Henry alone (or maybe not), dressed in all his rings and finery, his lungs and mind collapsing at the end of that final left. After Gus had been recaptured, I'd pulled Paula aside just as she was leading Kimberly upstairs. I regurgitated the scene in Henry's room, his confession. And maybe it was the blood leaking down my face, or the impending phone calls to the residents' offspring she had to make, but she cut me off with a guillotine-sharp: *Henry is ill.* Then she led a worried-looking Kimberly through the door, which shut behind them with a resounding *clunk.*

'Hey, man,' Ranjit said, taking a stab at levity, 'you look good for an OAP. What's your secret?'

'I'm just visiting.'

'Cool. Family or friend?'

'Mobile librarian.'

He busied himself with my dressings. 'Cool,' he said. 'Cool, cool.'

Would there arise an opportunity to pass a few words with Kimberly? Would that be inappropriate? Or would she smile at me again, as she had earlier? Either way, better she came back before Ranjit finished patching me up. That way, at least, my continued presence would be above reproach.

'And…we're…back…iiiiiiinnnnnnn *business,*' Ranjit said, prodding my wounds for the final time. The stinging had already greatly subsided, replaced by a deep, fuzzy ache. Ranjit began putting his equipment away. 'So where you headed now?'

'Home, I guess.'

'Taking it easy, yeah?'

'Something like that. Anyway,' – I waved my hands nebulously about my bandaged head – 'thank you.'

'Anytime,' he said, and strolled over to where James Stewart was still receiving treatment.

I lingered in the hallway. The toppled monitor had been removed, but a scattering of small brown pellets remained. The old lady was right, where *were* Gus's manners? The door Paula and Kimberly had disappeared behind was locked. Through the reinforced glass, I could see a flight of stairs but nothing more. There was no buzzer or intercom, no member of staff around to grant me passage. To prevent residents from wandering abroad, the main entrance was comprised of two sets of airlock-like double doors, the inner set of which were activated by a keypad on the wall. Paula had mentioned the four-digit code earlier, but after everything that had happened, I couldn't remember. But there was definitely an 8 in there somewhere, I thought. I again cast around for assistance – perhaps from the elusive Leanne – but I was quite alone. Outside, falling dollops of snow lent texture and depth to the darkness. It was lying quite thickly.

I tried some codes: 8-8…yes…8-8-something…4? I tried all ten permutations of the third digit, but the light on the keypad remained red. My finger hovered over the numbers as if I were on the verge of executing another plan of action, but I had no other plan of action.

Because you're a Mammy's boy, Alan. Just like Dad always said – a big, balding Mammy's boy who still needs his hand

443

holding. Well, in case you've forgotten, Mammy's resembled the
inside of a Hoover bag for some time now. And as for Kimberly
– you and I both know you don't got the moxie, kid. Not after
the last debacle.

I typed 1-2-3-4. No dice.

Not after the cuajada.

Of course, I knew being nice to clients was part of her job,
but over time I began wondering whether, to her with me,
it meant as much as it did to me, with her. I never made
an appointment, just shuffled in at the end of the day when
the place was empty (and after her assistant Gillian had
gone home), and she always smiled when I entered. A real
smile deepening the crowfeet around her eyes, even when
those eyes were sad, as they frequently were. Our chats as
she cut my hair were precious to me, and later, at home,
when I replayed them in my mind, I marvelled at the
fluidity with which we moved together from topic to topic.
Ordinarily, such exchanges would have been ersatz and
awkward for me – especially with women – but with
Corina, wonder of wonders, it was anything but.

Not that it strictly mattered. She was married and had
talked enough in the abstract about her husband Max for
me to deduce that they were reasonably happy. Slowly,
however, any mention of Max ceased and one day, yowling
in its absence, her wedding ring was also gone. It was selfish
of me, but I got my hopes up, and a churning anxiety rose
in tandem. Self-doubt, that nasty by-product of
opportunity: if Corina's marriage was at an end, then the
onus was now on me to drag my daydreams into reality.
To *do* something. Declare my love. Lay it all on the table.
I pep-talked myself before each visit – this was to be *the*

haircut I'd tell her, but each time I choked. Each time I smiled politely at the back of my own cowardly head in the hand mirror and shuffled home simmering with self-reproach.

Many haircuts followed in such fashion.

It wasn't until I overheard two ladies on the bus discussing the imminent closure of Corina's salon that my hand was forced, as I secretly prefer my hand to be. The time for decisive action was upon me, but what form would it take?

Cuajada.

She'd told me the story during one of my first appointments. Her auntie Bea lived in Spain, in one of those expat communities full of sunburned beer guts and five hundred peseta fry up shacks. Torremolinos, maybe, or the Costa Brava. Once a year, Bea had flown over for a visit, bringing with her bags of strange Spanish sweets and several boxes of something called cuajada. Cuajada – ('the *j* like this, Alan: *hhkkaa*, like you're clearing your throat') – was a powdered ewe's milk-pudding and, yes, Corina said, she knew it sounded rank, but you shouldn't knock it until you tried it. She and her brother Jim loved the stuff.

Bea died when Corina was eighteen. She just *went* at her local karaoke bar, and nobody even realised until it was her turn to do Anita Baker's *Sweet Love*. Some kind of aneurysm. Like snapping off a light.

It happens more than you think, Corina said. And she never ate cuajada again. They didn't do it in this country.

Ah, but the internet did. Even with shipping, it didn't come to much, and I was one mouse-click away from placing the order when a thought occurred: how much more special would it be if I made it myself? The traditional way?

Alan, you mother-*effing* genius you.

I had to go all the way to a farm in Great Ayton for the ewe's milk, and, perhaps it was the Spanish-language recipe I was following, but my first attempts were disastrous. The milk boiled over on the hob, and a penetrating sourness filled the house, got into my clothes and skin. But after eight or nine attempts, I had it…or something approximating it. Cuajada. It tasted alright – kind of like an earthy Angel Delight, with lumps. I ladled the mixture into an old ice cream tub and left it to set.

Corina looked even more pale and drawn than usual on her final day in business. 'You're a bit early, aren't you?' she said when I walked in.

And indeed I was. See, I always plumped for the same style – a simple short back and sides – but her impending closure meant I hadn't time enough to grow my hair to its required length. In desperation, I'd purchased a glossy celebrity magazine from Gary's (possibly the last transaction Gary ever made. His last words to me: 'See you next time'), in it found some Bright Young Thing on a red carpet, a perfect specimen with heaven-white teeth, waving to the unwashed from within a corona of flashbulbs. His hair was angular, severe, and, according to the accompanying text: "*OMG! So NOW.*" Inspecting myself in the mirror, I calculated I had just enough of my own hair remaining for Corina to be able to duplicate the style. She didn't smirk or laugh when I showed her the picture. There was no malice in her, no venal cruelty, and this was why I loved her.

During the haircut she opened up to me in a way she'd never done before. For the first time, she shared with me her fears and regrets, her hopes and dreams, and I glimpsed the dented beauty of her soul. In turn, I was thus emboldened to reciprocate with my own troubles. Our conversation was real, naked – I was sure she felt it too – and a weight lifted from me. The bleak future I worried lay ahead fell away, replaced by the possibility I could finally unleash the love of which I knew myself to be capable. For the duration of that haircut, at least, it all felt so mouth-wateringly close.

Plus, I still had my trump card – the cuajada! Literally up my sleeve! (Though I am stumped as to why I shoved the tub up my cagoule like that instead of, say, putting it in a carrier bag like a normal person. Perhaps I didn't want her guessing the contents, as I myself did to womens' shopping on the bus.)

My styling was nearing completion. Corina had shorn the sides of my head alarmingly close, and up top – what remained up top – had been swept asymmetrically to the right in a frozen, mousy-grey wave. Was I crazy, but did I actually look...*good*? At long last, was I now fashionable? She raised the hand mirror. The razored flesh at the back of my head was the blue-white of a plucked battery chicken.

I love it, I said.

When Corina went into the back to rinse her hands, I attempted to extract the tub from the cagoule before my courage failed me, but the box was wedged at an awkward angle and wouldn't budge. While I tugged at it with increasing vigour, the spiel I'd worked out began to jumble, the gist of which was: *Corina, I was recently looking for pudding ideas for a dinner party I'm having with friends* (yes, friends), *when I stumbled across this cuajada recipe. The name rang a bell, and I thought, 'Where have I heard that before?'*

*Then it came to me – hadn't you once mentioned enjoying it? Well, I thought I'd whip you up some…*at which point I'd give her the pudding and ask if, whenever was convenient for her, perhaps she wouldn't mind having a cup of, ah, tea with me. At least that was how it went in my head. I had not envisaged wrestling the unwieldy bulk out of my sleeve as sweat – hot and salty – trickled into my mouth.

Corina returned. 'What are you doing Alan?' she quite reasonably asked.

When the first globs of cuajada splattered onto the floor, the salon melted into a vortex of hysteria. Sensing Corina's disgust, I scuttled to the door with my cagoule clutched to myself as if I were a heavily pregnant woman whose waters had just broken. On the precinct, I almost knocked over a young woman who called me a far from inappropriate word, given the circumstances, but I didn't stop to apologise. I ran – limped – home, leaving globules of cuajada in my wake, much like Hansel and Gretel had once done in order to navigate a dark and scary world which wished to devour them.

'1348,' said a voice from behind me. Startled, I turned to see Kimberly.

'The year of the Black Death,' I heard myself say.

'What?'

'Ah, nothing.' Not trusting myself to spew more idiocy, I concentrated instead on punching in the code. The light on the keypad flashed green and the doors whined open on their robotic hinges.

'That's never happened before,' Kimberly said, looking at my newly bandaged head, my rapidly thinning hair. Her hazel eyes dropped to my cagoule. It was freshly torn where

I'd sewn it up after the cuajada incident. There was blood on it now, too.

I adopted what I hoped to be a breezy tone. 'Really, I'm pretty lucky if you think about it. I mean, how many people get to experience a predator up close like that? Only rodents, I suppose, but they don't live to write about it in their memoirs.'

'You're funny,' she said.

'Small birds, too. The occasional frog.'

Stop talking, Alan. Stop talking right now.

The doors finished opening. Freezing, snow-laced air swirled in to cool the sweat that had broken out on my upper lip.

'What will happen to Gus?' I said.

'Who?'

'The bird. What will happen to him?'

A strand of blonde hair tumbled down over her eye, and in that moment I was prepared to face down a hundred hawks just to be the one who got to tuck it back.

'I raised him,' she said. 'I've known him since he was an *egg*. They do anything to him over my dead body.'

'Birds of prey do tend to prey on things,' I said. 'Clue's in the title.'

'Aye, but as the boss-lady just yelled at me upstairs, all it takes is one complaint. One busybody wanting to know why Granddad's head looks like burger meat.'

I tried to keep up with Kimberly's brisk pace. We were halfway across the car park, the wind full in our faces, heading towards to the waiting van. The other bird handlers were huddled inside the cab, lit moodily by a single bulb. Looking around, I could see no mobile libraries parked anywhere.

'The aborigines,' I said, 'believed the moon had fire just like the sun, only the moon was too selfish to share. So the story goes a sparrowhawk flew up and stole it for them.'

'Who told you that?' Kimberly said.

'I read it somewhere.'

She smiled. 'You're really interesting.'

'You're interesting too.' Silence. Then I said, 'Well…I probably should…'

'Aye,' she replied, 'me too.' But she didn't move.

This is it, Alan! This is all you're going to get!

I opened my mouth without knowing what would come out. At the same moment one of the handlers honked the horn.

'Bye,' I murmured. I turned and limped towards the main road.

'Wait,' Kimberly said.

My heart leapt. She stood with her hands in her armpits for warmth, snow in her hair.

'Yes, Kimberly?' I said.

'You won't, will you?'

'Won't what?'

'Complain. You won't, will you?'

Top deck of the 551. Ten or eleven items in the woman's shopping bag: a probable microwavable chicken korma, a jar of sweet 'n' sour sauce, some chocolate digestives, and… could it be? Was that a box of *Pizzips!*? From my seat five rows behind, I judged the woman to be in her early thirties, her full lips rendered in burgundy, and a kink of black hair escaping from under her mustard bobble hat. With a death-mask blankness to her features, she stared out at the complex configurations of snow and streetlight shifting against the bus window. Knitted mitts obscured her ring finger, but for once I wasn't concerned. I had other things on my mind.

I'd recognised Mam's letters the instant they dropped onto the doormat last month; my whole life leaping out of that package to uppercut me. In the final year of her life, she'd spent hours propped up in bed composing long letters that were shrouded in mystery. Who was she writing to? And what information did she possess that could possible require so many pages to convey?

So I asked her.

Aunt Agnes, Mam said.

A satisfactory answer. Aunt Agnes had recently moved with her husband to Exeter. Yet…if Mam was writing to her sister, why did she only compose (and go out to post) the letters when Dad wasn't around?

Later, as she became weaker and her letter writing took on a greater sense of urgency, I got closer to the enigma. No longer able to make it to the post box under her own steam, she finally enlisted me into her confidence, and this was when I discovered that the addressee was not in fact Agnes, but something by the name of *Ananke Acquisitions*. This, of course, only ratcheted up my thirst, but Mam made me promise two things before engaging my services – ask no questions, and don't tell Dad.

I agreed, though it almost drove me crackers to do so, just as it did when, once or twice, a return letter arrived. My mother's name in bland, computer-printed type, the creamy caliper of the envelope; I *craved* steaming them open like they did in detective films. The urge over time becoming a bone-knit itch multiplied thousand-fold as my myriad questions jostled against my commitment to not rock the karmic boat while she died. Oh, that and my simple cowardice at being caught, of course.

You can imagine, then, how strange it was to be once more holding Mam's letters. They were bundled together inside a large padded envelope addressed to *Vincent Barr*, the sender apparently unaware of my father's recent incarceration and subsequent death. Aside from the letters themselves, there was nothing else inside except for a single sheet of paper on which was printed one sentence. Times New Roman, bold, all caps. An uncanny echoing of words Doug had once directed at me, about my father:

YOU DON'T KNOW WHO YOUR SON IS

The page was unsigned.

I turned my attention to my mother's letters. Her handwriting…her *f*s were like my *f*s, or rather, mine were like hers – looping treble clefs that stood apart from the rest of her somewhat squat and ordinary penmanship. She'd taught me the alphabet on the backs of old rolls of wallpaper.

Initially, the contents of the letters were puzzling. My brain simply refused to compute…but then, as I read the final one and the shock kicked in, I experienced an almost narcotic flood of relief which, for a while, outweighed even my astonishment. *I was not my father's son.*

Finally. Something that made sense.

Yet sense is not necessarily synonymous with peace. My entire life, I'd been the gritty chaff to my father's magnificent wheat, but now that the bonds of blood were apparently rescinded, was I now at liberty to simply *forget*? Was it really that simple? Our relationship had forever glinted with the dark, contra logic of an Escher staircase: me, climbing endlessly in his wake, never wanting to be like him, yet agonised that I could not. While Dad…well, who knows what he really thought of me? So, to hop suddenly off that Sisyphean cycle seemed a gross over-simplification, paradoxically requiring a strength I knew I didn't have by dint of being trapped in the cycle in the first place. And even if I *were* to somehow manage it, to who would I then turn? Henry? If Henry's involvement in those missing children were true, did I really want to attribute my anomalies to him?

The woman with the *Pizzips!* got off at the next stop. As she reached the stairs, she looked right at me. Seared with shame, I dropped my gaze. In fading black marker on the back of the seat in front of me, someone had written:

SCOTT ♥ BETH 4 EVA.

An empty pop can rolled about under the seats as we barrelled down the dual carriageway. I was the only person left on the top deck, and I could sense the estate and blocks ahead, in the dark, impending. We turned off at the usual place, down a gentle incline to the outskirts of the estate, and I wiped a gloved hand across the glass to see better the black bulks of derelict houses, the fenced-off building sites. Sounds like everything's a building site now, Ian had said, and I couldn't disagree. Drills and hammers now permeated my every waking moment. The very air rang with collapse. Maybe that was the root of my current malaise? Pop-psychologists could make something of it, probably.

The bus passed some Rowan-Tree hoardings: **IT'S**

WHERE YOUR HEART IS. I'd never felt that way about my home. Granted, everywhere I looked there were memories, but that was hardly the same thing, was it? Where was my heart? Not inside me, I knew that much. What beat there was its ghost. At the danger of sounding melodramatic, I sometimes felt that the real organ resided in a place I'd once glimpsed in a dream. Somewhere out in the fog…

We moved deeper into the estate and the houses began to show signs of life. Sad-looking Christmas lights glowed in windows of Sommers Road, at the end of which we would turn left onto Hollis Road, then onto the Crescent, towards my house. This left was so ingrained in me that my internal gyroscope took several moments to register we had in fact turned right. I struggled down the bottom deck. Except for me, the bus was entirely empty. I swung ape-like from a handrail and asked the driver to explain himself.

'The water main burst about an hour ago, and the whole of Hollis Road's flooded,' he said. 'So we're taking the scenic route.'

I crashed into a seat and peered out of the window. We appeared to be making a clockwise circuit of the estate, and soon the shabby Burn Estate terraces fell away to be replaced by the modern semi-detached homes of Moorside – double garages, pale festive lights twinkling tastefully in front-garden conifers; beautiful, spacious homes that had been built over the old waterworks, scene of my life's deepest terror and humiliation.

Do you remember that night, Peg? It was the first time we spoke.

After Frank Hulme and his friend left me at the well, after

454

night fell like a vat of tar, and the blood pumping from me went stony cold, I cried. This was it, *death*...yet the knowledge was entirely without epiphany. No life flashed before my eyes, no tentacle of calming white light telescoped towards me from the next realm. Instead, as I curled into a snivelling ball, my mind reacted to the shock by firing off on bizarre tangents. I imagined myself shrinking in size until the earth dry-pressed me into a sedimentary layer, so that millions of years in the future my final death throes would be fossilised like those of the dinosaurs, and just as academic to whoever exhumed them. My thoughts drifted further into the abstract, slipping into what felt like dream, and I let them slip, still aware – just – of the consequences of doing so. But then your voice cut across the grain of my consciousness.

Boy.

I opened my eyes, unsure as to whether the voice hadn't in some way been my own. I listened. The knotweed whispered around me.

Smell. You. A female voice unlike any female I'd ever heard.

I didn't move, didn't breathe.

Smell. Your. Blood.

Struggling upright, trembling, mewling, snot dangling from my chin, I said, 'Who's there? Where are you?'

Down. Here.

With sheeting horror, I realised that you meant *down the well*. My bladder betrayed me and fresh, shameful warmth spread over my crotch. The urine sang in my gashed thigh as I began dragging myself away from the hole.

Stay.

'Go away!' Maybe I was dead already? Maybe Heaven and Hell weren't metaphors after all, and my suspicions of them being such had earmarked me for the latter? Keeping my wounded leg stiffly out in front, I wobbled to my feet like a punch-drunk fighter several rounds beyond his threshold. To my left, the waterworks and the water tower – dark and portentous – reached into the night.

Where. I. Be?

'You're in England,' I said. 'Teesside. You're…you're down a well.'

River?

'I don't know. North somewhere.'

Show. Me.

'I can't…go yourself.'

RIVER. GONE.

'I'm sorry.'

LOST. I. BE.

'I'm so sorry,' I whispered.

AFRAID.

I took a step back.

COME. DOWN. HERE.

I felt your words in my head and wanted nothing else but to step into that black hole and let everything resolve itself. But then I thought about Mam. I couldn't do that to her. 'I'm sorry,' I said, 'but I'm going.'

Boy.

Each lurching step I took towards the knotweed was agony.

I. See. You. Again.

'So sorry!'

The last thing I heard you say: *HELP. ME.*

Only fragments of recollection after that: stumbling

through the knotweed, falling, cutting my palms on broken glass, everything going the wrong way down the plughole. Then I was under streetlights with vomit down my front, barely able to hold myself upright. Finally, I remember being on hands and knees, pawing weakly at the same blood-red front door I still live behind all these years later. A door which opened and basked me in warmth. My father's boots so close to my face I could smell the dubbing he rubbed daily into them. His voice above me and all encompassing, like that of God's on the First Day, giving light to His creation.

One word and one word only: *son*.

Daft, I know, but more than a year had passed since Ludwig's death and I still half-expected him to greet me at the door. But there was nothing but silence, darkness. Snow followed me inside. I tugged my bobble hat off gingerly, mindful of Ranjit's handiwork, and watched the snowflakes melt into the wool. I went further into the house, flicking on lights. In the backroom, I peeled off my gloves and shucked my coat. Removed my boots the way children do, by standing on a heel and wriggling the other loose.

My books, papers, and pens were everywhere. The coffee table, once the domain of my father's newspapers and ashtrays, his ale bottles and television remotes, was now where I did my work, such as it was. The dozens of holes Dad had drilled into the walls remained. I'd thought about filling them in, but wasn't sure how. I could still see the shield-shape outlined in nicotine, where Ludwig had been mounted until I'd taken him down and buried him in the allotment.

Here is what I don't understand: how could Dad, a man who – however misguidedly – had gone to such surreal lengths in order to preserve the memories of his beloved dogs, who planted a different species of rose on each of their graves, how could the same man have presided over a secret animal killing-field not five miles down the road from their bones? What superhuman feat of compartmentalisation permits such a scenario? That image in Doug's journals, of my father in underwear and welding goggles, descending into a mechanics' pit, it haunts me; as do the pictures the prosecution showed in court during his trial. The remains of greyhounds exhumed from the field by Rowan-Tree did not remotely resemble once-living creatures (and in the dock, Dad stared serenely into middle distance).

But then I think, are we not all thus conflicted? Exhibit A: the cuajada. Earlier, I left something out. I fudged the story, used the heat of my shame to make events just malleable enough to distort. You see, in Corina's salon, right at the crucial moment, when her exquisitely tired eyes met mine, my mouth fat with my practised words and my heart coursing with angst, I had deliberately wrenched the lid off that tub. What happened inside my cagoule was no accident – it was sabotage.

Meaning even this late in the game, I'm still finding ways of keeping myself here, in this house, on Vivienne Avenue.

I called the number from the old, tattered remains of the Lily Butler poster I'd torn off the alley wall on the way home. A man with a flat, serious voice answered on the third ring and listened to everything I had to say. At intervals, he made notes or asked questions. He got me to spell Henry's last name. He'd be in touch, he said, before hanging up.

I stooped at the hearth to check the fire. Not an ember in the grate and no logs in the basket. I'd have to get more from the washhouse. When I straightened up (issuing an Old Man *ooff* as I did so), I came face to face with Mam's urn on the mantelpiece, my speccy, elephantine head mooning back at me in the minute brass plaque screwed into its base. Her full name: JEAN PENELOPE ANNE BARR. I've never taken succour in her ashes; I dislike being so close to her in such an altered state. The urn itself was the size and shape of an egg cup and represented all of her Dad had been able to salvage from the rug after Doug's catastrophic New Year visit. That night had been important for me. Trying to uncover what had driven Doug to visit was where everything started, the guiding thread I'd wrap around my thumb as I stumbled into the labyrinth of my own history. But I failed. Unlike Theseus, somewhere along the line my thread snapped and I found myself alone in the dark with the Minotaur.

Next to the urn was a picture of my parents. It was taken in the late 1960s, before I was born; Dad still firmly in the rape-and-pillage of his Blackbeard Years, one sequoia-trunk arm casually yoking my mother, who, hair in an elaborate blonde beehive, gazed demurely into the camera. Over the years I must have clocked up hours studying this picture, scrutinising it for some encoded clue to their ensuing future, some ley-line thrum of my own eventuality in its emotional composition, but found nothing. As far as I could see, they were just young and happy. Maybe sometimes that's all that's required.

The washhouse keys were in my pocket, as usual. I snagged the torch from under the kitchen sink and unlocked the back door. Snow up to my ankles lay like primed canvas over the yard, and my boots crumped gorgeously as only boots in fresh snow can. The kennels stood empty against the back wall. After Ludwig, Dad had briefly got another dog – Amadeus – a gangling, shaggy monster sprung direct from the pages of *The Hound of the Baskervilles*. Amadeus' eyes had leaked a continuous stream of brown pus and, once Dad was imprisoned, I gave the creature to a shelter.

I unlocked the washhouse and scooped up an armful of logs, doing my best not to think about spiders. I walked back to the house in my existing footprints and began building a new fire on the ashes of the old one. There was only a handful of kindling in the pile and, looking around for something to burn, I saw on the coffee table beside my laptop and notebooks, stained with tea rings and *Pizzip!* sauce, The Document. The one I'd provisionally entitled *UXO*.

I'd started it some months earlier because, as I've said, I'd been convinced that Doug was my way in. Like Corina with her brother Jim's disappearance, I could almost *see* the obsidian threads tying it all together, thought the more people I talked to about that New Year's Eve, the more confused and contradictory things became. In fact, I'd been on the verge of throwing in the towel when Mam's letters arrived.

Reading them that first time, I felt so juiced I could taste pennies. So many new threads! Strong threads! Henry to my mother, my mother to the Great Una Cruickshank, and more – Stephan Santerre, I realised, had been the author of the article that first introduced me to Una. Online digging revealed that Una's life's work had been discovered by the property redevelopment company *Luxe*, the managing director of which was one Yohan Santerre, younger *frère* of Stephan, the influential collector, curator, and head of art-dealership *Ananke Acquisitions*, the man who'd championed and exhibited Una's work, and for whose correspondence with my Mam I'd acted as middle man.

Stephan died a few scant weeks before Dad. According to the obituary, he was survived by his wife and son, Aiden Santerre – 'Armitage Shanks' in some rags – who had, in 1989, been fined heavily in relation to the rave at the old waterworks. Was this, then, how my mother's letters had found their way back to me? Had Shanks been going through his deceased father's papers in much the same way as I'd be going through mine, stumbled upon Mam's correspondence and, having ground his axe all these years, posted them to Dad in revenge, unaware that he, too, had recently joined the choir invisible? I can only speculate. I decided to locate Stephan's original letters to Mam. They had to be in the house somewhere. I started my hunt in the loft. My search was long and spidery, and ultimately a failure in that I didn't find his letters.

I did, however, find something else.

It was in the deepest, darkest recesses of the double loft, at the bottom of a cardboard box that had once contained **McADAM'S HEARTY IRISH-STYLE STEW**. At first glance there was nothing special. Business ledgers mostly, packed with columns of numbers in Dad's rune-like hand, but also solicitor letters detailing his lost battle with Rowan-Tree over ownership of the field behind his garage. Below those, however, I found a small burgundy photo album filled with pictures of Mam as a girl. I'd never seen them before: there she was at maybe five years old, sat on her nana's knee, Mam and Aunty Agnes on the swings, Mam in her uniform on her first day of grammar school,

Mam in a crimplene dress, blowing bubbles into her limeade through a straw. At the back of the album was a single loose photograph tucked into the pages. Mam with another girl, both in their mid-teens, backdropped by varnished chipboard and decorative brass horseshoes. Mam was beautiful. Her bobbed hair effortlessly framing her face as she smiled the kind of easy smile that even I, inexperienced in such matters, could see was a heart-wrecker. Una was behind her. I don't know how I knew it was her, I just did. She was tall and pale, her wiry cloud of black hair almost a physical manifestation of her thoughts. She wasn't looking at the camera, instead she gazed at something beyond the frame, already uncoupling from this world, already fading away.

This isn't what I want to tell you about. I want to tell you about the letter I found crumpled right at the very bottom of the box. Not Stephan's letter, but one from the hospital. It was addressed to Dad, dated September 1993, nine months after Mam's death.

It was a sperm test. Dad had nine million sperm per millilitre of semen. Oligozoospermia. Or in laymen's terms: a low sperm count.

I put down *UXO* and picked up Dad's hospital letter. I read it for a final time, then screwed it into a twist and stuck it into the logs. I struck a cook's match, touched the flame to the tip of the paper. The fire consumed it greedily and spread to the rest of the kindling, licking at the logs.

Once the fire was roaring and Dad's room – my room – had heated up, I went to the kitchen and made myself a cup of tea. Then I sat down, opened my laptop, and started to write.

*

The book you have almost finished reading is the product of that writing. One night, many years ago, after I'd read to her the end of a Judith Krantz, Mam told me she used to write stories. When I asked her what they'd been about, she shrugged and said, *Just silly little things that I never showed anyone.*

Maybe you could write a new story? I said.

No, pet. No.

Why not? What could you write about?

The travel clocked ticked on her bedside table. Propped up in bed, surrounded by her pills and exhaustion, she said, I wish I knew.

So I decided to write the story for her, the only story I could think to tell: hers, which is also mine, and Dad's, and Jim's, and Corina's, and Doug's and Frank Hulme's and his boy's. And yours too, Peg. Especially yours. For so long I tried to follow the threads of our lives as they weaved together, but sooner or later they always snapped or snarled, and I became lost. Then I remembered what Corina told me in the salon, what Dad had said to her the night she'd confronted him over what happened to Jim – you either let the loose ends drive you mad, or you tie them together in whatever way that lets you keep going. So that's what I've done, tied them together as best I could. I used to fret about the truth, about swapping one fiction for another, but then, what other option do any of us have? Truth is a trap. It lures you deeper into the labyrinth of itself, always just out of reach, leading you past enough of your own failure and disappointment and humiliation and regret to convince you that you won't ever be strong enough to turn around, to head back.

Which is why I decided on a different path. Like with wrestling, the stories may be fictional, but the pain isn't.

Last month they tore down the precinct. Soon they'll do the same to this house. I accepted Rowan-Tree's offer. It was much less than what the house is worth, but *eff* it. Perhaps I'll take a long holiday. Australia, maybe. Check out Ayres Rock. But first I need to finish writing this. It's been a race to get the stories finished in time, but I'm almost done. This is the last page. I'll leave this manuscript in the Burn Pipe for you, Peg, because I want you to know that while the wrecking balls may be circling the last of this place, and while the final few souls who still keep your name in their hearts are scattered and gone for good, *I* still remember you. I still know you're trapped down there.

So I hope you find this, Peg. And I hope it brings you some solace until, like me, you find your way out and into the light.

Acknowledgements

Thank you to my parents John and Jaqueline, and to my sister Lauren. Thank you also to the rest of my family for their support and encouragement. Gracias to my friends – a million little things in this book are indebted to you all.

A huge thank you to my wonderful agent Veronique Baxter, whose faith in this book has meant so much to me. An equally large thanks to Richard Lewis Davies and all the team at Parthian, and especially to my editor Eddie Matthews, whose insights revealed aspects of the book I hadn't even considered.

Everyone in the writing department at the University of Chichester. I am particularly grateful to Stephanie Norgate and David Swann for granting me the opportunity to study there. I can say without hyperbole that it changed my life.

To those who critiqued sections of the book in progress: Hannah Brockbank, Donna Kirstein, Stephen Cass, Gillian Thompson, Mike Coot, Mark Wright, Paul Newton-Palmer, Jem Smith, Maureen Corfield, Corrina O'Beirne, Bea Mitchell Turner, Jocelyn-Anne Harvey.

For reading larger excerpts, or the whole manuscript – sometimes more than once – I am thankful eternally to Richard Buxton, Zoe Mitchell, Jacqui Pack and Tracy Fells.

Thank you to the Leeds Savages, and to SJ Bradley at Fictions of Every Kind. Mike Bonner for his police knowledge (any surviving mistakes are mine). Sam Byers for his friendship, encouragement, and help with the book after it was done. And an extra-special thank you to Emma Claire Sweeney.

Finally, the biggest thank you of all goes to my partner Susan Barker. Without your fathomless love, support, inspiration, and faith in me, this book simply would not exist.

Financial assistance from the Arts & Humanities Research Council was vital in the writing of this book.